ecpr PRESS

Series Editors:
Dario Castiglione (University of Exeter) and
Vincent Hoffmann-Martinot (Sciences Po Bordeaux)

just democracy

the rawls-machiavelli programme

Philippe Van Parijs

ecprPRESS

Front cover images
Photograph of John Rawls, circa 1969, with the kind permission of
Alec Rawls and Margaret Rawls
Painting of Niccolò Machiavelli, by Cristofano dell' Altissimo
(originally facing to the left)

First published by the ECPR Press in 2011

The ECPR Press is the publishing imprint of the European Consortium for Political Research
(ECPR), a scholarly association, which supports and encourages the training, research
and cross-national cooperation of political scientists in institutions throughout Europe and
beyond. The ECPR's Central Services are located at the University of Essex, Wivenhoe Park,
Colchester, CO4 3SQ, UK

Typeset by ECPR Press Printed and bound by Lightning Source

British Library Cataloguing in Publication Data A catalogue record for this book is available
from the British Library

Paperback ISBN: 978-1-907301-14-8

www.ecprnet.eu/ecprpress

Publications from the ECPR Press

ECPR Classics:

Beyond the Nation State: (ISBN: 9780955248870) Ernst Haas

Citizens, Elections, Parties: Approaches to the Comparative Study of the Processes of Development (ISBN: 9780955248887) Stein Rokkan

Democracy: Political Finance and State Funding for Parties (ISBN: 9780955248801) Jack Lively

Electoral Change: Responses to Evolving Social and Attitudinal Structures in Western Countries (ISBN: 9780955820311) Mark Franklin,Thomas Mackie, and Henry Valen

Elite and Specialized Interviewing (ISBN: 9780954796679) Lewis Anthony Dexter

Identity, Competition and Electoral Availability: The Stabilisation of European Electorates 1885-1985 (ISBN: 9780955248832) Peter Mair & Stefano Bartolini

Individualism (ISBN: 9780954796662) Steven Lukes

Modern Social Policies in Britain and Sweden: From Relief to Income Maintenance (ISBN: 9781907301001) Hugh Heclo

Parties and Party Systems: A Framework for Analysis (ISBN: 9780954796617) Giovanni Sartori

Party Identification and Beyond: Representations of Voting and Party Competition (ISBN: 9780955820342) Ian Budge, Ivor Crewe, Dennis Farlie

People, States and Fear: An Agenda for International Security Studies in the Post-Cold War Era (ISBN: 9780955248818) Barry Buzan

Political Elites: (ISBN: 9780954796600) Geraint Parry

Political Theory and Political Science (ISBN: 9781907301025) Martin Landau

State Formation, Parties and Democracy (ISBN: 9781907301179) *Hans Daalder*

System and Process in International Politics (ISBN: 9780954796624) Morton Kaplan

Territory and Power in the UK: Territory and Power in the UK (ISBN: 9780955248863) James Bulpitt

The State Tradition in Western Europe: A Study of an Idea and Institution (ISBN: 9780955820359) Kenneth Dyson

General Interest Books:

Parties and Elections in New European Democracies (ISBN: 9780955820328) Richard Rose and Neil Munro

Masters of Political Science (ISBN: 9780955820335) Edited by Donatella Campus and Gianfranco Pasquino

The Wit and Humour of Political Science (ISBN: 9781907301100) Edited by Kenneth Newton, Lee Sigelman, Kenneth Meier and Bernard Grofman

Please visit www.ecprnet.eu/ecprpress for up-to-date information about new publications

contents

| list of figures and tables

Figures

Tables

| foreword

TO THE MEMORY OF BRIAN BARRY (1936–2009)

With the exception of the new introductory essay, which presents the book's central idea, all the essays collected here have been reprinted without any substantive alteration. Some stylistic improvements have been made, bibliographical references have been added or updated, and a few cross-references have been inserted in footnotes. Each essay is preceded by a brief preamble that sketches the context in which it was originally prepared. The full references of the original publication feature in the Acknowledgements.

This volume is dedicated to the memory of Brian Barry. This may seem an odd choice, especially for the second half of the book, as he was not exactly a friend of either the European Union or of plurinational democracies. He even described Belgian politics as 'nauseating to all concerned' (Barry 2001: 312). However, Brian Barry was probably the first political philosopher to devote an article to democracy in divided societies, in one of the first issues of the journal of the ECPR. He was also one of the sharpest thinkers I ever knew, and one of the first-rate academics I have ever met most fervently committed to the cause of social justice. Moreover, he was my first and very conscientious DPhil supervisor when I arrived in Oxford in 1974; he became much later one of my most formidable philosophical allies in the advocacy of an unconditional basic income, and shortly before he died, he asked his wife Anni to hand over to me, after his death, the DPhil gown his parents got made for him.

There is no better choice for the dedication of an ECPR book on 'just democracy' than one of the most insightful European thinkers ever on both justice and democracy.

| acknowledgments

I am most grateful to Dario Castiglione, who encouraged me to gather these essays and gave me useful advice in the process; to Jacque Woolley for her help in preparing the final manuscript; to the publishers of the original versions of the essays for having granted permission to reprint them; to Kris Deschouwer, co-author of two of them and co-spokesman of the Pavia Group, for smooth and fruitful collaboration in both writing and action; and to many commentators and critics, for insightful feedback, only some of which is explicitly acknowledged below.

CHAPTER 1. THE RAWLS-MACHIAVELLI PROGRAMME

This introductory chapter has not been previously published. It incorporates some material from A. Reeve and A. Williams (eds), 'Hybrid Justice, Patriotism and Democracy. A Selective Reply', *Real Libertarianism Assessed. Political Philosophy After Van Parijs,* Basingstoke: Palgrave Macmillan, 201–16

CHAPTER 2. JUSTICE AND DEMOCRACY: ARE THEY INCOMPATIBLE?

English version in *Journal of Political Philosophy* 4 (2), 1996, 101–17, translated from French by David W. Lovell, reprinted with permission of Wiley-Blackwell. Original French version in *Revue européenne des sciences sociales* 97, 1993, 133–149; reprinted in G. Haarscher and M. Teló (eds), *Après le Communisme,* Bruxelles : Editions de l'ULB, 1993, 161–70; and in P. Van Parijs, *Sauver la solidarité*, Paris: Cerf, 1995, 27–60. Portuguese version in *Estudos Avançados* (Sao Paulo) 23, Janeiro-Abril 1995, 109–28. Spanish version in *Contrastes* (Malaga) 1, 1996, 239–58. Greek version in G. Haarscher and M. Teló (eds), *Metaton kommunismo*, Athens : Papazissis, 1997. Dutch version in P. Van Parijs, *Solidariteit voor de 21e eeuw*. Leuven: Garant, 1997, 59–75.
The text of this chapter is based on talks presented at the Université libre

de Bruxelles, the CNRS (Paris), the Société Philosophique de Montréal, the Université Laval (Québec), the Université de Lausanne and the Universitat Autonoma de Barcelona. I am grateful to the organisers of these meetings (respectively, Guy Haarscher and Mario Teló; Jean–Marc Ferry and Dominique Wolton; Robert Nadeau, François Blais, Gérald Berthoud and Giovanni Busino; Toni Domènech and Angeles Lizón) and to participants in them (especially Luc Bégin, Monique Canto–Sperber, Jocelyne Couture, George Fletcher, André Lacroix, Guy Laforest, Maurice Lagueux, Hervé Le Bras, Jean Leca, Anne Legaré, Claude Lefort, Kai Nielsen, Hugues Poltier, Lukas Sosoe, Françoise Thys–Clément, Daniel Weinstock as well as numerous anonymous others) for their stimulating remarks.

CHAPTER 3. CONTESTATORY DEMOCRACY VERSUS REAL FREEDOM

Original publication in I. Shapiro and C. Hacker-Cordón (eds), *Democracy's Value*, Cambridge: Cambridge University Press, 1999, 191–8.

The text of this chapter is based on a comment on Philip Pettit presented at the conference 'Rethinking Democracy' (Yale University, 28 February - 2 March 1997).

CHAPTER 4. THE CHILDREN'S VOTE, AND OTHER ATTEMPTS TO SECURE INTERGENERATIONAL JUSTICE

Original publication as 'The Disfranchisement of the Elderly, and Other Attempts to Secure Intergenerational Justice' in *Philosophy and Public Affairs* 27 (4), 1998, 292–333, reprinted with permission of John Wiley and Sons, Inc.

The text of this chapter is based on talks presented at the University of California(Davis), the University of Arizona(Tucson), Virginia Commonwealth University (Richmond), New York University, the Massachussetts Institute of Technology, the Università Cattolica del Sacro Cuore (Milano), at the 1998 annual meeting of the September Group (Cambridge, Mass.) and at the 1999 Oxford Political Thought Conference. I am most grateful to the organisers of these events (especially John Roemer, Tom Christiano, Peter Vallentyne, Frances Kamm, Josh Cohen, Andrea Villani, Robert van der Veen and Dario Castiglione) for their critical comments as well as for these opportunities to elicit precious feedback; to Vittorio Bufacchi, Axel Gosseries, Gerd

Grözinger, Wayne Norman, Claus Offe, Kenneth Shepsle, Quentin Skinner, Peter Vallentyne, Stuart White, Andrew Williams and Erik O. Wright for insightful written comments or suggestions; to Bruce Ackerman, Paul-Marie Boulanger, Axel Gosseries, Gerd Grözinger, Klaus Hurrelmann, Silvano Möckli, Claus Offe, Stein Ringen and some of my Louvain students for useful material; and to the Program on Ethics, Politics and Economics at Yale University, its director, its registrar and its students for the stimulating setting it provided for most of the preparation of this article.

CHAPTER 5. SHOULD THE EUROPEAN UNION BECOME MORE DEMOCRATIC ?

Original publication in A. Follesdal and P. Koslowski (eds), *Democracy and the European Union*, Berlin and New York: Springer, 1997, 287–301, with kind permission of Springer Science and Business Media.

The text of this chapter is based on talks presented within the framework of the Oslo workshop on 'Democracy and the European Union' and the Louvain workshop on 'The normative foundations of federalism'. I am most grateful to the participants for stimulating exchanges, and to Renaud Dehousse for instructive written comments on an earlier version.

CHAPTER 6. POWER-SHARING VERSUS BORDER-CROSSING IN ETHNICALLY DIVIDED SOCIETIES

Original publication in S. Macedo and I. Shapiro (eds), *Nomos XLII. Designing Democratic Institutions* , New York: NYU Press, 2000, 296–320.

The text of this chapter is based on a comment on Donald Horowitz, 'Constitutional Design: an Oxymoron?' presented at the annual meeting of the American Society for Political and Legal Philosophy (San Francisco, January 5–6, 1998). I am grateful to Don Horowitz for the stimulation provided by his paper, his reactions to my verbal comments and the part of his work I took this opportunity to read, and to Paul Janssens for checking (and correcting) my interpretation of the political history of Belgium.

CHAPTER 7. MUST EUROPE BE BELGIAN?

Original publication in *The Demands of Citizenship*, C. McKinnon and I. Hampsher-Monk (eds), London and New York: Continuum, 2000, 235–53, reprinted by kind permission of Continuum International Publishing Group. Reproduced in K. Hinrichs, H. Kitschelt and H. Wiesenthal (eds), *Kontingenz und Krise. Institutionenpolitik in kapitalistischen und postsozialistischen Gesellschaften*, Frankfurt: Campus, 2000, 59–78; and in F. De Rynck, B. Verschuere and E. Wayenberg (eds), *Re-Thinking the State*, Mechelen: Kluwer, 2009, 85–102. Italian version in M. Ferrera (ed.), *Nuova Europa e nuovo welfare*, Bari: Cacucci Editore, 2001, 121–49. Dutch version in S. Gatz and P. Stouthuysen (eds), *Een Vierde Weg ? Links-liberalisme als traditie en als oriëntatiepunt*, Brussel: VUB Press, 2001, 285–314.

The text of this chapter was prepared within the framework of the inter-university research project 'The New Social Question' directed by Bea Cantillon (Belgian Federal Government, Prime Minister's Office, Federal Office for Scientific, Technical and Cultural Affairs). It is based on talks presented at All Souls College (Oxford, May 1998) and at the Conference 'The Historical Perspectives of Republicanism and the Future of the European Union (Siena, 23–27 September 1998).

CHAPTER 8. BELGIUM RE-FOUNDED

Original publication in F. De Rynck, B. Verschuere and E. Wayenberg (eds), *Re-Thinking the State* , Mechelen: Kluwer, 2009, 99–102, followed by a comment by Harry Van Velthoven.

The text of this chapter is based on the final part of the Robert Vandeputte lecture delivered at the Hogeschool Gent on December 18th 2008 under the title 'Naar een nieuwe sociale en federale staat'.

CHAPTER 9. ELECTORAL ENGINEERING FOR A
STALLED FEDERATION

Pre-publication as lead piece in *Electoral Engineering for a Stalled Federation*, Re-Bel e-book no.4, Brussels, July 2009, 6–19. Forthcoming in *Power-Sharing in Deeply Divided Places* (B. O'Leary and J. McEvoy (eds)), Philadelphia: University of Pennsylvania Press.

The text of this chapter was co-authored with Kris Deschouwer. The authors are most grateful to Brendan O'Leary for careful and insightful editing and to the Andrew Mellon Foundation for support rendered through the Sawyer Seminar for Power-Sharing in Deeply Divided Places.

CHAPTER 10. ANYTHING (EVEN) BETTER THAN THE PAVIA PROPOSAL?

Original publication in *Electoral Engineering for a Stalled Federation*, Re-Bel e-book no.4, Brussels, July 2009, 40–8.

The text of this chapter was co-authored with Kris Deschouwer. The authors are most grateful to Laurent de Briey, Don Horowitz, Bart Maddens and Brendan O'Leary for their thoughtful critical comments.

chapter one | the rawls-machiavelli programme: political institutions as instruments of social justice

Suppose you discover that there is a conflict between justice and democracy, which should you choose? This is the simple question that triggered the inquiry reflected in the present set of essays. You may dismiss this as a non-question, because your notion of justice is so comprehensive that it entails democracy, or because your notion of democracy is so rich that it encompasses justice. It is sound intellectual policy, however, not to make our concepts too fat. Fat concepts hinder clear thinking and foster wishful thinking. By packing many good things under a single label, one is easily misled into believing that they never clash.

I have therefore opted for a thin definition of democracy as a form of collective decision-making that combines three elements: free voting, universal suffrage and majority rule. On close inspection, each of these elements requires further clarification and turns out to be a matter of multi-dimensional degree. Furthermore, once a plausible conception of social justice is spelled out, albeit only in rough outline, the interesting question turns out to be, not whether democracy or justice need to be given up when they clash, but how democracy should be structured and constrained in order to best serve the objective of social justice. We don't just need democracy. We need just democracy.

Optimal or maximally just democracy, in this sense, is certainly not maximal democracy. A 'democratic deficit', therefore, need not be a lamentable defect. It may be a sensible condition of the most effective pursuit of sustainable social justice. What should optimal democracy look like? This question is most unlikely to admit of a universal answer. Rather, it calls for a set of place- and time-specific conjectures about the likely effects of various possible democratic designs. The formulation and critical discussion of such conjectures forms what I shall here call the Rawls-Machiavelli programme.

This programme has two components. The first one consists in spelling out what one should regard, on due reflection, as a defensible characterization of a just society. This can – and in my view must – be done broadly in the spirit of John Rawls' (1971) *A Theory of Justice*, though without taking the nation state as the self-evident frame of reference. The second component consists in reflecting on which, among the millions of ways in which political institutions could be organized, provides the most promising way of securing social justice so characterized, given what political agents are or can feasibly be made to be. This can be understood as an intellectual enterprise akin to Niccolò Machiavelli's (1517) in his *Discorsi sopra la prima Deca di Tito Livio*, though obviously replacing, as the standard of effectiveness, conduciveness to the greatness of Rome by the propensity to foster the realization of social justice in our societies and in our world.

The essays collected in this volume all fit into this Rawls-Machiavelli programme but they fall far short of implementing it in systematic fashion. Most of them illustrate its potential and its limits by discussing specific issues. The longest essay addresses the challenge of how to structure and constrain our democracies so as to best (or least badly) serve the requirements of intergenerational justice. The optimal shaping of Europe-wide democracy is a concern present throughout the volume, not only in the essays explicitly devoted to it. And several essays, including all the most recent ones, focus on the specific problems that arise in the context of ethnically divided countries. In these essays, I predictably pay special attention to the predicament of my own country, Belgium. This is so in part because my familiarity with is history and current situation boost the confidence with which I feel I can use it to illustrate problems that arise far more widely. In addition, this reflects my growing involvement, along with fellow Belgian academics from both sides of the language border, in a public discussion about the country's institutional future that has been growing both in intensity and in philosophical interest.

The same holds for this Rawls-Machiavelli programme as for any other research programme: the proof is in the pudding. The essays collected here are no more than a very modest foretaste of the prospective outcome of a well-informed, critical and imaginative justice-driven instrumentalist approach to political institutions. For the sake of those who may be tempted to dismiss this approach without tasting any of its output, however, it may be useful to briefly deal with two principled objections to it.

Firstly, universal suffrage, which is part of my thin definition of democracy, is a minimal interpretation of political equality. Is it not obvious that something like political equality should be part of any plausible conception of justice? Democracy, in this light, would not be a contingent tool for justice, but a necessary component of it. There are two interpretations of this objection.[1] On the first one, the right to vote is part of the possibilities, the opportunities, the real freedom that justice (as I understand it) requires should be sustainably distributed in maximin fashion, i.e. so as to maximize the pos-

---

1.   Both of these objections are forcefully articulated by Thomas Christiano (2003).

sibilities of the worst off.[2] But the possibility of casting a vote every so many years, possibly to no avail, is a very small thing relative to many other things one might wish to do with one's life, indeed so small that the requirement of universal suffrage, and more generally of political equality, could easily be overridden if deviance from it could sustainably yield a distribution of life chances more favourable to the worst off.

On a second and more persuasive interpretation, the reason why universal suffrage matters to justice, has nothing to do with the fair distribution of opportunities. Justice is here understood as being not only a distributive matter, but also a matter of equal respect, of equal dignity, of equal recognition. Once such a view is adopted – as I now believe it must be [3] – it seems that no just political system can deprive some categories of the right to vote or deliberately give some categories greater weight in the voting procedures. Or at least it cannot do so without a special justification consistent with equal dignity. As argued in some of the essays in this volume, it may be possible to justify, for example, an over-representation of smaller ethnic groups or of those most likely to care for the interest of the young or the unborn. Justice as dignity, however, is inconsistent with denying voting rights to some members of a society throughout their lives. On this basis, it can be said that no society can be just without being democratic for intrinsic and not just for instrumental reasons. I am now willing to say that, as Rawls no doubt was, but given the extreme thinness of this democratic constraint, this concession hardly shrinks the space within which the Rawls-Machiavelli programme can operate. Knowing that, for intrinsic reasons, a just polity must be a democracy leaves wide open the question of which, among the countless democratic setups, is, for instrumental reasons, the just one.

A second objection to the Rawls-Machiavelli programme challenges the philosophical arrogance it seems to entail. Who do we think we are, political philosophers, to feel entitled to decree what justice demands and shape democracy accordingly, rather than modestly let the democratic will determine what the content of justice should be? Political philosophers, and the institutional engineers they might inspire, are fortunately not in a position to despotically impose their personal conception of justice and the corresponding institutions. A democratic majority must decide. But this must not stop political philosophers from telling that majority what it should decide and why, including as regards institutions that will modify its own functioning and lead

---

2.   Very roughly characterized in this way, a conception of distributive justice of this sort will be assumed throughout. A specific version of it is articulated and defended in Van Parijs (1995).

3.   In Van Parijs (2011: chapters 4–5), I make room for this dimension, absent from Van Parijs (1995), in order to tackle what I regard as the trickiest aspect of 'linguistic injustice'.

it to take decisions different from what it otherwise would. As argued at some length in connection with intergenerational justice (see Chapter 3), this task is not self-contradictory, or possible only when it is not useful. But for it to make sense, the conception of justice to which it appeals must be defensible with arguments that embody an equal respect for each citizen's conception of the good life and an equal concern for their interests. This is the case for the conception of justice as 'real freedom for all' and other conceptions in the liberal-egalitarian family to which appeal will be made throughout. No reason, therefore, to shy away from arguing for bold justice-inspired institutional reforms and trying to persuade political actors to go for them. This is not a manifestation of philosophical hubris. This is an essential part of what our societies and our world can expect from their political philosophers and from the latter's active interaction with a broad range of social scientists.

With short-sighted, media-dominated and increasingly volatile electorates, with effective decision-making needing to operate on an ever larger scale, the sort of thinking illustrated in these essays is more important than ever. Rather than yielding to populist calls for 'more democracy', we shall have to think carefully about how the structure of collective decision at the various levels can be designed to best serve a conception of social justice defensible before all. However inchoate the present essays may be, I strongly believe that they are illustrative of an intellectual endeavour that must be intensified and amplified if a concern for social justice is to have a major impact on the future of our societies and of our world.

chapter two | justice and democracy: are they incompatible?

In February 1992, I was invited to give a talk on democracy at the University of Brussels' Seminar in European Political Theory. I had just published a book whose title was a question, 'What is a Just Society?' (Van Parijs 1991), and I had just completed the last full draft of another book, whose title summarized my answer to that question: 'Real Freedom for All' (Van Parijs 1995). Hence, I focused naturally on the relationship between democracy and justice. In the process, I gave a first rough formulation to the central thesis of this set of essays, i.e. the view that democratic institutions should be treated as sheer servants of social justice. This view was inspired, in particular, by reflection on an intriguing feature of the Indian Union's impressive political system.

ॐ

It happened some months ago, in a peculiar village on the banks of the Volga. After a long series of toasts at the end of the meal to mark the completion of the Summer School in which I had participated, a man in his sixties, Professor of Philosophy at the Academy of Sciences and active collaborator of the Gorbachev Foundation, came up to me. 'You are Belgian', he said to me and had I been Canadian or Swiss, or even Spanish he would doubtless have spoken much the same. 'You know that for us, living in the former Soviet Union, Belgium represents something important. Because it constitutes a rare example of a multi-national state which has succeeded. At the Gorbachev Foundation we were and remain very attached to the Soviet Union, not because it was soviet but because it was a union. And we believe that only such a union can guarantee not just an effective protection of the minorities within its diverse regions, but also a higher degree of solidarity between its more prosperous and its poorer regions'.

Listening to him speak, I felt myself becoming more and more embarrassed (as no doubt I would too, had I been Canadian) thinking of the most recent vicissitudes in the chronic and ever-present disputes which characterise the multi-national state which he believed was so successful. At this point, I was thinking in particular of the demand to secede from the national social security system that had been forcefully made by a collection of Flemish cultural organisations. According to these organisations, each of the two peoples which make up the Belgian state should have the right to fashion, according to its own preferences and with its own resources, all interpersonal transfers, and it was thus urgent to put an end to the current system which transferred each year from Flanders (Dutch speaking, more prosperous and more populated) to Wallonia (French speaking, less prosperous and less populated) from 3 to 4 per cent of their respective Gross Domestic Products (GDP).[1]

The connection between these two examples (and a handy point of departure for this essay) is that both the dislocation of the USSR and the possible breaking up of the Belgian social security system move us away from implementing a conception of justice that involves a strong solidarity across the frontiers between peoples, while at the same time - rightly - appealing to a concern with achieving more democracy. For a people's right to determine its fate and to fashion its social policies in its own way is closely linked with what is customarily meant by the ideal of democracy. This double example thus enables me to sketch the thesis that I will try in a moment to substantiate by using two further illustrations: contrary to the misleading impressions

---

1. Close to two decades later (2011), the federal social security system is still in place and the overall size of the inter-regional transfers from the Flemish Region to the Walloon Region (and now also to the Brussels Region) has increased further, but is expected to shrink, mainly as a result of faster ageing of the Flemish population.

conveyed by political rhetoric, the relation between democracy and justice, very far from expressing a pre-established harmony, is on the contrary highly problematic.

1. WHICH JUSTICE, WHICH DEMOCRACY?

Before going any further with these illustrations, I must define what I mean here by justice and what I will call democracy. As I believe not only in the virtues of Ockam's razor, but even more in those of a conceptual trimmer – I hate fat concepts into which one sinks and becomes entangled – I will offer in both cases a deliberately simple, even simplistic, definition. I will define democracy as the combination of majority rule, universal suffrage and free voting. Of course, each of the elements of this definition requires further specification. But since my argument is largely independent of their exact characterization, I will not dwell on this semantic matter, except to stress that this is a purely procedural definition of democracy: what makes a society democratic is that public decisions are (ultimately) taken according to a procedure which satisfies the three conditions mentioned, and not that these decisions are conducive to some specific substantive result.

Further, I will define justice as the maximinning of material conditions, possibly subject to satisfying certain constraints, such as respect for fundamental liberties. What makes a society just, in other words, is that thanks to its institutions the conditions of the least advantaged among its members are made (lastingly) better than what would have happened if other institutions (satisfying the same constraints) had been chosen. In this characterisation of justice, I deliberately use the indeterminate notion of material condition, which can be specified for example in terms of income, potential income, wealth, standard of living, endowments, resources, capabilities, social and economic advantages, etc. For simplicity, however, I will suppose here that net monetary income constitutes an adequate index of this material condition. It is the maximin, applied to this variable, which constitutes the criterion of justice. However, an argument analogous to the one presented here applies *a fortiori* to more egalitarian conceptions of justice (that is, to conceptions which imply that a worsening of the condition of the worst-off can lead to more justice if it produces a greater equality of conditions), and also, though more weakly, to more aggregative conceptions of justice (that is, to conceptions which imply that a worsening of the condition of the worst-off can lead to more justice providing it gives rise to an improvement in the average situation). The maximin will consequently be used here as a privileged member of a larger family of criteria of distribution.

Even if one takes account of these caveats, the conception of justice put forward here remains particular and controversial. On the one hand, it is a liberal conception of justice, in the sense that it makes no appeal, in deciding what is just, to some particular conception of the good life; instead, it is intended to be compatible with equal respect for the various conceptions of the good life which co-exist within our pluralist societies. This first limitation is scarcely a problem, in the sense that the great majority of contemporary conceptions of justice are also liberal in this sense. But the conception of justice proposed here is not simply liberal. It is also solidaristic, i.e. it requires an equal concern for all citizens, an equal consideration of the interests of all members of society. Solidaristic conceptions contrast with entitlement conceptions, which regard justice as nothing other than the absence of any violation of individual natural rights, presumed to exist prior to all social institutions[2]

The choice of a solidaristic perspective – and in particular of the maximin of material conditions adopted here as its most plausible interpretation – can be justified in at least two ways. First of all, along with the conceptions of Rawls, Sen, Dworkin, and many others, the conception of justice to which I am personally committed is liberal-solidaristic in the sense indicated; it is thus natural that, in my thinking about the relations between justice and democracy, I should pay this interpretation a privileged attention. In addition, it is also intrinsically more interesting to explore the relation between democracy and solidaristic justice than the relation between democracy and justice as entitlement. For according to those who support the latter conception, democracy most often constitutes an obvious threat for justice, understood as respect for pre-defined individual rights, and their whole institutional strategy consists in strictly limiting the exercise of democratic power, sometimes to the point of practically annihilating it, so as to guarantee to the individual protection against the oppression by the majority. That there are strong tensions between democracy and this sort of justice is nothing to be surprised at, and has moreover been forcefully emphasized by numerous authors[3]. But when by contrast justice is conceived as equal concern for all members of society, would we not expect that democracy (in the sense indicated above), by according to each an equal weight in the outcomes of voting procedures, supplies justice with a steadfast ally? We shall see that this is not so, and that between solidaristic justice and democracy the presumption of a pre-established harmony will not withstand analysis[4].

2.　Van Parijs (1991, chapter 10) articulates and discusses more systematically the various families of conceptions of justice summarily characterised here.

3.　The locus classicus is Hayek (1960, chapter 7), which cites some earlier formulations of this tension between democracy and liberalism by Jose Ortega y Gasset, Hans Kelsen and others.

4.　If the definition of solidaristic justice were to include the equal distribution to all of the right to

2. MAXIMED VERSUS MAXIMIN

To understand a first tension between democracy and justice as defined here, let us begin by supposing that democracy operates through an electoral system in which two parties confront each other trying to obtain a majority which will permit them to govern; that the voters are motivated by their personal self-interest, itself exclusively determined by the level of their income; that they are costlessly and perfectly informed of the implications of the programmes of both parties and hence that they vote for the party whose programme maximises their income; that the only question to be settled is the fixing, between zero and 100 per cent of the flat rate of taxation upon incomes that will be used to finance an equal unconditional basic income paid to everyone; and that the total of incomes is not influenced, even after a time lag, by the level of that rate.

In this extremely simplified model, where are the dynamics of democracy leading? The answer is clear: everything depends on the respective levels of the median income and of the mean income[5]. If the median voter – the one whose vote is required to obtain just over 50 per cent of votes and whose preferences are therefore decisive – earns a gross income greater than the mean income, each one of these two parties will have an interest in proposing a zero rate of tax, and thus a distribution of net incomes identical to the distribution of gross incomes. For all strictly positive rates will leave the median voter with a net income closer to the mean income, and thus smaller than what he would receive in the case of a zero tax. If by contrast the median voter earns a gross income smaller than the mean income, each of the two parties will have an interest in proposing a tax rate of 100 per cent, and thus a strictly egalitarian distribution of net incomes, since for all rates below that the median voter would receive a smaller net transfer. The rate of 100 per cent is of course also – in both cases – the rate for which the smallest incomes are maximised. Now, one universal feature of the distribution of gross incomes in capitalist countries is that it is skewed upward, so that the mean income lies beyond, and often well beyond, the median income. It is therefore the second of the above-mentioned cases that is relevant. In the context of the model described in the preceding paragraph (and represented in Figure 2.1), therefore, there

---

vote and freedom of speech – as is the case in Rawls (1971), for example – it is clear that this tension would vanish (a non-democratic society would be unjust as a matter of definition), or rather that it would have to be reformulated as an internal tension between different components of justice as equal concern. (See pp 2–3 above for a brief discussion of this possibility.)

5.   This section is of course inspired by (the most elementary version of) the economic theory of democracy, whose origins go back to Downs (1957). See, for example, Ordeshook (1986) for a survey of the literature.

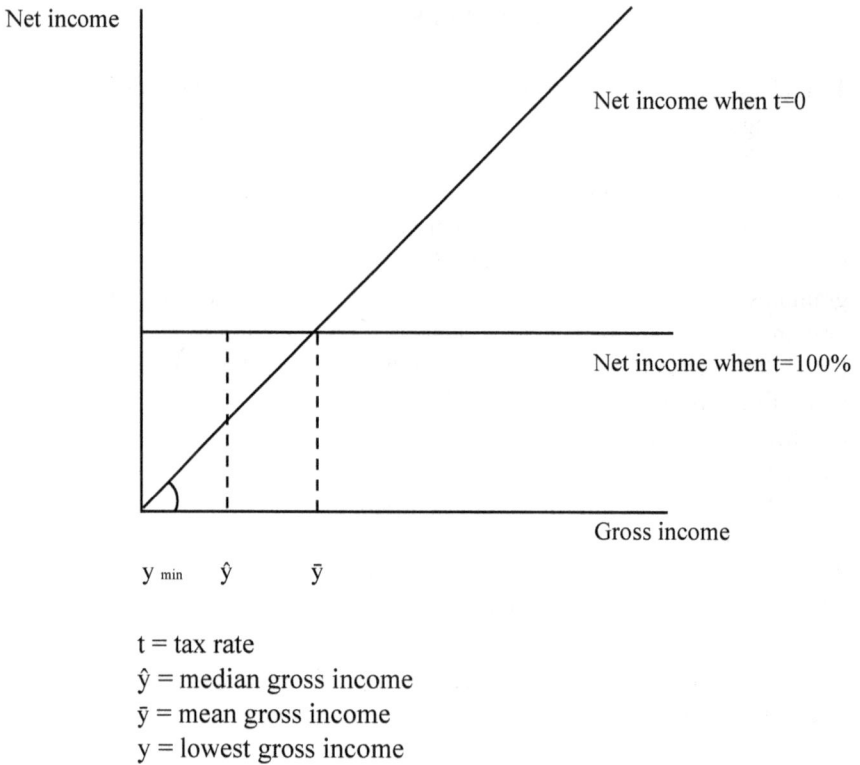

t = tax rate
ŷ = median gross income
ȳ = mean gross income
y = lowest gross income

Figure 2.1: Net incomes when gross incomes are assumed to be insensitive to taxation

is no tension between what justice requires and where democracy leads. The maximisation of the median income, secured by the democratic process, coincides with the maximisation of the minimum income, which is demanded by justice as equal concern for the condition of all.

The model of Figure 2.1, however, rests on the very restrictive assumption that the total income yielded is in no way affected, even in the long term, by the manner in which that income is distributed. Even when fully anticipated by the economic agents, the payment to all of an unconditional basic income absorbing the whole disposable income, for example, would not diminish one's eagerness to seek a job, to muster effort, to save or to make risky investments, nor the capacity of talented persons to exercise their talents. When one abandons that highly unrealistic assumption to take into account the dynamic effects of taxes and transfers, the harmony between justice and democracy breaks down. True, a tax of 100 per cent still raises both the minimum income and the median income to the level of the mean income. But the mean

Net income

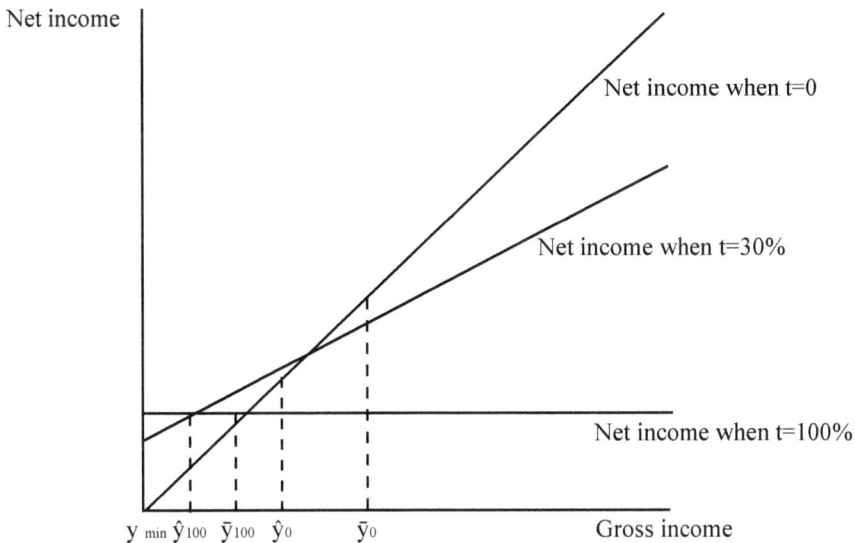

Net income when t=0

Net income when t=30%

Net income when t=100%

y_{min} $\hat{y}_{100}$ $\bar{y}_{100}$ $\hat{y}_0$ $\bar{y}_0$ Gross income

t = tax rate

$\bar{y}_0$ = mean gross income when t=0

$\hat{y}_0$ = median gross income when t=0

$\bar{y}_{100}$ = mean gross income when t=100%

$\hat{y}_{100}$ = median gross income when t=100%

y_{min} = lowest gross income

Figure 2.2: Net incomes when gross incomes are assumed to be negatively affected by taxation (example)

income (gross or net) with a tax of 100 per cent is no longer equal to what it would be in the absence of any tax. It has every chance of being considerably smaller, and even smaller than the net median income and the net minimum income would be for lower rates of taxation. Neither a concern for winning the favours of the median voter nor a concern for serving the interests of the least advantaged would therefore lead to advocating a tax rate of 100 per cent.

Moreover, and this is most important for our topic, there is now no reason why these two concerns would lead to selecting the same rate of taxation. Figure 2.2 shows three hypothetical curves that represent the distribution of net income corresponding to tax rates of zero, 30 and 100 per cent, when the dynamic effects (ignored in Figure 2.1) are taken into account. We can see there that the mean income (and thus the total) is slightly smaller when the rate is 30 per cent than when it is zero, and considerably smaller when it is 100 per cent. Of the three rates, however, it is still 100 per cent which is the best from the point of view of maximin, as the positive effect on the minimum income of the equalization (when passing from 30 to 100 per cent) more than compensates the negative effect of the reduction in aggregate income. From the point of view of the median income, by contrast, the opposite is true, and 30 per cent is consequently the preferred rate. The order of preference corresponding to the two points of view thus ceases to coincide, and there is no longer any reason to expect that the optimal rate of taxation will be the same according to the two criteria. In the situation partially described in Figure 2.2, for example, it is quite possible that the median income would be maximised for a tax rate of 25 per cent, while the minimal income would be maximised for a rate of 75 per cent. The reassuring convergence between the maximed of democracy and the maximin of justice has well and truly disappeared.

Of course, even after having relaxed the assumption that aggregate income is insensitive to the rate of taxation, the model still remains strongly unrealistic. The parties may be many and their electoral programmes multidimensional, the tax may be progressive and the transfers strongly differentiated, the personal interest of the voters may be far from reducing to the level of their net income, and their perception of the impact of the various platforms from the point of view of that personal interest may be burdened by a high level of error and/or uncertainty. Lifting these assumptions, however, considerably complicates things, without doing much to raise hopes of abolishing, or even attenuating, the divergence that was pointed out. Quite to the contrary, in removing at least some of the most unrealistic assumptions, we can expect a further deepening of the gulf that separates the actual functioning of our democracies from the realisation of justice as maximin.

Thus, if one takes account of the fact that it is necessary to make the party and its candidates known to the voters, that one must convince them that the electoral platform of the party is closer to their interests than that of its opponents, and sufficiently so to make it worth the trouble to get out to vote, and especially if one takes account of the fact that to do all that effectively requires a lot of money, then our assumption of the income maximisation of the median voter becomes clearly less plausible than the rival assumption of the income maximisation of the owner of the median dollar, as a predictor of the electoral platform of the parties. And in that case, we do not even need to appeal to the dynamic considerations discussed above for the gulf between maximed and maximin to deepen. The (gross) median dollar, indeed, has every chance of hiding in the pocket of a voter whose gross income not lower but far higher than the mean income. In this case, consequently, and even excluding (as in Figure 2.1) all negative effects of taxation on the aggregate income, the democratic dynamic leads, under our simplified assumptions, to selecting a zero rate of taxation, and thus one that lies as far as possible from a rate of

100 per cent which, under our assumptions, maximin requires one to choose[6].

Whether we deviate from the overly simplified initial model by one or the other of these two roads – by bringing in dynamic considerations or economic power – the pre-established harmony between justice and democracy obviously evaporates. Instead, there emerges a profound tension, to which I shall return in a moment. But before that, I would like quickly to discuss a second tension, quite different from the first.

3. DEMOCRACY AGAINST MIGRATION

Let us apply a conception of justice of the type adopted here to the world level. It is clear that the disparities of condition related to being a citizen of one nation rather than another constitute massive injustices according to such a conception. How can they be reduced? Hesitation is out of place: abolish the borders that hinder the free movement of capital towards the poorest countries and the free migration of workers towards the richest countries. Is this what democracy leads us to? It is certainly not what a brief glimpse of the evolution of the political fate of migrations over the course of the last century would urge us to think[7].

When international disparities began to widen because of the emergence of industrial society, the capitalist nations were far from being democratic. Politically, neither the influx of foreign workers nor the exodus of capital was then a problem. The bourgeoisie, who exercised a direct control over political power, had little to fear and much to gain, from the influx of a cheap and eager work force, which they did not even risk having to put up with in their fashionable suburbs. The borders, consequently, could remain wide open. It was only after the first world war that the requirement to obtain an entry visa, which made its appearance in the course of the nineteenth century, was generalised across the industrial world. Why suddenly this general closing of borders, new to the history of mankind? Essentially because of the

---

6. Among the other complications worth pondering about in the present context is the gap between the actual and the expected impact of various electoral programmes. If the voters are typically the victims of a static illusion, which makes them neglect the dynamic impact of the redistributions, that are being contemplated, does the median voter not have a tendency to promote, in the belief that it serves his personal interest, redistributive policy which serves much more the interests of voters poorer than him? Conceivably. But isn't instead the tendency nowadays – as a result of the spectacular collapse of European communism but also because of the uncertainty induced by an ever deeper immersion in the world market – towards an overestimation by the electorate of the negative consequences of strongly solidaristic policies?

7. This section is based on several of the contributions contained in Barry and Goodin (eds) (1992).

conjunction of two factors: first, the deepening of the inequality of conditions on a world scale which derives from the expansion of capitalism and
the demographic and ecological developments more or less directly linked
to it; second, the growth in the political power of the working class and its
organisations, closely related to the progressive implementation of universal
suffrage. In short, the closing of borders was the joint product of capitalism
and democracy. While capitalism generates migratory pressures, democracy
provides those who would suffer from these migrations in both their incomes
and living environment, with the ability to stem them.

If this very stylised outline is (albeit approximately) correct, it is the very
extension of democracy that constitutes the main obstacle along one road–
perhaps the only significant one – towards more justice on the world scale.
Here, too, we are far from a pre-established harmony between justice and
democracy, since it is the very deepening of democracy which creates an increasingly robust obstacle to the realisation of justice as maximin of conditions at the world level. And the spread of democracy to all the nations of the
world – which is different, of course, from the advent of a world democracy –
will not diminish, but indeed will contribute to, the strength of that obstacle[8].

4. DEMOCRATIC ENGINEERING

Once aware of these two, quite different, tensions, what conclusions can we
draw? I shall propose two: one rather crude, the other more refined.

If we cannot assume a pre-established harmony between justice and democracy, if instead there exists between them – and for deep-rooted reasons –
some acute conflicts, we must ask which of the two it is preferable to sacrifice.
My reply to that question is clear: let us stick to justice, and sacrifice democracy. Indeed, the latter is not part of an ideal that it is important to pursue[9]. It

---

8. According to this analysis, while capitalism and democracy are jointly at the source of the closing
of borders, it is democracy, not capitalism, which is (here) in conflict with justice as maximin.
For while it is capitalism that generates a very unequal development, it is democracy that blocks
a wider distribution of the fruits of that development through migration. This analysis of the
relations between capitalism, migration and global justice is of course still very schematic. See
Van Parijs (1993a, chapter 7) and Van Parijs (2007a) for somewhat less summary treatments.

9. This purely instrumentalist conception of democracy is of course far from being new. One finds it
for example in Schumpeter (1943: 242): 'Democracy is a political method ... incapable of being
an end in itself, irrespective of what decisions it will produce under given historical circumstances. And this must be the starting point of any attempt at defining it.'; in Hayek (1960: 106,
117): 'However strong the general case for democracy, it is not an ultimate or absolute value and
must be judged by what it will achieve. It is probably the best method of achieving certain ends,
but it is not an end in itself ... The danger is that we will mistake a means for ensuring justice for

only constitutes an institutional instrument which it is legitimate to deviate from *if* the pursuit of the ideal requires it. I stress the 'if' because while more democracy may take us further from justice, less democracy (need it be said?) does not necessarily bring us closer to it[10].

This first conclusion is without doubt somewhat too crude. Perhaps it treats the venerable theme of democracy too swiftly. But above all, it does not address the really important question. For as regards the conception of justice adopted here, it is difficult to see how a non-democratic procedure (one which does not satisfy the three minimal conditions set forth) could offer the best guarantees. This does not necessarily hold for other conceptions of justice. Thus, the American neo-liberal economist Henry Hazlitt (1968) proposed, in order to dramatically weaken the electoral pressure to increase social transfers, withdrawing the right to vote from all citizens in debt with respect to the state: the recipients of social benefits could only regain the right to vote when they had paid more in taxes and contributions than they had received in benefits[11]. This negation of universal suffrage no doubt reduces the tension between the 'democratic' process and justice as Hazlitt and other neo-liberals understand the latter, but it further widens the gap which separates that process from justice as maximin. To pursue the latter effectively, it is highly unlikely that we need ever renounce one or other of the three conditions which define democracy, and most probable on the contrary that rigorously respecting them – notably by extending the right to vote to immigrants and lifting administrative obstacles to the effective participation of the least advantaged in elections – constitutes a crucial precondition to all significant progress in that direction. The most relevant question is thus not whether justice requires democracy in the sense indicated. It is rather to know which, among the numerous set-ups for collective decision-making which satisfy the three minimal conditions, is the most capable of ensuring the implementation

---

justice itself'; and, in most systematic fashion, in Dworkin (1989), who distinguishes detached conceptions of democracy, which justify it without any reference to its consequences, and dependent conceptions, which propose by contrast a consequentialist justification of democratic institutions. Even diversely interpreted, justice constitutes only one of the ends by reference to which dependent (or instrumental) conceptions of democracy can conceivably be specified. Peace and growth, for example, constitute further possibilities. But in Dworkin as in Hayek, it is by reference to justice that democracy is made instrumental, as it is here.

10. This is why, as Norman (1990: 119) suggests, it may be politically expedient, in circumstances where it can contribute to discrediting them, to strike at some undesirable reforms by denouncing their anti-democratic nature, even if the basis of their undesirability has nothing to do with their not being democratic

11. One finds a sketch of the same idea in Hayek (1960: 105) where he notes that 'it is also possible for reasonable people to argue that the ideals of democracy would be better served if, say, all the servants of government or all recipients of public charity were excluded from the vote.'

of the conception of justice adopted here.

To resolve, or at least markedly reduce, the first of the two tensions discussed above, for example, it is essential that the set-up chosen should permit the emergence of a public debate through which all the parties concerned can make their positions and arguments heard and above all influence, from the sole fact that they are known to listen, the contents of the declarations and the tenor of the decisions. Only the existence and the liveliness of such a debate can generate and ceaselessly regenerate throughout society a sense of justice that conforms to the conception of justice adopted here. Moreover, they alone are capable of making democracy an institutional mechanism which enables this sense of justice to fashion the laws that society gives itself and, through those laws, its actual functioning. Not only does democracy thus institutionalised appear in this case as a promising means of pursuing the realisation of a solidaristic conception of justice. But it is very difficult to find any other plausible basis for the hope of significantly bringing the way in which material resources are distributed between the members of our societies significantly closer to justice as maximin.

The general thesis that I have thus tried to formulate, illustrate and thereby support, is that, in reflecting and acting on democratic institutions – the electoral system, referenda, decentralisation, the balance of powers, the recruitment, remuneration and rotation of elected officials, the financing of election campaigns, etc. – what is at stake is not the elaboration and pursuit of a democratic ideal which would make sense in itself. The aim should not be, for example, in the name of democracy as an end in itself, to design an electoral system which will produce an assembly as 'representative' of the people as possible, statistically speaking, nor to build a system of collective decision making which will produce choices as close as possible to the 'popular will', i.e. to the true preferences of the majority of citizens. No: when in search of optimal combinations – between independence and submission of the elected to their electoral base for example, or between the law of the majority and constitutional constraints, or between governmental stability and the expression of minorities – democratic engineering should not be guided by an autonomous democratic ideal – equality of power between all citizens, the implementation of the general will, etc. – but by an ideal of justice, in relation to which any democratic ideal that one might wish to formulate constitutes, at best, a sheer instrument.

This thesis and the contrast which underlies it may be usefully clarified by another illustration, very different from those introduced so far. In 1931 there took place in London the second Round Table Conference to decide the political future of India. Among the participants figured B.R. Ambedkar, a brilliant lawyer and the political leader of the Untouchables. With the support of the British, it was agreed that the Untouchables would not participate in the general elections but choose their own representatives.[12] Gandhi was so incensed by this decision that he began a hunger strike. Ambedkar gave way and accepted a compromise – the Poona pact – whereby 148 seats were assigned to the Untouchables, but without dividing the electorates. In each one of the constituencies concerned – the number of which corresponds approximately to the proportion of Untouchables in the total population of India (15 per cent) – candidates from the Untouchable caste alone can stand, even though the latter constitutes, in each of these constituencies, only a minority of the population. In the other constituencies, the seats are in principle open to members of all the castes, although the Untouchables are *de facto* practically excluded from them (they currently occupy three out of a total of more than 400).

The system conceived at that time still functions more than half a century later. And the fact that it was preferred to Ambedkar's proposal probably constitutes one of the key factors behind the astonishing persistence of (formal) democracy in one of the planet's most crowded, vast, poor and divided countries. For the dynamic of the two electoral systems is profoundly different. If, in the context of the system actually adopted, a party wants to have a chance of capturing the seats reserved for the Untouchables, it is compelled to recruit from among the Untouchable elites and thus to fashion its electoral platform accordingly. Of course, such a system deprives the most radical among the Untouchables of parliamentary representation – which helps us understand the passionate disagreement between Ambedkar and Gandhi. But at the same time it is probably closely linked to the remarkable fact that, for a half century now, the Untouchables have been enjoying an astonishing range of measures of positive discrimination. Hence it does not seem absurd to conjecture that the system adopted has strongly contributed, not only to the stability of the democratic institutions, but also to the realisation of a solidaristic conception of justice[13].

The most general empirical hypothesis suggested by this analysis is that, from the point of view of the conception of justice which I am committed to, a democratic dynamic embracing all categories of the population – as is the case, with regard to the cleavage considered here, in India's current system – is preferable to the mixed dynamic that combines electoral competition within each category and power relations– in the best case, diplomacy – between the various categories, which would have prevailed in India if Ambedkar had car-

---

12. One solution of this type is apparently in force today for the four seats in New Zealand's Parliament that are reserved for the (geographically dispersed) Maoris (Nagel 1993: 11).

13. For further details and qualifications, see Deliège (1993) and Jaffrelot (1993).

ried the day[14]. This hypothesis may be true or false. But to know which is the most appropriate democratic set-up, it is this type of hypothesis that we must assess. Is it not anti-democratic to deprive the (non-untouchable) majority of the right of eligibility in the constituencies reserved for Untouchable candidates? It certainly is. But who cares? What matters is to evaluate objectively, in the light of the most relevant empirical evidence and theoretical analysis, the impact that can be expected, in terms of social justice, from the various possible set-ups.

5. GLOBALISING DEMOCRACY

This approach can easily be extended to the twofold example with which I began. When deciding whether we must keep a federal level or not and, if so, what powers must be attributed to it, what mode of political representation must be adopted there, etc., the question that must be asked – in the case of the ex-Soviet Union as in the case of Belgium (or Switzerland or Canada or Spain) – is not what would be most democratic. The important thing is rather to identify the distribution of powers which has the best chance of promoting the realisation, on the largest possible scale, of the conception of justice to which we are committed.

That task, needless to say, is difficult and complex, and it branches out rapidly into multiple sub-questions. With respect to this twofold example, I shall therefore do no more than express a (perhaps too) simple and (perhaps too) strong conviction that I have developed while casually observing the situation in Belgium and in Europe. It is that from the vantage of the conception of justice adopted here, it is essential that key decisions about the distribution of resources – and also about fundamental liberties[15] – should be taken by a federal

---

14. In the United States, it is gerrymandering, the ad hoc redrawing of electoral boundaries, which has been adopted to try to ensure a significant representation for scattered minorities (particularly Blacks) despite the first-past-the-post system. But this solution holds little attraction from the point of view of a solidaristic conception of justice – and no doubt contributes notably to explaining the pitiful performance of the richest nation on the planet in matters of social policy. As Douglas Rae (1993: 14) notes, the solution has as its inevitable side-effect that the number of members of Congress who have practically no Blacks in their constituencies is being maximized: 'it frees the majority of incumbents from anxiety about the needs and perceptions of African-Americans. Surely, this is not what we need if we are to achieve better and fairer outcomes nationally'.

15. As noted at the beginning, the maximinning of conditions can be subjected to the constraint of a strict respect for fundamental liberties. And a central task of democratic engineering – for example, in the choice between monist democracy, dualist democracy and rights foundationalism, to borrow Ackerman's terminology (1991) – will consequently consist in determining the optimal status and contents of constitutional protections. The hypothesis outlined here, concerning this

parliament whose members directly represent the citizens of the federation and not the federated entities, and where all would be done, for example at the level of the method of voting, of the constitution of parliamentary groups, of the relations with the media, etc., so that the decisive cleavages are more ideological than national[16]. The important thing, in other words, is that the dynamics be such that the policies adopted would not be a sheer compromise negotiated between the representatives of the various national components[17], but that they would be subjected to the constraint of having to be justified by way of arguments that appeal to the citizens of the whole federation[18]. What this conviction illustrates, once again, is the answer I am offering to the question posed in the title. If there is a compatibility between democracy and justice, it is not by virtue of a happily pre-established harmony between the two ideals. It can only be as a result of laborious, ingenious, sometimes frankly Machiavellian, institutional engineering, aiming not only to establish or to preserve democracy, but above all to select, among the innumerable democratic set-ups, those which have the best chance – sometimes still very feeble – of rendering our world a little more just – or at least a little less massively unjust – than it is today.

This holds in particular for the most resilient tension, illustrated by the example of migration, which confronts democracy at the level of nations (be it of all nations) and solidaristic justice at the world level. That this is indeed a tension which should arouse our concern is not unanimously admitted. For many argue that between justice within a nation and justice on the world scale, there is a radical difference. Whereas within one nation a solidaristic conception makes obvious sense, between the nations, on the other hand, justice only demands rules of international trade securing the equivalence of the goods exchanged, a fair division of the surplus of mutually advantageous coopera-

---

component of a complete conception of social justice, is that fundamental liberties have more chance of being adequately determined (by the standards of this conception) and effectively protected if that determination and that protection are carried out by a larger entity than if they are carried out by smaller and thus probably more homogeneous entities in racial, linguistic or religious terms.

16. In the same vein, the Indian example discussed in the preceding section suggests that if one day the European Community had to choose its President by direct elections, it might for example be advisable to impose each time (and by rotation) the member state(s) of which all the candidates must be citizens, with each European citizen of course each time enjoying the right to vote. (See section 5 of Chapter 5 .)

17. In the manner of the Council of Ministers of the European Community, of the Conference of Presidents of the Confederation of Independent States, or of the so-called 'dialogue of community to community' which sometimes threatens to short-circuit the national Parliament in Belgium.

18. The importance of this distinction between arguing and bargaining is usefully stressed by Jon Elster (2000) in the context of a comparative analysis of constitutional assemblies.

tion and an assistance in the case of famine or of catastrophe[19]. When applied to the twofold example just discussed and above all when extended to the case of migration, the point of view adopted here presupposes on the contrary that this dichotomy is illegitimate, that the solidaristic conception can legitimately apply across the borders of nations, and that if democratic institutions which are capable of lending credibility to such an extension do not exist, one should fight to put them in place. The only borders which constitute anything other than a temporary pause, imposed by pragmatic imperatives, in the progress of globalisation (as opposed to sheer diffusion) of democracy and, thereby, of a solidaristic conception of justice, are the borders of mankind itself.

The realisation of this vision implies neither drastic centralisation nor massive uniformity. Providing systematic use is made of the principle of subsidiarity, the realisation of a solidaristic conception of justice and, therefore, the putting into place of institutions which make the latter possible are, on the contrary, ever more essential to protect the diversity of cultures against the pressure towards uniformity which stems from the growing hold of the world market. For a solidaristic vision of global justice does not require that one should rush to break down frontiers and thus to allow the migratory flux to rapidly erode differences. That would be a very crude way of contributing to the world maximin of conditions on a world scale. Much as the necessity of tackling the causes of vagrancy played a crucial role in the pre-history of the Welfare state, i.e. of those institutions which aimed to implement equal concern at the national level, so it is from the need to stabilize the vagrants of our era, the transnational migrants, that we can expect a decisive impact in the establishment of the institutions required to realise something like equal concern at the world level. And, just as in the context of individual nations, such institutions should include a system of transfers as individualized, as unconditional and as high as possible.

Is this utopian? Of course it is – and this is precisely the central theme of this essay – as long as appropriate democratic institutions have not been established. But isn't the very establishment of such institutions utopian? Is it not already too ambitious to want simply to preserve, deepen and generalise democracy within nations? Is a multinational democracy, as John Stuart Mill (1861: chapter 16) believed, not bound to remain, if it ever comes into existence, extremely precarious? Perhaps so. And in this case the tension between justice and democracy illustrated by the example of migration will persist in all its acuteness. World justice and democracy will always be incompatible.

---

19. One finds some variants of this view, for example, in the above-mentioned document by Flemish cultural organisations which I discuss in Van Parijs (1993b), but also in the formulation that Rawls (1993, 1999) gave to the extension to the 'law of peoples' of his conception of justice as fairness. See also the discussions in Rawls and Van Parijs (2003) and in Van Parijs (2007a).

But perhaps not. For all of us, people of the Earth, often through grief and conflict, are becoming ever more aware that we share the same surface to walk and dwell on; that we live, directly or indirectly, from the same natural resources; that our wastes are discharged into the same air and water; that our goods and services are contending in the same markets; in short that we are bound, for better and worse, by an ever tighter interdependence from which there is no escape but through further involvement. If barbarism and chaos are to be avoided, this can only be through the establishment, no doubt laborious and meandering, of true democratic institutions beyond the national level.

Hence, the failings and difficulties of multi-national states should not make us give up. Instead, they should educate and guide us. For the sake of the man who came up to me on the bank of the Volga and for the sake of many others across the world, what needs doing today is try differently what has not succeeded and dare to try what has not yet been. What is at stake here is, for sure, the reconciliation of democracy and justice. It is perhaps also our very survival.

chapter three | contestatory democracy versus real freedom

In February 1997, a major conference on democracy was organized at Yale University (see Shapiro and Hacker-Gordon (eds) 1999a, 1999b). I was invited to comment on Philip Pettit's contribution and was pleased to have this opportunity to reflect, in connection with the themes of the conference, on the relationship between his 'republicanism' and my own 'real libertarian' political philosophy. After clarifying the difference between our respective central notions of 'real freedom' and freedom as 'non-domination', I argued that the plea for contestatory democracy which follows from a concern for freedom as non-domination implies a presumption in favour of a level of government less and less able to pursue effectively the realization of an egalitarian conception of social justice.

ॐ

Since the mid-seventies, the United States and a number of other industrial-ized countries have experienced a dramatic increase in income inequality and a steep fall in the standard of living for the lower layers of the income distri-bution. These trends are, in a plausible sense, the outcome of greater freedom. They are also, in an even more plausible sense, a deadly threat to the freedom of many. To tackle this threat, to reverse the underlying trends, democracy is essential, but not any form of democracy. Philip Pettit's (1999) contribution to this discussion is helpful, not just because it helps clarify the conceptual relationship between freedom and democracy, but because it also makes us think about how to reshape our democracies to preserve or create as truly free a society as is possible. I warmly welcome this, as political philosophy has never been for me an idle game played for the pleasure of making subtle distinctions and smart points, but a crucial part of the urgent task of thinking what needs to be done to make our societies and our world less unjust than they are, or even simply to avert disaster.

I fully agree with Pettit that making our democracies more contestatory is urgently required, not as an aim in itself, but in order to promote freedom. Yet, I also believe that making them as contestatory as possible would, under present circumstances, handicap their pursuit of the ideal of freedom in the most defensible interpretation of that ideal. To explain, some preliminary con-ceptual clarification is in order.

1. THREE DISTINCTIONS

On the freedom side, Pettit's key distinction is between freedom as non-in-terference and freedom as non-domination, also called republican freedom. How does this distinction relate to the old (and often confusing) distinction between negative and positive freedom? How does it relate to my own favou-rite distinction between formal and real freedom, at which Pettit (1999: 167 fn1) briefly hints. If positive freedom is interpreted (as it is by Pettit 1999: 164) either as psychological self-mastery or as political participation, it defi-nitely lies outside the scope of both Pettit's and my distinction. Both of these interpretations rather operate within the domain of negative freedom, broadly understood as not being prevented from doing what one may wish to do. But they differ in the cut they make between different characterizations of what counts as freedom-restricting.

Though a variety of negative freedom in the broad sense just stated, *re-publican freedom* is crucially distinct from negative freedom in the narrower sense of absence of interference, i.e. absence of intentional coercion or ob-struction. Republican freedom is the absence of domination, i.e. of 'the capacity to interfere on an arbitrary basis' or 'without regard to [the interferee's perceived interests]' (Pettit 1999:165). There can be domination without interference (when the capacity is left unused) and there can be interference without domination (when it is not arbitrary).

Republican freedom, so defined, is not strictly more demanding than formal freedom, characterized along standard libertarian lines as the existence of a consistent and well enforced system of property rights which incorporates universal self-ownership. This is not because any law is coercive and 'coercion, under standard views, is a form of interference' (Pettit 1999: 168). Property-rights-protecting legislation is not formal-freedom-restricting even if it is, in this plausible sense, coercive. The reason is rather that there can conceivably be non-arbitrary, and hence non-dominating, government interference in breach of the citizens' self-ownership, for example in the form of conscription for the defence of the republic. The extent to which a concern with republican freedom will fall short of guaranteeing formal freedom to all is crucially dependent on what counts as non-arbitrary power, or power that is 'forced to track the interests and judgements of those on whom they are imposed' (Pettit 1999: 170). And so is *a fortiori* the extent to which the promotion of republican freedom can be relied upon to give citizens, at the highest level enjoyable by all, the *real* freedom – the actual possibility, encompassing the means and not just the right – to do what they may wish to do.[23] Conversely, no degree of formal or real freedom for all citizens entails, by definition, that they enjoy republican freedom.

2. CONVERGENCE?

In the light of these distinctions, it is clear that the ideal of freedom is conceptually different, depending on whether it is interpreted in terms of republican freedom for all or in terms of real freedom for all (in a sense that incorporates but does not reduce to formal freedom). But this conceptual distinction would be of negligible practical importance if a strong convergence could safely be expected between the requirements of the ideal under both interpretations. Whether this is the case hinges on substantive implications of the key criterion of 'non-arbitrary power' which enters the definition of republican freedom. The quickest way of spelling them out is to turn to the link Pettit's (1999) central thesis establishes between republican freedom and contestatory democracy.

---

23. This rough characterization will suffice for present purposes. For a detailed discussion of real freedom and its metric, see Van Parijs (1995: chapters 2–4) and the essays by Brian Barry, Peter Vallentyne, Robert van der Veen and Andrew Williams in Reeve and Williams (2003).

When freedom is understood as non-domination, democracy, understood as collective rule, is neither necessarily inimical to freedom, nor necessarily freedom-friendly. But it can be made more freedom-friendly as a matter of necessity, according to Pettit, by being shaped on a contestatory model. The latter is one of two models of democracy that could block, or at least sharply reduce, the possibility of an elective democracy degenerating into collective tyranny, arbitrary power exercised by the collectivity over its members. The first and most straightforward of these models is *unanimitarian democracy*, which gives each citizen a veto on any public decision. But this model is of purely academic interest:

> The reason is that no vetoing scheme of things has the remotest chance of being instituted; it is a wholly infeasible mode of public decision-making. (Pettit 1999: 178).

The second model, *contestatory democracy*, does not share this defect. It consists in

> a procedure that would enable people, not to veto public decisions on the basis of their allowable, perceived interests, but to call them into question on such a basis [...] in a forum that they and others can all endorse as an impartial court of appeal'.

This model is far more feasible than the first one to the extent that, in actual fact, 'it empowers people in their assertion of their perceived interests, but does not set them up as dictators with an individual capacity to negate any public decision' (Pettit 1999: 180). Democracy is here defined not as government by the people (collectively) but as contestability by the people (distributively) and therefore as intrinsically freedom-friendly if freedom is defined as the absence of arbitrary power, which it is in the essence of contestability to undermine.[24]

Pettit (1999: 185–7) describes a number of illustrative features of how a contestatory model would work in practice. One crucial feature is 'the requirement that parliamentary democracy be deliberative and that governmental decisions should be generally open to inspection, justified by documented reasons.' To make contestation possible, legislation must take place in a context of debate to which all sides are represented, and only those reasons which are acceptable in such a debate can be recognized as relevant.

---

24. I interpret the necessity of this connection as a conceptual rather than factual one. Pettit emphasizes the conceptual possibility of domination by private agents (and hence republican unfreedom) even under a fully contestatory democracy. But can anything establish the presence of political domination (and hence of politically generated republican unfreedom) apart from the observation of a departure from the procedures of contestatory democracy?

Pettit is not explicit about the set of socio-economic institutions that would be likely to emerge from such a process. But other theorists of deliberative democracy (e.g. Gutmann and Thompson 1996, Cohen 1997) have allowed themselves to sketch the substantive principles that can be expected to systematically underlie the resulting legislation. Unsurprisingly, the tracking of both the interests and the opinions of all turns out to plausibly lead, in a pluralist society, to liberal-egalitarian principles involving both a strong protection of fundamental liberties and a strongly egalitarian (be it maximin) distribution of the means each is given to pursue her conception of the good life. Once the notion of an acceptable or compelling reason is duly specified and a number of uncontroversial empirical facts are taken into account, it seems that any well-functioning contestatory democracy should gently converge on a set of institutions that will express adequate concern for all its citizens' formal and real freedom, and the contestatory model of democracy should therefore be just about as congenial to the real-libertarian as to the republican-libertarian.

3. A TRADE OFF?

This expectation of a convergence is comforting, but it should not blind us to the possibility of a conflict between the optimal realization of republican freedom and the pursuit of the greatest real freedom for all. Let me illustrate this possibility with one example, that is particularly close, for reasons that will soon be obvious, to some of my current concerns. Pettit (1999: 182) mentions that there are cases in which contestatory democracy will hardly be less paralysing than giving everyone a veto:

> There are many social divides such that people on different sides will not be willing to have their rival views on certain issues decided by any independent process. [...] In such cases, the promotion of freedom as non-domination will require us to look at possibilities of secession for one or another side, or to explore the prospect of separate jurisdictions for the different groups, or to think about a federal structure in which each gets its own territory.

In particular, in a linguistically heterogeneous polity, with limited or sometimes no knowledge of each other's language, there is a strong fear that the weaker voices will not be heard, that the debates and arguments that hold sway in the minority-language areas will simply be ignored.

In recent negotiations on the future shape of the European Union's institutions, this was for example one of the reasons given by the Swedish government in favour of maintaining a veto right at the Council of Ministers for each member state, however small its population: the purpose is not, it was argued, that minority interests should enjoy absolute protection but that arguments should be heard (see Gustavsson 1997: 7). As such a veto right is often paralyzing, some alternatives have been proposed that would precisely exemplify the move from a unanimitarian to a contestatory model, in the sense of enabling member states ' not to veto public decisions on the basis of their allowable, perceived interests, but to call them into question on such a basis and to trigger a review' (Pettit 1999: 180). For example, the 'alarm bell mechanism', which is already used in some federal systems, would enable a member state to get a decision suspended and reconsidered on another occasion when it can plausibly argue that some of its vital interests are at stake.[25]

Yet, in the light of the recent experience of a multilingual country such as my own, Belgium, it is overwhelmingly clear to me that a smoothly running contestatory democracy is far more difficult to achieve in a linguistically heterogeneous polity: the screening of proposals and arguments so that they are acceptable to every citizen, not just to those who happen to speak the speaker's language, the ability to get one's voice heard, to effectively scrutinize legislative and administrative processes and the disposition to accept verdicts as impartial are all systematically weakened in such a context. Republican freedom, therefore, is far safer in a unilingual republic, and if it were the overarching aim, I could not think of any persuasive argument in favour of preserving or developing multilingual states such as Belgium or the European Union.

But republican freedom is not the overarching aim. In my view, it is just an important means, not to something other than freedom, but to a conception of justice as maximin real freedom. And this aim may justify getting along with less republican freedom than could be durably achieved. In my example, dismantling the Belgian federal state so as to enable each of its linguistically more homogeneous components to achieve greater republican freedom would mean splitting up a common social security system that redistributes massively from richer to poorer areas. It would also mean conferring to the components a fiscal autonomy that would soon lead (for reasons exacerbated by the peculiar geographical situation of largely francophone Brussels surrounded by Flemish territory) to cut-throat fiscal competition and hence also far lower redistribution within each of the components. For the sake of real freedom for all, or any other substantive principle of justice, the scales at which one locates the democratic process, contestatory or otherwise, are of

---

25. For example, since 1970, Belgium's constitution gives each linguistic community the power to force reconsideration of a decision if three quarters of its parliamentary representation find it detrimental to its interests. See Dehousse (1994: 121–3) and Karmis and Gagnon (1996: 457–8.)

crucial importance. Nothing guarantees that the scales that such a conception of justice recommends that we select are also the ones that are optimal for the sake of republican freedom. When there is a conflict – as I believe there is in my example – the choice of scales should be made with a view to the sustainable achievement of justice, while doing one's best, on each of the selected scales, to make democracy as contestatory as possible.

4. STRUGGLES AHEAD

Let us return against this background to the growing inequalities which I mentioned at the beginning of this chapter. Should we simply accept them as the necessary correlates of economic freedom or of efficient incentive structures? I militantly believe that our concern for freedom, properly interpreted, should make us resist this pitiful shrinking of the agenda. We do not need to claim that reducing inequality would not affect incentives. There are strong efficiency-based arguments in favour of more equality, but many of them stress the effect on overall capacities (to become or remain healthy and skilled) rather than on incentives.[26] Moreover, even if there were a net cost in terms of overall growth, this would not need to make a fairer distribution of resources unachievable. Making democracy more contestatory is certainly part of the answer, for example, especially in the USA, by making the voices of the poor less inaudible compared to wealthy campaign sponsors.[27] Once the effects of this massive wealth bias will be under check, one can reasonably hope, for the sake of a fairer distribution of real freedom, that the US political system will have acquired the capacity to react to the crisis of the welfare state, not through running it down, through making it ever stingier and more selective, but through universalizing its provisions, for example as regards health care and child benefits.

But making democracy more contestatory, promoting republican freedom for all, is not enough. The growth of factor income inequality in advanced democracies is a deep-rooted trend. I am not sure much can or should be done to reverse it. But I do believe that much can and should be done to prevent this gross inequality from translating into net inequality, post-tax-and-transfer inequality in standards of living (in a broad sense that encompasses not

---

26. See e.g. Glyn and Miliband (eds) (1994) and Bowles and Gintis (1998).

27. The liberty-based constitutional argument that has so far blocked any attempt to impose significant limits on campaign spending provides a crystal-clear example of how a totally implausible notion of freedom can undermine the prospects of a free society, and there is now plenty of good argument around (e.g. Dworkin 1996 and Okin 1996), it seems to me, to blow up the constitutional blockage.

only consumption, but also security, environmental quality and participation in social and economic life). However, how much this 'much' is crucially depends on the democratic capacity to get hold of an increasingly concentrated economic rent in order to permanently distribute it widely across the whole population, not only in cash but also in the form of expenditure on education, public health, the environment, etc. This in turn depends on the extent to which the payers and recipients of this economic rent are able to play off against each other the redistributive polities. The easier and cheaper it is to move a commodity, a business, a deposit, a highly skilled worker's work place or residence, from one jurisdiction to another, the weaker the grip of the democratic will, contestatory or otherwise, on the resources that can help make freedom more real for all. In a context in which technological and institutional impediments to mobility keep melting, this prompts a strong case for limiting the fiscal autonomy of individual states in existing federations and for scaling down the fiscal autonomy of the nation-states in order to build up a supranational redistributive authority.

This sounds most freedom-unfriendly in at least three ways. It would bridle the collective freedom of each state. It would diminish the richer people's freedom to protect their wealth and incomes from what they regard as confiscatory taxation. And it would arguably depress the overall level of republican freedom, as important decision-making powers are moved away from the people's contestatory reach to a more centralized, less accountable level. Yet it is for the sake of freedom that we should move that way as fast as we can, for the sake of freedom as tangible, real freedom for all, the only freedom that matters to justice as such and for which the other freedoms I have discussed are sheer means.

chapter four | the children's vote and other attempts to secure intergenerational justice

'The median age of voters in Japan will reach 65 within the next ten years. We should seriously consider giving children a vote and having their parents use it on their behalf.' This proposal, briefly stated in a letter published by the Economist on January 1st, 2011 (Aoki 2011), is the sort of proposal I was keenly looking for during the term I spent as a Visiting Professor at Yale University in the Spring of 1998. I wanted to work out the implications of the approach to democracy sketched out in Chapters 2 and 3 by considering an aspect of social justice particularly tricky for democracy to handle: justice towards the generations who are too young to vote or as yet unborn.

Thanks to the University library's remarkable resources in various languages, part of the work involved turned out to consist in a fascinating scanning of the dustbin of the history of ideas, in search of proposals actually made to make democracy less oblivious of the just claims of the young and of future generations. Some of these proposals are ludicrous, such as the one that inspired the title under which this chapter was originally published ('The disfranchisement of the elderly and other attempts to secure intergenerational justice'). Other proposals are far less so, including the family of proposals that inspires the title I adopted for the present edition of the same text.

My (rather qualified) defence of such a proposal had one unexpected consequence. In March 2004, I was invited to discuss the idea at some length on Italian TV, along with Philippe Schmitter, Elisabeta Galeotti and the prorector of the Catholic University of Milan, Luigi Campiglio, who subsequently published a book in its defence (Campiglio 2005). To my amazement, the reference to a 'Rawls-Machiavelli programme' in my piece had prompted the TV team to cover the background of the studio with poster-size pictures of both Rawls and Machiavelli, whose intimidating smiles followed us patiently as we were debating enthusiastically a radical extension of the suffrage.

In 1970, a visiting professor at the University of California, San Diego, got very impatient at the conservative retirees flocking into Southern California and trying to impose their values, with Governor Ronald Reagan's help, upon the University of California's emancipated students. So impatient was he that he published in *The New Republic* an article charmingly entitled 'Disfranchise the Old'. Here is its trenchant conclusion:

> There are simply too many senile voters and their number is growing. The vote should not be a privilege in perpetuity, guaranteed by minimal physical survival, but a share in the continuing fate of the political community, both in its benefits and its risks. The old, having no future, are dangerously free from the consequences of their own political acts, and it makes no sense to allow the vote to someone who is actuarially unlikely to survive, and pay the bills for, the politician or party he may help elect. [...] I would advocate that all persons lose the vote at retirement or age 70, whichever is earlier. (Stewart 1970: 20–2).

One generation later, the concern that the elderly are becoming politically too powerful has taken, in a number of countries, unprecedented proportions. The main fear is no longer that the elderly may be animated 'by a desire to see old prejudices vindicated' (ibid.), that they may use their electoral strength to impose their values. It is rather that they may use it in excessive manner to benefit their unavoidably short-term self-interest. Such a fear has found countless expressions in the last two decades[1], in some countries far more and earlier than in others, and sometimes no doubt in an overblown sensationalist form.[2] I shall not attempt to assess to what extent such fears are justified. I shall simply take for granted that there is a problem of this sort,[3] and use the

---

1. Here are just a couple of typical formulations: 'In an aging population, the great danger is that the electorate will become more and more focused on the short term, for there will eventually be fewer and fewer voters who are parents of young children and more who are concerned with having the state provide either for their own aged parents or for themselves in retirement.' (Longman 1987: 143). 'But the elderly are growing both richer and more numerous, and unless something is done to curb their expanding political power, programs to benefit them may yet become untouchable.' (Bayer 1997)

2. Binstock (1994) describes and denounces some aspects of this in the USA. Several other essays in Marmor et al. (1994) reflect on why this issue became more salient in the USA than in Canada. The age-inclusiveness of Canada's health-care system (in contrast to the restriction of Medicare to the elderly) and the far greater inequality among the elderly in the USA (and hence the conspicuous affluence of some of them) are likely to have played an important role.

3. In doing so, I put myself in good company: 'For example, there are sensible proposals for what should be done regarding the alleged coming crisis in Social Security: slow down the growth of benefit levels, gradually raise the retirement age, impose limits on expensive medical care for only a few weeks or days, and finally, raise taxes now, rather than face large increases later. But as things are, those who follow the 'great game of politics' know that none of these sensible

latter for illustrative purposes in order to stimulate thinking on the following more general question. Suppose we know what social justice is, what political institutions should we attempt to put into place in order to achieve it as closely and safely as possible?[4]

1. FOUR ASSUMPTIONS

More precisely, I shall make four basic assumptions, one of a normative nature, three of a factual nature, which jointly cause the illustrative problem to arise. Firstly, I shall adopt a conception of intergenerational justice that requires each generation, each birth cohort, to make sure the situation of the next generation – somehow measured, on a per capita basis – is no worse than its own. This requirement follows, for example, from a general conception of social justice as a liberty-constrained maximin. According to this view – one version of which I present and defend in *Real Freedom for All* (Van Parijs 1995) – social justice demands that, subject to the protection of certain individual rights, the worst off should be as generously endowed with socio-economic advantages, resources, opportunities, real freedom (or whatever other magnitude is chosen to express a person's 'situation') as is sustainably feasible across successive generations.[5]

Secondly, I shall assume that, to an extent that may vary greatly from one industrialised country to another, unchanged socio-economic institutions are leading to a major injustice (as characterized) being inflicted to future or younger generations. One dimension of this impending injustice relates to the depletion of natural resources and long-term environmental damage. It has become clear enough that the way of life of the industrialised countries is

---

proposals will be accepted.' (John Rawls 1997: 773).

4. I found the intergenerational dimension a particularly interesting aspect of this more general question, but the fact that this chapter focuses on it should not be taken to imply that I regard other aspects – for example, justice between wealth or skill categories, or between genders, ethnic groups or regions – any less important. See the other chapters in this volume for an exploration of some of some of these other dimensions.

5. Along these lines, see e.g. Rawls (1971: 284–93), Hartwick (1977), Barry (1977), Van Parijs (1995: 38–41). The conception of intergenerational justice that follows from this view is significantly different from the more generous 'solidaristic' conception of Léon Bourgeois (1902), which requires each generation to improve the situation of the next one just as previous ones contributed to improving its own situation. It is also crucially distinct from the meaner 'equal exchange' conception which provides much of so-called 'generational accounting' with a simple ethical ideal of equal 'benefit ratios' (see e.g. Auerbach et al. 1991 and Kotlikoff 1993). But those who are committed to either of these alternative conceptions of intergenerational justice should find the considerations below no less relevant to their concerns.

not sustainably generalisable to the whole of mankind, and hence that major changes are required to plausibly meet the requirement that 'as good' be left for the next generation, as patterns of consumption and production spread throughout the world. A second dimension of impending injustice stems from the fact that, as life expectancy keeps growing and medical techniques become more sophisticated, old-age pensions and medical care for the retired absorb a share of the Gross National Product (GNP) that rises rapidly. Even if this share rose so steeply that people of working age would end up far worse off than retirees, intergenerational injustice, as characterised, would not necessarily be present. No more may be involved than each cohort treating itself to a more comfortable old age in exchange for a more Spartan youth. But this thought cannot provide much relief if the resulting shifting of burdens to the active population is unsustainable – as is emphatically argued for a number of countries. Subjected to taxes and social security contributions whose revenues are disproportionately geared to the old, it is claimed, men and women of working and procreating age increasingly find that they lack the money and/or leisure to have the children who will pay for their own pensions.[6] It is not just that the bag gets bigger: the swelling of the bag makes the carrier shrink. It is therefore possible – indeed perhaps, as we shall see, politically unavoidable – to postpone the adjustment, but not indefinitely. Hence, whether smoothly or brutally, cohorts will stop being compensated for their rougher youth by a cosier old age, and the growing burden of the older age group for the younger one will reveal its underlying nature: that of an injustice between successive cohorts.

Thirdly, I shall assume that the political feasibility of a reform that would prevent such injustices is exceedingly problematic, given how our democracies are currently organised. Why? The age of the median elector – the person who is exactly in the middle when people entitled to vote are ranked from the oldest to the youngest – has kept rising steadily and is expected to keep rising. In a typical West European country such as Belgium, the age of the median elector was about 41 in 1980. It has now become 45 and is expected to rise to 56 by 2050. Between now and 2050, the gap between the median elector's age and the standard retirement age of 65 is therefore expected to shrink from 20 to 9 years, while the remaining life expectancy at 65 is expected to rise from 14 to 21 years.[7] Hence, the median elector – whose preferences power-hungry

---

6. As pointed out by Offe (1993: 9), in countries in which pension levels are highly sensitive to the completion of a full working career, this phenomenon is further amplified as a result of women giving up the idea of having (more) children because of a cost in pension rights far more than proportional to the immediate loss in earnings.

7. Figures and 1998 estimates for Belgium (assuming an unchanged minimum voting age of 18) have been kindly provided by Paul-Marie Boulanger and André Lambert (ADRASS, Ottignies).

parties are out to satisfy – will soon be expecting to spend in retirement well over two thirds of her remaining life.[8] And the significance of this rising trend in the median *elector*'s age is further strengthened by a strong and widely documented correlation between voting turnout and age, which makes the median voter systematically older than the median elector.[9] Unsurprisingly, political entrepreneurs have seized the new opportunities arising from this conjunction of factors. In some countries using proportional representation, new parties targeting the elderly have sprung up or are threatening to do so and thereby exert electoral pressure on established parties, who have had to readjust their platforms in order to retain the traditionally most reliable segments of their electorates. In corporatist countries, separate trade unions for the retirees have set themselves up and claimed a direct voice in the various bodies competing for policies that directly affect the aged. In lobby-prone countries, powerful organisations have had no difficulty raising adequate funds to put pressure on governments, representatives and public officials in order to promote the adoption and implementation of aged-friendly policies.[10]

Fourth, I shall assume that age-differentiated self-interest affects voting behaviour to a significant extent. To this assumption, which is simply taken for granted in the alarmist literature on intergenerational justice, it has been

---

The estimates are based on the assumptions of 1.55 children per woman, a net immigration of 0.1 per cent per year, and a life expectancy gradually rising to its 'natural limit' of 90 years.

8. Bear in mind that, in some European countries, the average effective retirement age for men and women was well below 60 in the 1990s. Moreover, between the time of a particular election and the time at which it has an impact on age-sensitive policies, there may be a considerable time lag. With a median electoral age of 56, an average retirement age of 58 and a 3-year policy lag, an absolute majority of the electorate can expect to be in retirement at the time their votes produce their effects.

9. In Switzerland's 1991 national election, for example, the turnout was 52 per cent among the over 65s, while it was only 30 per cent among those aged 18 to 23, and 44 per cent among those aged 24 to 39 (Möckli 1994). In the 1992 US national election, the turnout was 70.1 per cent among the over 65s, while it was only 38.5 per cent among those aged 18 to 20 and 45.7 per cent among those aged 21 to 24 (Price 1997: 82).

10. In the USA, the lobby of the elderly has been a mass-based movement since the mid-1960s (Pratt 1976: chapter 4). It is far better organised than the family lobby, for example, despite the fact that there are nearly twice as many households with children as households of retirees (see Levy and Murnane 1992). With over 33 million members aged 50 or more, the American Association of Retired Persons (AARP) is the biggest organisation in the USA with the exception of the Catholic Church. One out of four registered voters is a member of it, and it can count on the involvement of 350.000 active volunteers (Price 1997: 88–9). It may be true that, in the USA for example, the enactment of the major old-age policies is 'attributable for the most part to the initiatives of public officials in the White House, Congress, and the bureaucracy', rather than to the lobby of the elderly (Binstock 1994: 165). But by no means does this prevent the ageing of the electorate from significantly affecting the content of the platforms that candidates feel they have to put forward or the content of the policies which incumbents feel they can get away with adopting.

objected that party preference hardly varies among age groups: in the USA, for example, the over-60s share their votes between Republican and Democrat presidential candidates in pretty much the same proportions as younger voters (Binstock 1994: 164–5). But this is a weak challenge, as this lack of correlation may simply reflect the fact that candidates were driven to converge to the same positions on age-sensitive issues. A more powerful challenge arises from surveys that show that the degree of support for the old-age pension system is about the same (and very high) among all age groups.[11] However, as long as the system is believed to be sustainable, the simple fact that we shall all be old one day (if not too unlucky) suffices to reconcile these data with the assumption.[12] On the other hand, even US data show a significant negative correlation between age and attitude towards expenditure on education (Day 1990: 48), and surveys in countries in which cash transfers for the young are more developed than the USA similarly reveal a sharp decrease in support for such programmes as age increases.[13] Moreover, voting at referenda on long-term ecological issues – such as whether or not a country should abandon nuclear energy – has been shown to be strongly related to age.[14] Hence, there is at least some *prima facie* evidence showing that age-related self-interest affects voting behaviour. Moreover, this impact is likely to grow as a result of a decline in the identification of older people with the interests of younger people. Such a decline can be expected in part because geographical and social mobility loosens the ties between generations, in part because both the proportion of households currently without dependent children and the proportion of people who are and will remain childless keeps increasing.[15]

---

11. This appears to have been the case throughout the1970s and 1980s in the USA. See Day (1990: 41–52): 'older people are nearly indistinguishable from younger adults (both middle-aged and younger categories) on most issues – including age policy issues'.

12. Support for the US social security system (versus private old-age insurance) may of course also reflect, apart from age-group-sensitive interests, ideological stances about redistribution that are unevenly distributed across birth cohorts, depending on the economic and cultural contexts in which each of these grew up. This might upset any simple correlation between attitudes on transfer systems for the elderly and age-related interests even if the latter were certain to have a significant causal impact. (On the relevance of generations as cohorts on political attitudes in Germany, see Metje 1994.)

13. According to a 1982 Belgian survey, for example, support for higher pensions went up monotonously from 61 per cent among the under-25s to 80 per cent among the over-65s, while support for higher child benefits peaked at 52 per cent among those 25 to 34 and dropped to 31 per cent among the over-65s (Boulanger 1990: 979).

14. In Switzerland's September 1990 national referendum on this issue, 47 per cent of all those taking part voted in favour of the proposal (which was therefore rejected), compared with 57 per cent among the voters aged 30–39 and 64 per cent among those aged 18–29 (Möckli 1993).

15. In the USA, the proportion of households with children under 18 has declined from over half to

The conjunction of our first two assumptions implies that some urgent action needs to be taken in industrialised societies in order to prevent major intergenerational injustice. The conjunction of our last two assumptions implies that we cannot reasonably expect such action from their democratic systems, because of the growing weight of increasingly selfish elderly voters. If we care about intergenerational justice, what should we do? Reshape our democratic institutions in such a way that our last two assumptions become less true, i.e. in such a way that older members of the electorate either possess less power or exercise it less selfishly.

2. TESTING THE RAWLS-MACHIAVELLI PROGRAMME

This institutional engineering for the sake of intergenerational justice can be viewed as a facet of a more general social-justice-guided consequentialist research and action programme, which could be described as a combination of 'Rawls' and 'Machiavelli'. The 'Rawls' component refers to a publicly defensible vision, an explicit conception of social justice – including intergenerational social justice – that articulates equal respect and equal concern, typically in the form of a liberty-constrained maximin. Unlike the real Rawls, however, the 'Rawls' component of the programme I shall here illustrate does *not* stipulate anything by itself about political institutions – not even universal suffrage – and it does not assume any sharp dichotomy between self-interested economic behaviour and sense-of-justice-guided political behaviour.[16] The 'Machiavelli' component, on the other hand, refers to an approach to political institutions that aims to shape them in such a way that those acting within them will end up generating the 'right' collective outcome, even though they may be moved by little else than their own private concerns. Unlike the real Machiavelli of the first few chapters of the *Discorsi*, however, this 'Machiavelli' component of the programme to be discussed does not try to design the rules of the political game so as to foster the greatness of the city, but so as to promote the achievement of social justice, as defined by the 'Rawls' component.[17] Bearing in mind this exegetically unwarranted trimming, the

---

slightly over a third between the 1950s and the 1990s (Levy and Murnane 1992).

16. See Rawls (1971: 60–1, 223–4) on the (slightly qualified) immunity of universal suffrage and eligibility from consequentialist consideration, and ibid. (1971: 199, 359–61, 454) on the sharp contrast between the motivational assumptions required within market and democratic institutions. In a less than ideal political world, however, Rawls (1971: 57, 198) allows this contrast to loose its sharpness.

17. See Machiavelli (1517: 81–92) and Skinner (1981: 64–71) for clear formulations of this conse-

two components slot perfectly into each other and their combination defines the programme, which it is the central purpose of this article to test, using intergenerational justice as an illustration.[18]

This test will be twofold and can be spelled out as follows. Suppose we know what social justice is ('Rawls') and are worried about the ability of our current democratic arrangements to deliver, for example along the intergenerational dimension, what social justice requires. How much potential is there for improving our polity's performance in this respect, not through high-minded preaching but through shrewd tinkering with features of the constitution or other measures that will improve the outcomes of the political process, without relying on the moral improvement of citizens and legislators ('Machiavelli')? This is a factual question, partly empirical – to be settled, insofar as it can be, by assessing the comparative and historical evidence on the impact of potentially relevant features of democratic design – and partly speculative – to be settled, as far as it can be, by examining arguments about the possible impact of more or less dramatic alterations, as yet untried, of the way our democracies are organised. The desire to find the best possible, unavoidably tentative answer to this question is the main motive behind the present inquiry. What is the point of dreaming up a splendid vision of the just society if our collective decision-making institutions are ill-suited to turn into reality anything resembling that dream? By raising questions more than providing answers, the main purpose of this chapter is to illustrate the research programme – social-justice-guided constitutional engineering[19] – which is prompted by this concern. From this angle, the programme will be successful if it turns out that the prospects for 'Rawlsian' social justice can be made significantly brighter through the use of 'Machiavellian' thinking. Fruitfulness in this sense defines the first test to which the programme is being subjected.

Unavoidably, however, the programme will at the same time be put to a distinct, philosophical test. For by giving the 'Machiavellian' component total freedom to come up with any arrangement that would further the achieve-

---

quentialist approach to constitutional design, formulations of which can also be found in Hume (1741: 42), Mill (1861: 298) and indeed Rawls (1971: 57, 198).

18. John Roemer made me aware of the fact that this programme could be viewed as a special case of the intellectual ambition behind so-called implementation theory – the attempt to design pay-off structures in such a way that the individual agents' behaviour will generate the socially preferred outcomes – at least providing one allows these outcomes to be characterised in non-welfarist terms. Unlike implementation models with neat behavioural assumptions, however, our Rawls-Machiavelli programme moves in the messy world of people 'as they are or can realistically be made to be', on the look out for context-dependent local institutional improvements.

19. I shall be using the term 'constitutional' throughout in a broad sense that encompasses all the rules of the political game, including those (such as some electoral rules or the rules which govern the funding of political parties) which are not part of a country's constitution but of its ordinary laws.

ment of the goals defined by the 'Rawlsian' component, one runs the risk that what it comes up with as its best bet will turn out to be, in reflective equilibrium, impossible to stomach. What is being put to the test of our considered judgements, in other words, is an uncompromisingly consequentialist approach to political institutions, in which democracy itself, however thinly defined, should not be taken for granted and in which anything goes, as long as the expected outcomes are the best we can hope for. The strategic inquiry, therefore, is simultaneously a philosophical inquiry. Picking the intergenerational dimension for illustrative purposes, this paper also investigates whether the ruthless consequentialism inherent in the programme generates any outcomes which one should be embarrassed by.[20] Put differently, watching the programme at work may make us deny it our support on two distinct grounds: because it proves fruitless, unable to generate any promising non-trivial proposal, or because it proves repugnant, prone to make recommendations inconsistent with some of our considered moral judgements.

3. AGE-DIFFERENTIATED POLITICAL RIGHTS

How could our democratic institutions be altered in order to reduce the weight of the older generation? A first family of proposals consists of various ways of tinkering with the age condition for the exercise of political rights. One might first think of the right of eligibility, the age limits for access to public office. Just as 'parity' has been proposed for genders (Jansen (ed.) 1986, Gaspard *et al.* 1992) and quotas for minorities (Rule and Zimmermann 1994, Reynolds and Reilly 1997: 98–9), one could conceive of introducing a statutory parity for the young and the old, or quotas for the various age groups in representative assemblies. One could, for example, require proportional representation for the under-25s (Phillips 1995: 63), or have a general system of age quotas (Offe 1993: 16), or introduce a maximum age limit for holding an elected office (or lower that limit if there is already one in place). But this is hardly promising. Not because age quotas, unlike gender or ethnic quotas, would not serve the separate aim of equalising opportunities. Nor mainly because quotas for the young would propel to the legislature people who have had little time to find out what the world is like, while the exclusion of the older would deprive the political system of the services of experienced, less ambitious and hence less corruptible people who still have a lot to offer. But fundamentally

---

20. I thereby pursue the inquiry I undertook, along other dimensions, in Chapters 2 and 3. The uncompromising justice-consequentialist approach tested in this way is akin to the one sketched by Arneson (1993).

because a strategy focused on representatives would not address the problem, which is not the ageing of the representatives (whose average age may well have declined in many countries) but the ageing of the electorate: whether old or young, those who want to be elected or re-elected will have to promise and do what the ageing electorate wants them to do.

The first family of proposals on which I want to concentrate therefore consists, more narrowly, in the age-differentiation of the right to choose, not of the right to be chosen. Its crudest member is the one advocated in the opening quotation: simply strike off the elderly's suffrage. But one can think of smoother methods than political death at age 70. If the objective is to reduce the median age, it is of course also possible to work from the other end. Minimum voting age was still around 25 in many countries at the end of World War II. It is now down to 18 in most of them.[21] But some countries have gone further. In Brazil and Nicaragua, voting starts at 16, in Iran at 15, and in 1994 Nelson Mandela (unsuccessfully) proposed to go even further by fixing the voting age at 14 in the newly democratised South Africa[22]. In Western Europe, Germany is at the forefront. Since 1992, politicians from all parties are advocating the lowering of the minimum voting age to 16. In 1994, both the Greens and the (East-German) PDS included the proposal in their manifestos for the national elections. Several *Länder* have since implemented the proposal for local elections: Lower Saxony since 1995, Schleswig-Holstein and Saxony-Anhalt since 1997. Moreover, some academics and politicians have been arguing in favour of generalising this measure to all elections and even of considering a further lowering of the voting age to 14.[23] Economic dependence and the inability to fully understand what is at stake cannot be prohibitive obstacles, they argue, for otherwise the electorate would be much slimmer than we currently allow it to be. Nonetheless, there are obvious limits below which it would be unreasonable to proceed, and the expected impact of any lowering of the age threshold of voting rights is strongly dampened by the low turnout of younger voters.[24]

---

21. Minimum voting age is still 19 in Austria and 20 in Switzerland (Vallès and Bosch 1997: 53).

22. See Vallès and Bosch (1997: 44), Perrin (1997), Ludbrook (1996: 19).

23. For a presentation and discussion of these ideas, see Hurrelmann (1997), Hurrelmann and Palentien (1997), Palentien (1997), Hattenhauer (1997). The lowering of the suffrage to 16 was also proposed by a New Zealand Royal Commission in 1986, by the UK's Liberal Democrats in the late 1980s and by the Australian Youth Organisation AYPAC in 1994 (Ludbrook 1996: 18–19). More radical proposals for the extension of suffrage to all children had been made for example by John Holt (1974: 118) and Hubertus von Schoenbeck (1980). Many more modest proposals can also be found. For example, Campiglio (1997: 199) suggests that teenagers should have their own representatives (themselves not older than 30) with a political agenda restricted to 'the problems of the young'.

24. See Feist (1992: 51) for Germany, Möckli (1993: 15) for Switzerland, Price (1997: 82) for the

Instead of working either at the top end or at the bottom end, one can work at both ends at the same time. This is in effect what is being done in a very differently motivated proposal by Friedrich Hayek (1973: 19–21). His aim is to make the members of the legislative assembly independent representatives of prevailing opinions of right and wrong, rather than spokesperson for particular interests. He therefore proposes that they should be elected every year, for a fixed and non-renewable term of 15 years, among the people who reach the age of 40 in that year and by them. Since it would permanently block the median age at 40, this would be highly effective for our present purposes, on the background of an expected rise of the age of the median elector from 41 to 56 (see above). It would certainly be more effective than lowering the minimum age to 16 and even than introducing a maximum age at 70, while sounding less risky than the former and less discriminatory than the latter. Countless variants can be imagined with a similar impact. For example, candidates of any age could be elected for renewable terms of a standard four-year length, but by an electorate consisting exclusively of those who have become 18, 38, 58 or 98 since the last election. (Since the over-98s are very few, the median age should be about the same as in Hayek's formula.) Any such formula looks less shockingly discriminatory towards the elderly than one in which they simply lose the suffrage at some given age, presumably because at each election some of the younger age groups are also disenfranchised. But whichever variant is chosen, the proposal implies reducing – not necessarily to one, as in Hayek's formula – the number of occasions on which each citizen's interests and views are allowed to express themselves through elections. And the fact that holes are being made in the electorate all over should of course not blind us to the fact that people are *de facto* from a certain age deprived of any electoral weight.[25]

Altering the franchise – whether at the top, at the bottom or both – may be the most obvious but it is by no means the only way in which electoral weight can be shifted between age groups. A fourth proposal relies on the introduction of plural voting.[26] It amounts to making the weight of a person's vote age-

---

USA. Voter turnout is particularly low among those aged 16 to 18 in Brazil (Offe 1993: 9).

25. Another, very different, way of working from both ends at the same time would consist (as suggested to me by Axel Gosseries) in introducing a competence test below and beyond a certain age, in such a way that a significant proportion of the under 18s would be enfranchised and a significant proportion of the over 70s disenfranchised.

26. As pointed out to me by Stuart White and Andrew Williams, an analogous effect could be achieved by attributing political power to an age-stratified random sample of citizens (at referenda or in assemblies), whose sampling bias favours younger age groups. (The coefficient of overrepresentation must equal the weight of one's vote in the parallel case of plural voting.)

sensitive, for example by giving one extra vote to the under-60s,[27] or by giving a weight of 2 to the vote of an 18-year old and having that weight reduced by 1 per cent every year (Möckli 1993: 13), or, most consistently perhaps, by making the number of an elector's votes proportional to her remaining life expectancy, each elector being entrusted with a proxy vote for her future selves (Grözinger 1993: 1265). It obviously makes a big difference whether these future selves are chopped up in small or big chunks, i.e. whether the remaining life expectancy is to be measured, say, in months or in half-centuries. To keep things simple and moderate, one additional vote could be given for each quarter of a century of remaining life expectancy. Under current conditions in the USA, for example, this would mean being given three votes at 18, losing one at about 27 and losing another one at about 55.[28]

But let us think this through. If the underlying principle is that people should be empowered to influence decisions in proportion to the extent to which they are likely to have to bear the consequences of these decisions, then there is no reason not to differentiate further. For example, the average remaining life expectancy of American women reaches 50 years at the age of 30, and 25 at the age of 57, while that of American men is already down to 50 at 24, and to 25 at 52. If implemented, therefore, the proposal would give one more vote to women than to men in the 24–30 and 52–57 ranges, thereby further increasing female majorities in Western electorates. As this is unlikely to stop men from grabbing far more than an equal share of elected positions (and presumably paying the associated toll in reduced life expectancy), perhaps one should not feel sorry for them. However, it is not only gender but also the level of education, for example, which is strongly correlated with life expectancy. As the level of education is nearly as easy to ascertain as a person's gender, this suggests introducing through quite a different path the plural voting advocated by Mill (1861: chapter VIII): if you have a degree, you'll get more votes, because this creates a presumption, not that you are more competent, but that you will live longer and therefore should care more for the future. Why not?

There is, however, another, equally obvious but far more awkward implication. In the USA, while white males reach a remaining life expectancy of 50 years at the age of 24 (and white females at 31), black males reach that same threshold at the age of 16. It follows, under the above proposal, that black males should never be entitled to three votes, reflecting the fact that they cannot expect to live over half a century as they reach voting age. Our

---

27. Claimed by Lefèvre (1997) to have been unsuccessfully put to a referendum in a Swiss canton.

28. These are figures for 1994 derived, as are the figures in the next paragraph, from Wright (1997: 396).

'Machiavellian' component has no difficulty perceiving that such racial discrimination can hardly be expected to boost a country's political potential for maximin policies, and the 'Rawlsian' component is bound to say that this is simply unacceptable. But this need not kill all variants of the proposal. The fact that unequal socio-economic conditions cause statistically identifiable categories of people to enjoy different average life expectancies cannot be allowed to justify giving a lesser electoral weight to the victims of these inequalities. But this need not prevent age – as a proxy for every category's life expectancy in the absence of those inequalities – from being a legitimate criterion of differentiation. In the most promising variant, therefore, voting rights should shrink at the same pace, irrespective of race, education and gender.

A fifth option consists in modifying the age structure of electoral power without touching the electorate, through working on the discrepancy between being entitled to vote and actually voting. I mentioned before that younger electors tend to vote in lesser proportions than older ones. To cancel or reverse this disproportionality, one could think of introducing asymmetric compulsory voting, with the younger voters paternalistically fined if they do not show up at elections, while the older electors would be exempted from this obligation.[29] If asymmetric incentives are thought to be cleaner than asymmetric coercion, one could design a suitably age-sensitive tax-and-subsidy scheme: while a poll tax would discourage the older from voting (without disfranchising them), a poll fee would bribe the young into voting (without obliging them to). A more subtle variant relies on the conjecture that the age of the candidates and of the elected may affect who, among the electors, will actually vote. The younger voters' comparatively low turnout may be partly caused by their feeling alienated from a political system run by people they do not regard as being of their own kind. Age quotas among the candidates and the elected may therefore matter after all, not for their own sake, but because of their indirect impact on the median voter's (as distinct from the median elector's) age.[30]

---

29. Similarly, in Nasser's Egypt, both men and women had the right to vote, but only men the obligation (Abukhalil 1994: 131), and in Belgium, where voting is compulsory for Belgian citizens at all elections, EU citizens now entitled to vote for local councils and the European Parliament are only subjected to this obligation if they choose to register as electors.

30. A further option, suggested to me by Erik Olin Wright, would remove altogether the problem that arises from the young turning up in lesser numbers. It consists in giving each age group a weight proportional to its total size in the electorate, rather than to the fraction of it that actually votes: 'one could have a vote-inflater attached to each vote that is a function of the proportion of the age group in the electorate which simply multiplies the vote of a given 18-year-old, so that the total of 18-year-old votes is proportionate to their number in the population. (If 50 per cent of 18-year-olds vote and 66 per cent of 25-year-olds vote, then each 18-year-old vote gets a weight of 2 and each 25-year-old vote a weight of 1.5).' This vote inflater technique is likely to create a

A sixth possibility arises if each age group elects its representatives, or takes part in referenda, in separate constituencies. Use can then be made of the requirement that the adoption of a law requires not only an overall majority, but also majorities in some or all of the age groups. This sort of device has been in use as a form of minority protection in some ethnically divided societies, where a majority among the representatives of each ethnic group is required on issues sensitive to community relations (in Cyprus in 1960–63, in Belgium since 1970). Analogously, one could require each age group to elect its own representatives – possibly but not necessarily among candidates belonging to it. When issues which are of special importance for the long term are being voted on in Parliament, a law could be adopted under this proposal only if, in addition to an overall majority, it obtained a majority among the representatives of the younger group. For the same sort of issues, a special majority among the younger category of voters could similarly be required at referenda (see Möckli 1994: 12).

A final option leaves voting weights and voting rules unchanged but targets the public funding of election campaigns. Using the common method of public funding based on party scores at the previous election, one could require people below a certain age to cast their votes separately (though not for separate candidates), and distribute public funds among political parties according to electoral performance in that category only. Alternatively, one could use the voucher system for campaign spending advocated by Bruce Ackerman (1993) and distribute vouchers exclusively to electors in the lower age group. Depending on the level of this public funding and on the extent to which private resources can be used, concurrently with it, to fund political parties and election campaigns, this measure would either only provide a very mild corrective to the overwhelming control of political sponsoring by older people or make parties and candidates completely dependent financially on the support of the young. The closer one moves to the latter extreme, the more parties and candidates will be induced to pay particular attention to the interests of the younger, even if the electoral rules, as such, are strictly unchanged.

---

self-regulating dynamics favouring the equalisation of turnout rates – since my vote matters more if I belong to an age group with a low turnout, candidates and parties will be particularly keen to get my vote out – but even if it did not, the younger electors' lower turnout no longer translates into a lesser political weight. Even with a small number of age categories, the ex post calculation of inflation rates obviously makes for some sizeable complications. But the fact that this proposal, unlike those mentioned in this paragraph but like those mentioned in the next one, requires a separate counting of the votes cast by each age group should not be a prohibitive obstacle. What about extending the technique to the gender or ethnic or class divide?

4. THE CHILDREN'S VOTE

Disfranchising the elderly, it thus turns out, is only one, and not exactly the most promising, of at least seven different ways in which one can imagine altering the balance of electoral power between the various age categories. But our potential arsenal is still far from exhausted. Instead of concentrating on electoral power's relationship with the electors' age, one can focus instead on its relationship with parenthood.[31] The simplest element in this second family of proposals can be – and has repeatedly been – presented as the introduction, at long last, of genuine universal suffrage: every member of the population is given the right to vote from the very first day of her life.[32] This can easily be achieved without requiring minor children to cast votes themselves. As for so many other things of far more momentous importance to their personal fates, one can simply entrust their parents with the responsibility of doing so on their behalf, by granting them proxy votes.[33] The expansion of the electorate that would result from giving one proxy vote per child is huge, though not quite as dramatic in today's ageing Western societies as it would have been a generation ago. In the USA, for example, this extension of the suffrage would have meant an increase of the electorate by half in 1960, but only by one third in 2000.[34]

To my knowledge, this proxy vote for children existed only briefly and in a very restricted form: in the inter-war period, each father of four children or more was given a second vote in the French protectorates of Tunisia and

31. Here again, and for reasons analogous to those spelled out in connection with the first family of proposals, the focus is on the electorate rather than the representatives. Introducing a parents' quota among the latter (a possibility mentioned, though not endorsed, by Claus Offe 1993: 10) would be just as inadequate as the quota for the young mentioned above (indeed, even more so, as no analogous impact on turnout can be expected). It would leave electoral pressures unchanged, while not guaranteeing a better defence of the interests of parents and their children. Indeed, these interests may be far more effectively defended by an energetic childless person trying hard to tap the parents' votes than by some of the latter's overstretched, exhausted peers.

32. As pointed out by Sauvy (1945: 214), there are countries, including France, in which the size of a constituency is measured (for the sake of seat allocation) by the size of its population, not of its current electorate, and extending the suffrage to all children would be consistent with this practice.

33. Even without giving parents extra votes, our electoral systems are arguably already assuming now that children's interests are represented through their parents: 'Their parents have the vote, and we trust them to use it (at least in part) to protect their children's interests as well as their own. [...] There is nothing illegitimate, in those circumstances, in letting such others speak on the child's behalf.' (Goodin 1996: 843). Moreover, in some countries at any rate, parents are entitled to vote on behalf of their children qua shareholders (Löw 1997).

34. In 1960, 35.7 per cent of the US population was under 18; in 2000, only 25.7 per cent is expected to be (Wright 1997: 276).

Morocco.[35] However, it has been repeatedly discussed for over a century, especially in France, and mostly with pro-natalist motivations. The earliest proposal of this sort seems to have been made, shortly after Prussia's victory over
France, by a certain Henri Lasserre (1873), 'the universally known historian
of Notre-Dame de Lourdes'. In his proposal, every French citizen, whatever
his or her age or gender, is given one vote, with the (male) head of each family exercising this right to vote on behalf of his wife and each of his children
(Toulemon 1933: 108–9). The proposal was hardly noticed, however, except
by the philosopher Gabriel de Tarde (1892), who took it over enthusiastically, as a way of enforcing a concern for the interests of younger and unborn
generations.[36] The first law proposal was made in 1910 by the deputy Henri
Roulleaux-Dugage and seriously discussed by the *Assemblée nationale* only
in 1923. The latter first decided to couple the introduction of the proxy vote
for children and that of women's suffrage, and next took them jointly into
consideration with a large majority (440 against 135). However, the Poincaré
government was not very keen and procrastinated. New elections took place
in 1924, followed by a financial crisis that wiped both proposals off the agenda until women's suffrage, on its own, was introduced in 1946.[37] Since the end
of World War II, it was picked up again by the socialist political thinker and
demographer Alfred Sauvy (1945: 213–14), sympathetically expounded in
Adolphe Landry's (1949: 634) classic treatise of demography, unsuccessfully
proposed, in the late 1950s, by General de Gaulle's Prime Minister Michel
Debré (Westoff 1978: 56) and recently revived by Jean-Marie Le Pen's right-
wing Front national.[38]

---

35. See Toulemon (1933: 121–2). A de facto approximation to a more general form of parental vote
is the plural voting system that was in place in Belgium between 1893 and 1910. Universal male
suffrage was combined with an extra vote for married (or widowed) men, providing they were
also taxpayers, and most of these married men (given that the average number of children per
family was then larger than now and life expectancy shorter) had at least one non-voting child at
home (see e.g. Carstairs 1980: 102).

36. 'For while children mean future and hope, women are above all the children's mothers, and the
interest of the nation is that its statesmen should worry, not about the present generation, on which
the thought of adult men usually gets stuck, but about posterity' (Tarde 1892:414).

37. See Toulemon (1933: 115–39, 217) for a fascinating detailed account of this 'near miss'.

38. The Front national's web site phrases the proposal as the attribution of extra votes to families
in proportion to the number of minor children. Support in France is broader than the extreme
right, however: just before the 1997 general election, the conservative representative Christine
Boutin (from President Chirac's Gaullist party) gathered the support of 123 members of the
French Assembly from various parties around a proposal that included, in vaguer terms, some
sort of family vote. In Belgium, the extreme right Flemish-nationalist party has also picked up
the idea: 'Children, on whom policy exerts a great influence, are not democratically represented.
Therefore, the Vlaams Blok advocates that parents should vote on behalf of their children until
they reach majority.' (Annemans et al. 1998: 9)

In Germany, the idea seems to have been first aired by a political scientist from the University of Bayreuth (Löw 1974). But it only started being seriously discussed in the 1990s, first at the initiative of the Christian-Democratic representative Wilfried Böhm (in July 1992), soon supported by the conservative archbishop of Fulda Johannes Dyba and by the youth section of Bavaria's Christian-Social Union. Support, however, has by no means been confined to the Christian right. Proposals along these lines have also been made, for example by the family affairs spokesperson for Bavaria's Social-Democratic party (Schultz 1992) and by the justice minister for the city of Berlin, Lore Maria Peschel-Gutzeit (1997), also a Social-Democrat. Furthermore, in July 1993, the all-party Children's Commission of the National Parliament unanimously asked the government to look into the feasibility of introducing a proxy vote for children.[39] Outside France and Germany, nothing resembling a serious discussion has come to my attention. However, a number of scholars seem to have hit upon the idea independently, including the Norwegian sociologist Stein Ringen (1996), the American political scientist Paul Peterson (1996), the economic consultant Alexei Bayer (1997), the Italian economist Luigi Campiglio (1997: 198–9) and also, years earlier, Harvard University lecturer Manuel Carballo (1981).[40]

Let us now turn to specifics. Some of the proposals – from Lasserre (1873) and Toulemon (1933) to Carballo (1981), Grözinger (1993) or Löw (1997) – go all the way to 'genuine universal suffrage', granting one extra vote for each minor child. One at least, adopted in 1930 by the French Republican Party, goes beyond this, by allowing parents to keep the extra votes even after their children have become voters themselves.[41] Others – such as Ringen (1996) – stop at conferring one extra vote as soon and as long as there is at least one

---

39. For further details, see Suhr (1990), Grözinger (1993), Löw (1993, 1997) and Hattenhauer (1997), as well as the proceedings of a conference on the subject gathering left-of-centre academics and activists at the Akademische Akademie Arnoldshain (Grözinger and Geiger (eds) 1993).

40. In his short piece in the Boston Globe, Carballo (1981) writes: 'I am left with an uncomfortable sense of imbalance in our political system. In a society all too ready to live for the present, how do we create a political force for our children's pensions?' Here is his answer: 'My proposal is quite simple. Give parents a vote weighted by their number of minor children. Two parents with two children get four votes. One parent with one child gets two votes.' According to Harvard University's web site, 'throughout a life dedicated to public service, Carballo was committed to serving the poor, the vulnerable and the public at large', so much so that Harvard's Kennedy School of Government set up a Manuel Carballo Memorial Prize to encourage 'innovations for improving the quality and effectiveness of programs to serve the poor and disadvantaged'. This is worth remembering, just in case anyone tried to disparage the idea by exhibiting such embarrassing supporters as France's Le Pen or Germany's Dyba).

41. Article 8 of the law proposal by Sallies et al. of the Fédération républicaine, gives each father as many extra votes as he currently has minor children, and one extra vote for as long as he lives (Toulemon 1933: 217).

minor child in the household. Others still – such as several of the proposals discussed in France in the 1920s and the one actually implemented in Tunisia and Morocco – reserve the extra vote to large families. Whether one or more proxy votes are awarded to a family, the question arises of which of the parents should receive them. The pioneering proposals by Henri Lasserre in 1873, by Gabriel de Tarde in 1892 and by Henri Roulleaux-Dugage in 1910 and 1923 gave them all to the father, as does the Front national's. Stein Ringen (1996), on the contrary, gives all extra votes to the mother: his empirical research on the allocation of family budgets (Ringen 1997) establishes that mothers, on average, can be trusted to take their children's interests to heart far more than fathers can. At a time at which the lower age limit for voting was still 21, Alfred Sauvy (1945: 213) proposed that mothers would vote for their children up to age 10, and fathers from 11 to 20. Grözinger (1993: 1264–5), instead, proposes that fathers should vote for their sons and mothers for their daughters, on the basis of empirical evidence showing gender-specific electoral preferences. Somewhat more complicated to administer is the strictly egalitarian one, which gives half a vote to each parent (Hattenhauer 1997: 16). The compromise adopted in 1930 under feminist pressure by the French parents' vote lobby is close to this, while dispensing with half votes: it gives one vote to the father for each of his children of odd rank, and one vote to the mother for each of her children of fair rank (see Toulemon 1933: 132–3, 137, 216, who endorses the proposal himself). More sensible, no doubt, would be the symmetric proposal giving mothers proxy votes for their children of rank 1, 3, 5, etc., and fathers for the others. The resulting significant pro-mother bias could easily be justified using Ringen's argument quoted above.[42]

Further details need to be filled in. Most obviously, each of the formulas listed above has to make provisions for cases in which one at least of the two parents has died or disappeared. These provisions may or may not generalise to cases in which at least one of the two parents is not entitled to vote, because of being a foreign national or below 18 or in prison. Most importantly, for the large and growing proportion of children whose parents are alive and entitled to vote but do not live together, how much of a sharing of parental responsibilities should there be for both parents to be able to claim their chil-

---

42. Alternatively, one could restrict the same assignment formula using the children's rank order, not among all children born in the family, but only among those of them who are still under voting age. Not unlike Sauvy's scheme mentioned above, this variant could be interpreted as making fathers and mothers take turns in being a proxy for their children (except the first one) as these grow older (even though, for the sake of administrative simplicity, it may be better to sever the individual proxy link between parent and child and simply give the mother one more vote than the father if they have an odd number of minor children). Note too that this variant involves a much greater bias in favour of mothers: at any one time, mothers would have at least as many votes as fathers in all, not only in most households.

dren's votes? And if adoptive parents are given proxy votes, why not also step-parents?[43] There is an obvious trade off between on the one hand the scheme's ability to track each parent's concern for their children's welfare and to distribute votes accordingly, and on the other its administrative simplicity, uncontentiousness and unintrusiveness. Given that what is at stake here is not the effect of the decision on the welfare of any particular child, but the scheme's general effect on policy, it is clear that the second set of considerations should prevail and that the scheme should therefore operate on the basis of very rough and simple presumptions.

The choice among the many variants of the family vote, or parent's vote, or children's proxy vote, obviously depends on the objectives that are being pursued. Four main distinct objectives feature in the justifications given for the proposals.[44] Firstly, from Lasserre (1873) to Peschel-Gutzeit (1997), pro-natalist considerations are conspicuously present: to halt demographic decline, it may help to publicly express in this way the consideration society owes to those who secure its future and even more to give families the political power that will enable them to successfully push for child-friendly and hence birth-promoting policies. Secondly, irrespective of any demographic impact, the proposals are often advocated on the ground that, by correcting the overrepresentation of small households, they would make it possible for policies to be adopted that more closely approximate what inter-household distributive justice requires (see e.g. Ringen 1996). Thirdly, they would have as a consequence – it is sometimes claimed – to optimally locate the peak of the average person's electoral power at 'an age at which he is still young enough to muster enthusiasm, yet already old enough to possess experience' (Toulemon 1948: 114).[45] Finally, they are justified, particularly today in green circles, on the ground that, by increasing the influence of those with 'a deeper sense of the community's permanent interests' (Landry 1949: 634), they would increase the time horizon of the electorate or, as Grözinger (1993: 1261) puts it, reduce 'the dictatorship of the present over the future'. Obviously, this fourth justi-

---

43. In the USA, nearly a third of all children were not living with both their parents in 1995 (see Wright 1997: 284). Several of these difficulties are articulated by Claus Offe (1993: fn 3).

44. Note that all of these justifications, in the interpretation I give them, are consequentialist. It would be absurd to claim that this unequal distribution of voting rights among adults according to the number of their children is just in itself: what about those who could not find a partner, for example, or those who cannot have children, or those whose children have died? It can only be shown to be just (if at all) by virtue of its indirect effects on the distribution of resources.

45. See Tarde (1892: 419): 'The reform I am dreaming of would have the indisputable advantage of making the numerical weight of a person's vote proportional [...] to his physical or mental strength and to his civic importance throughout his life. [...] The electoral peak would be the 45–50 age slice, i.e. the culmination point, not of imagination and love, but of experience and political capacity among most men.'

fication is the one most closely related to our present concerns. It crucially relies on the empirical conjecture that on average adults with minor children in their household care about a more remote future more than other adults do.

5. POPULATION POLICY

This empirical conjecture suggests a third, quite different but no less plausible, family of proposals. Consider the following three highly stylised conjectures about relevant voting behaviour: (1) Voters are guided by their own self-interest. (2) Voters are guided by an abstract sense of intergenerational justice. (3) Voters are guided by their own self-interest and that of their children, grandchildren, etc. No doubt many of us would find this third conjecture the most plausible one, to an extent that may vary greatly from one time or country to another. If this third conjecture is the one that best approximates reality, there is less reason to worry about an ageing electorate, providing a large proportion of the latter actually have children.[46] But as mentioned before, in some countries at any rate, the proportion of adults who never have children is on the increase, even when average family size is pretty stable.[47] In order to lengthen the time horizon of the electorate, and thereby of governments and legislators, it would be useful to identify ways of increasing the proportion of voters who can be moved by a concern for their descendants. This must be achieved, however, without boosting total population too much. It would not make sense to create an electorate more favourable to the younger or unborn generations using a means whose side effect is to harm the latter's prospects.

The controversial area of population policy therefore forms another promising corner of our 'Machiavellian' arsenal, at least providing it contains le-

---

46. One may wish to replace the most plausible conjecture (3) by the following variant: (3) Voters are guided by their own self-interest and that of the other people with whom they actively interact outside market relations and with whom they thereby develop close emotional ties. As persuasively pointed out to me by Erik Olin Wright, the extent to which the elderly are firmly integrated into multigenerational communities – not just multigenerational kinship structures – then becomes of decisive importance: 'If the elderly live in settings where children and young adults help them and interact with them, then [they] will develop a stronger sense of obligation towards future generations.' Even more than the child-spreading policies to be considered in this section, packages of policies (housing, town planning, public transport, social services, health care) that encourage socially active generationally mixed neighbourhoods – rather than segregated old people's homes and condominiums – could then be expected to boost the political potential of intergenerational justice.

47. In the USA, the proportion of childless women in the 40–44 range has increased from 10.2 per cent to 17.5 per cent between 1976 and 1994, while the total fertility rate went up from 1.8 to 2.0 children per woman in the same period (Wright 1997: 282).

vers that can affect the distribution of children between households. That some tools at a government's disposal can have a deep and lasting effect on fertility draws some plausibility from a number of fairly spectacular facts. A textbook case is provided by the comparison between fertility rates in East and West Germany in the 1955–1985 period. Initially, the East and West German trends ran closely parallel to each other , with the number of children per woman going up from about 2.2 to 2.4 between 1955 and 1965 and then steeply down to about 1.5 by 1975. In May 1976, the East German government introduced an explicitly pro-natalist policy package including half a year of maternity leave at full pay, and another 32 weeks on sick benefit as from the second child. The fertility rate soon jumped up from 1.5 child to about 1.9 in 1980 in East Germany, while the West German rate kept declining to 1.4. After that date, both rates declined again in parallel, but with the East German rate consistently remaining about 0.5 child above the West German rate (Büttner and Lutz 1990: 540–3).[48]

The problem with these pair-wise comparisons is that many other potentially relevant variables have behaved differently in the two countries over the period. Hence, inferring from the striking covariation of fertility rates and family policies to the existence of a causal link is far too hasty. To try to correct this defect, one can lump together countries and years and check whether any correlation between policy and birth rates emerges. When this is done, for example by Blanchet and Ekert-Jaffé (1994: 92–3) for 28 countries in the 1970–1982 period, no correlation emerges. But there is no lack of ways of explaining away this negative result: for example, low fertility countries can

48. Less clear-cut, but still quite spectacular, is the case provided by Italy and Sweden swapping positions in the European fertility league between 1970 and 1990. Italy went down from about 2.4 children per woman in 1970 to 1.7 in 1980 and 1.3 in 1990, while Sweden went first down from 1.9 in 1970 to 1.7 in 1980 and then up to 2.1 in 1990 (far above the European Union average of 1.5). It is hard to resist the temptation to relate this swapping of positions to a number of striking policy differences. Child benefits are generous and kept pace with inflation in Sweden, but now hardly exist in Italy, where annual government expenditure on children outside education is about $400 per capita, compared to $1800 in Sweden (1992 figures). Italy's maternity leave of 20 weeks at 80 per cent of pay is not bad at all on European standards, but no match to Sweden's full year (or more) of parental allowances (for either mother or father) with a 70 to 90 per cent rate of salary replacement – probably the world's most generous scheme. Moreover, the world of work is so organised that the rate of women's participation in the labour force is 85 per cent in Sweden (with two fifths in part-time jobs), double the corresponding Italian rate. (See Chesnais 1996: 730–3, Gauthier 1996: 174–5). Note, however, that since 1990, the difference has been shrinking, with total fertility rate down in 1995 from 1.3 to 1.2 in Italy, but from 2.1 to 1.7 in Sweden (Chesnais 1996: 730). Note too that Italy has a particularly developed pre-school system (with over 85 per cent of the children between 3 and school age in subsidised institutions compared to 80 per cent in Sweden (Gauthier 1996: 181) and that Italy, unlike Sweden, has a tax credit system for dependent children. For this reason, the difference between Sweden and Italy is less sharp than non-educational government expenditure figures suggest.

plausibly be expected to introduce generous benefits as a pro-natalist policy (negative feedback link) and greater affluence may generate both relatively more generous benefits and lower birth rates (spurious correlation). These interactions can be controlled for, as much as they can, through multiple regression analysis. And then, the relationship reappears. For example, using data for 22 industrialised countries in the 1970–1990 period, a more differentiated set of family policy indexes, and dynamic regression analysis, Gauthier and Hatzius (1997) produced results suggesting that an increase in benefit levels for a two-child family by 1 per cent of average earnings would boost the number of children by nearly 4 percent.[49] As the current levels of benefits vary widely across countries,[50] this strongly supports the view that there is plenty of room of manoeuvre for effective demographic policy.

Our concern, however, is not to revive demographic growth or to slow it down. It is to spread whatever number of children is being born as widely as possible among all households. Econometric results of the type cited above are relevant to the extent that they strongly suggest – not beyond any doubt, but far more than introspection, anecdotal evidence or casual observation of trends and correlations could do – that some effective policy tools should be available for this objective too. Further results can help identify the nature of the most effective among these tools. For example, when a broader index of child benefit was used, so as to include tax relief for dependent children, the relationship between benefit level and fertility ceased to be significant. 'This may reflect the higher 'visibility' of cash benefits as couples may be less aware of tax relief opportunities when deciding when to have a child. Besides, low-income families, who are likely to be most responsive to transfer payments, will benefit relatively less from tax relief if marginal tax rates increase with income.' (Gauthier and Hatzius 1997: 305) For a given cost, therefore, it is clear that one should go for cash benefits rather than tax allowances.

---

49. Gauthier and Hatzius (1997: 302) show that a 25 per cent increase of the benefits given for the first two children would raise total fertility by 0.01 child per woman in the short run, by 0.07 in the longer run. Given that, in the countries considered, the average level of benefits for a two-child family was about 5 per cent of average earnings and that the average total fertility rate was 1.71, this implies that a benefit increase by 1 per cent of average earnings increase births by nearly 4 per cent. Earlier, using data for 11 European countries in the 1969–83 period, Blanchet and Ekert-Jaffé (1994: 93) came up similarly with a significant and positive regression coefficient between the total fertility rate and a family policy index consisting of a ratio of the weighted average of child benefits to the average wage: a 25 per cent increase in the latter index increases the total fertility rate by 0.04 child per woman. (The total fertility rate in a given calendar year is the expected number of children per woman, with each woman experiencing each year between the ages of 10 and 50 the probability of giving birth exhibited in the current calendar year by women in the corresponding age categories.)

50. In the case of families with average earnings and two children, from 0 per cent in Italy or the USA and 0.3 per cent in Spain to 10.4 per cent in Belgium or 11.3 per cent in Austria (Gauthier 1996: 166)

Further, it turns out that 'at the margin, increasing assistance for the first child by a given amount has a greater effect on fertility than for subsequent children' (Gauthier and Hatzius 1997: 300).[51] This is good news for our strategy of getting people to have at least one child. We should not rejoice too quickly, however. In the data set that produced the result, no birth-specific fertility variable was included, and one cannot, therefore, rule out that the significant positive impact may be due, not to otherwise childless households deciding to have children, but to households otherwise with one or more children ending up with an additional one as a result of having the first one earlier (Gauthier and Hatzius 1997: 301). Nonetheless, this kind of result provides strong support for a presumption in favour of cash benefits targeted at the first child, [52] or possibly in favour of other tangible benefits – housing subsidies, for example – the value of which decreases with the rank of the child.[53] Using such policy

---

51. This is not necessarily a blow for those countries – such as France or Germany (see Blanchet and Ekert-Jaffé 1994: 90) – which chose to pursue pro-natalist aims by generously focusing benefits on the third child: focusing on the third child is so much cheaper than focusing on the first that it may well yield better pro-natalist value for its money, despite the greater demographic impact of a given per-capita increase of the benefit for the first child than for the third.

52. The presumption might seem to be, more specifically, in favour of benefits targeted at poorer households, since it is hard to imagine how the demographic impact could not be greater, for a given cost, if benefits were concentrated on lower-income families than spread more thinly over all families. But one must realise that it is a serious mistake to reason about redistribution schemes in the same way as one reasons about other expenditure programmes (a point well put, for example, by Shaviro 1997). Whereas the cost of these programmes matches an opportunity cost in terms of other things one could have done with the same resources, increasing or decreasing the 'cost' of a redistribution scheme is more appropriately described as a shifting of the profile of marginal and average net tax rates applying to the various components of the population. In particular, rather than as a 'cheapening' of an expenditure programme, the phasing out of benefits as family income increases is more appropriately described as the subjection of households with children, and hence de facto in most cases their female secondary earners, to a higher effective marginal rate of taxation than childless households: any additional euro earned is not only subjected to the explicit rate of tax but also to the rate of benefit withdrawal. There might conceivably be reasons for taxing mothers at a higher marginal rate than other workers, but they are most unlikely to have anything to do with the encouragement of a first birth.

53. An econometric study by Ermisch (1988: 571–5) on the basis of individual British Census data for 1971–1985, shows that higher hourly wages for women (relative to men's weekly wages) and higher housing costs (relative to the cost of living) were the main factors behind the increase in the proportion of women remaining childless. Leaving aside, for the moment, the influence of wages, his results suggest that doubling housing costs would add another 7 per cent of childless women, while reducing average family size by 0.16 child only, and doubling the (rank-independent) child benefits would reduce the proportion of childless women by about 3.5 per cent, while increasing average family size by 0.17 child. If the aim is to reduce childlessness (or stem its progress) rather than to increase (or maintain) average family size, child benefits look less appropriate a tool than keeping housing costs down, as the latter has a much more powerful effect on childlessness than on average family size. However, acting on housing costs (rents, mortgage interest rates, housing subsidies) may well just be a clumsy, distortionary, truly costly way of providing implicit child benefits at a decreasing rate as family size increases. The same asymmetric effects should

instruments should enable us to help enlist, in the service of intergenerational justice, the electors' spontaneous concern for the interests of their progeny.

6. GUARDIANS

A fourth family of proposals aims to foster the achievement of intergenerational justice by strengthening the direct grip of a concern for it on political decision-making. How can this be achieved? One can of course invite the voters to drop a veil of ignorance over the particular generation they belong to. But it is most doubtful that, in the secrecy of the voting booth, the most powerful and high-minded eloquence will have any lasting impact on whether or not the ageing voter will cast her vote for the candidate who was most adamant about protecting the vested interests of the elderly. In a representative democracy, however, where governments and legislators have a significant degree of discretion and need to publicly justify the stance they adopt, the legislative assemblies may be a more appropriate locus for action. To help secure intergenerational justice, various people and organisations have proposed to set up a position of 'guardian' for the interests of younger or unborn generations.[54] This 'guardian' could be an appointed officer, or an expert commission, or a full-scale institution, whose views must be heard by the government and/or the legislative assembly whenever a decision is about to be taken with an irreversible long-term impact that can be presumed to be considerable.[55]

While conceding that there may be nothing else on offer to protect the interests of distant generations, one may be tempted, in 'Machiavellian' spirit, to dismiss such devices as idealist day-dreaming. But the following analogy may make them appear in a different light. In matters of intragenerational justice, some surveys suggested that there was hardly any difference between

---

therefore be expected from increased cash benefits if they were focused on the first child, rather than rank-independent.

54. See, for example, Birnbacher (1988: 265–8), Offe (1993: 15–16), Stone (1994: 134–5), Scorer (1994: 239).

55. In the more ambitious versions, the 'guardian' would be empowered to take governments to court on the basis of clauses in a constitution or in an international treaty which protect future generations against both the governments' actions and their inaction. This may be thought to be question-begging, as it presupposes that the constituent or treaty-endorsing bodies are sufficiently driven by a sense of intergenerational justice to enshrine some features of what it commands in legal clauses that can be enforced even against governments and assemblies. However, while it is obvious that this device could not work on its own, it could nevertheless prove quite effective by virtue of the fact that representative assemblies may be willing to adopt principles in a certain form and at a certain time, which they may be under pressure to abandon when confronted with specific issues.

the content right and left voters gave to the ideal – some form of equality of opportunities – but that there was a significant gap between their respective perceptions of the extent to which distributive justice, so conceived, was realised in actual fact.[56] The same may well hold, *mutatis mutandis*, for intergenerational justice. People of all ages may be officially committed to non-deterioration as a minimal condition of intergenerational justice, while differing significantly, and in a way that strongly correlates with their age, on whether or not the current pension system is viable or on whether or not the use of nuclear energy generates long-term risks. In this context, the summoning up of expert evidence by the 'guardian' of the interests of younger or unborn generations may well play a significant role, at least as long as one can rely on the scientific community's professional ethos and discipline to provide a sufficient guarantee of independence. An astutely institutionalised guardian, therefore, is not something the 'Machiavellian' component of our programme would dismiss out of hand, not because of any equivalent of an electoral weight the guardian may be given, but because of the ability she may have to effectively challenge and discredit self-serving beliefs.[57]

7. THE PROGRAMME AT WORK

Whether by listening to current debates, by foraging through the dustbins of the history of ideas or by exercising one's own imagination, it is thus possible to come up with a whole range of possible reforms that may bend the operation of the political system in the required direction. By looking and thinking harder, one could certainly come up with far more. But I doubt that this would take us beyond variants of the four families of options sketched above, and for our purposes, in any case, no more is needed. No rushing to firm proposals, though. The literature on constitutional design is replete with horror stories about unintended, sometimes even disastrous and sadly irreversible consequences.[58] It is a central part of the Rawls-Machiavelli programme to screen the alternative proposals carefully, whether in isolation or in interac-

---

56. See Swift et al. (1992, 1998).

57. The sheer fact of systematically bringing the intergenerational issue into the open may also exert a civilising influence on the monopoly-power-wielding generation through a mechanism that does not rely on belief formation. However strong the self-interested pressure on the representatives of this generation, they may shy away from publicly dismissing a perfectly audible strong case on behalf of the unrepresented (whether other countries or future generations) out of anticipated shame for the moment these will find out that their interests were deliberately ignored.

58. See, for example, Curtis (1998), Horowitz (2000a).

tion, checking the possibility of counterproductive unintended effects. Some of these effects may concern intergenerational justice itself, irrespective of any other dimension of social justice. Here are three examples.

With the exception of the last one, all proposals mentioned above crucially rely on the assumption that voters are, to a large extent, guided by their self-interest and the interest of their children, and they aim to promote intergenerational justice, not by making voters or their representatives more public-spirited (as the fourth family tries to do), but by shifting electoral weight in favour of those whose interests are at risk of being insufficiently taken into consideration. But, one might wonder, will not the very nature and justification of such proposals strengthen the legitimacy of self-seeking political behaviour at the expense of whatever public-spirited motives did exist? The net effect on the prospects for intergenerational justice would then be unclear, as the effect of the weakening of the older categories of the electorate would be offset by the effect of their now feeling entitled to go for the unbridled pursuit of their self-interest.[59]

This is a relevant objection, which must not be rejected out of hand. People need to be taken as they are or can feasibly be made to be, not as elementary economic textbooks posit they are. There is no need to assume that voters are strictly selfish, let alone to make them more selfish than they currently are or to waste precious moral resources that we should be keen to put to good use. Historical precedents offer some reassurance, however. True, granting suffrage to women might be said to have relieved male family heads of their duty to represent their wives' interests. But there is little doubt that whatever was lost in this way for the purpose of giving women's interests fair consideration was far more than offset by the power shift in their favour from which this loss is supposed to have resulted. So, perhaps, negative side effects can be avoided through a careful phrasing of the justification for the proposed electoral reforms: they are less about shifting the balance of power between self-interested individuals than about giving a stronger guarantee for the inclusion of younger people in the operative definition of the common good or about

---

59. This concern is expressed by Offe (1993: 21–2) in connection with the proxy vote for children. That there is ground for concern is strongly substantiated by the virulent attack on the 'civil servant' (versus self-interest-seeker) conception of the elector by the most articulate advocate of the parents' vote André Toulemon (1933: 179–89, esp. 184–5): 'When voting, the elector does not attempt to hide that he defends his interests and nobody blames him for it; quite the contrary, in order to catch his votes, the most honest and even the wisest candidate endeavours to show the elector that his interest, well understood, commits him to accept his programme and his person. Whoever would tell the electors 'Vote for this programme, even though this will be in your interest neither now nor later; free yourself of the selfishness that is natural to any well born creature', would rightly be considered a madman or an imbecile; for it is obvious that the electors have indisputably the right to vote in defence of their interests [...].'

giving greater weight to those who can more easily imagine what fairness to the younger or the unborn may mean.

Consider, secondly, any of the proposals – tinkering with the age conditions or introduction of the parents' vote – that amount to giving less political power to the older portion of the electorate. This may be an improvement for the fair consideration of the interests of the younger among those currently living, but a definite deterioration for more remote unborn generations. For while the elderly have less to lose from any mismanagement of the planet's resources, they also have less to gain from the persistence of a way of consuming and producing that jeopardises the welfare of mankind generations hence, and may therefore be, on average, more receptive to bad news about long-term damaging impacts and hence more capable of the sort of impartiality that fairness to remote generations requires.[60] Clearly, assessing this argument requires not only empirical evidence about age-differentiated voting motives, but also a more refined elaboration of our normative conception of intergenerational justice: what does it require when keeping the situation of the next generation at least as good as ours can only be achieved at the expense of making it impossible for the situation of more remote generations to reach that level?

Thirdly, consider, more specifically, the proposal to extend the relevant time horizon by distributing proxy votes to parents in proportion to the number of their children. Might this number not be inversely correlated with the time horizon of the parents? For example, owing to procreation incentives built into the structure of some welfare states, poorer families may have, on average, more children and, being subjected to more pressing needs, have a more short-term orientation on policy issues. Or the sheer fact of having a greater number of children may reflect a disregard for the overcrowding of the planet and hence for the (per capita) welfare of future generations. Under such circumstances, the extension of the suffrage through proxy votes for children would still mean that the interests of younger people would be expressed by the people who most care for them, but as the number of proxy votes given to a person would tend to increase with the short-termism of her interpretation of these (as well as her own) interests, the net effect may be a shortening rather than a lengthening of the time horizon of the electorate as a whole.[61] Here

---

60. The possibility of this counterproductive effect was pointed out to me by Andrew Williams. It is arguably documented by the fact that in the 1990 Swiss referendum on the abandonment of nuclear energy, support went down monotonously from 64 per cent for the 18 to 29-year-old category to 32 per cent for the 50 to 59-year-old category, but went up again to 46 per cent for the over 60s (Möckli 1994).

61. This possibility displays a standard case of fallacy of composition. If, for any particular type of person (in terms of propensity to care about the future), votes are distributed according to the

again, empirical evidence is needed to assess this puzzling conjecture. If the latter turned out to be true, the radical proposal of genuine universal suffrage would clearly become unwise, even though the favourable impact of a more modest scheme that would give, say, no more than one proxy vote to each mother or father of minor children under voting age would not be in doubt.

The screening of counterproductive effects should not be narrowly focused on intergenerational justice, however, as intragenerational dimensions of social justice may be badly affected by reforms aiming to better protect the interests of the younger or the unborn. A first illustration of this possibility has already been provided above, in connection with the idea of giving people proxy votes for their future selves in the form of a life-expectancy-sensitive plural voting. The implied intragenerational shift of electoral power away from disadvantaged categories – manual workers, racial minorities – makes this idea unpromising for the achievement of social justice as a whole, however effective it may be for the sake of lengthening the electorate's time horizon.

Secondly, consider the parents' vote proposals. While protecting better the interests of the younger, they also increase the electoral power of those who have children, or more children, at the expense of those who do not, whether because they could not have them or because they would not. Indeed, when the parents' vote was nearly adopted by France's National Assembly in the 1920s, a recurrent argument was that out of the eleven million electors, seven million had no children or only one and made their interests prevail over those of the remaining four million, who bore the burden of bringing up the bulk of France's children (Toulemon 1933: 126). But by distributing votes in proportion to children, is injustice not going to swing the other way, not of course because an unequal distribution of votes is inherently unjust, but because the new majority will be able to use its newly gained electoral power to subsidise, at the expense of the childless, the way of life they had the capacity and desire to choose?[62]

Thirdly, consider the proposal of an extended maternity leave at full pay and without loss of pension rights, all at the employer's expense. This would

---

number of children, the overall time horizon is lengthened. Also, if there were no correlation between type and number of children, such a proportional distribution of votes would lengthen the time horizon. But if there is a strong correlation, voting power is being shifted across types as well as within types to such an extent that the net effect may be a shorter overall time horizon.

62. More contingently, having more children may also be strongly correlated, in some countries, with membership of religious communities – say, Mormon, Hassidic, Amish, catholic traditionalist, or Islamic fundamentalist – which tend to adopt political attitudes – for example, in favour of state-imposed morality or against state-organised social policy – inimical to other dimensions of the full ideal of social justice (understood as some liberty-constrained maximin). The parents' vote would boost the power of these communities and may therefore, under certain demographic and institutional conditions, badly damage a country's overall political potential for social justice. This possibility too must be paid the attention which Erik Olin Wright convinced me it deserves.

considerably reduce the opportunity cost of having a child by enabling work-ing mothers to take several months off work without incurring any fall in their incomes, and should therefore boost the propensity to have children.[63] If it turns out that this boosts population growth too much, the measure can easily be fine-tuned through targeting the first birth. Moreover, the proposal can also be expected to have the side effect of depressing women's wages relative to men's, as a fall in the demand for the labour of women at child-bearing age would unavoidably follow from the employers' obligation to pick up the full bill of maternity leaves. This would also make it relatively more attractive for not (yet) (full-time) working women to have children rather than to enter the full-time work force – an expectation borne out by empirical evidence.[64] We here seem to be exceptionally lucky: the measure produces a side effect which, far from subverting the explicit objective, further con-tributes to its achievement. But we must not get carried away. Statistical dis-crimination against women would unavoidably take significant proportions on a free labour market – either in the form of unequal pay or, if equal-pay rules were strictly enforced, in the form of unequal unemployment rates – if employers were subjected to the above-mentioned obligation. When this is taken into account, concern with intergenerational justice may still justify, for child-spreading reasons, the provision of material support after the birth of at least the first child.[65] But, whatever the variant, the bill should be footed by society at large, or by all firms, rather than only by those firms that happen to employ pregnant women – or, in the more restrictive variant, women pregnant with their first child.[66] Most of the impact on male-female wage differentials

---

63. Note, however, that in the most extensive cross-country study 'maternity leave (duration and benefits) did not appear to be significantly related to fertility' (Gauthier and Hatzius 1997: 304) – contrary to what was suggested by the East/West-Germany and Italy/Sweden comparisons (Büt-tner and Lutz 1990, Chesnais 1996).

64. Ermisch's (1988: 571–5) estimates for the UK suggest that a 35 per cent increase in women's hourly wages relative to men's (similar in magnitude to the increase in the 1971–85 period) would add about 7 per cent to the (then) current 16 per cent of childless women and depress average family size by 0.3 child from its current level of 2.0. Note, however, that, in Gauthier and Hatzius's (1997: 300) cross-national study, women's wages display a slightly significant positive relationship with fertility levels, which suggests that the opportunity cost of large families, for given women's wage rates, may be very different depending on the extent to which being the mother of more than two children means giving up one's career altogether (availability of child care and part-time jobs, extended parental leave with a right to return, etc.).

65. Though possibly at a flat rate (irrespective of a woman's current wages and past career) and rather in the form of benefits not contingent upon the interruption of work (so that they can, for example, be used to top up wages in order to improve one's housing rather than to enable one of the parents to stay at home).

66. An alternative way of removing the side effect (suggested to me by Andrew Williams) would consist in enforcing substantial paternity and maternity leaves of equal length. This would get rid

should thereby be avoided. However fortunate this reinforcing side effect might have looked for our narrowly defined objective, the effective pursuit of our overall objective requires us to do without it.

These six examples illustrate the sort of activity the Rawls-Machiavelli programme consists in: both imaginative and reflective, fearless but cautious, combining tireless fact finding, informed guesswork, special attention to interdependencies and a constant reminder of the overall goals. For it is crucial that the 'Machiavelli' component should not go about its business in too rash, too heavy-handed a way. It must not only take the time to consider possibly counterproductive effects with respect to some partial objectives, such as intergenerational justice. It must also pause to talk things over with the 'Rawlsian' component in connection with the broader set of goals that make up the full picture of a just society. Even when this is done, the best package one can ever hope to come up with will never be a recipe valid for all times and places. The effectiveness of any combination of proposals is contingent on a large number of factual assumptions, only a small subset of which has been touched upon above. It can therefore be challenged as more data become available, or as the causal factors of political or procreative behaviour are subjected to a more subtle analysis, or as the details of the particular society concerned are being further specified. No particular combination of constitutional rules (and of policies affecting the latter's operation) can be identified with absolute certainty or claimed to be universally optimal. Yet, by shaping political institutions in the light of whatever little or much can be known about their consequences in a specific historical context, one can serve the cause of social justice far better than if one simply accepted whatever political institutions happen to be in place or if one only tried to make them as 'democratic' or 'efficient' or 'legitimate' as possible. Indeed, taking such steps before it is too late may prove of crucial importance to prevent social justice from turning ever more into a sheer dream, as the rules of the political game inexorably drive our societies away from anything resembling it.

---

of the gender bias, but might further contribute to the shrinking of the number of families with at least one child (by strengthening the base for the male partner's veto power), thereby killing the solution at the same time as the defect in the solution.

8. FATAL TROUBLE?

This is, at any rate, the conviction that underlies the Rawls-Machiavelli programme. But beyond quibbling about the crucial factual assumptions of any specific proposal the programme generates, there are a number of general objections that seem to threaten its very core. One of them applies to any package that includes a change in the rules of the political game. The problem, so it is often pointed out when constitutional engineering is being contemplated, is that the people who have the power to change the rules owe whatever power they possess to the very rules they are expected to change. This certainly accounts for the fact that significant changes in the rules of the game do not happen very often. But as recent history has reminded us with gusto – from Russia to Japan and from Italy to New Zealand – they do change now and then, and sometimes quite dramatically. Those involved in the Rawls-Machiavelli programme should not expect the political system to be receptive to their advice as soon as they utter it, but they can meaningfully aim to be ready for those rare opportunities, for example when outside pressure for a change is mounting and a vigorous case one way or another may make all the difference, as governments and legislators feel they have to change something in order to deflate the pressure, but are at a loss as to which way to go.

Moreover, some significant shifts in the institutionalised balance of political power may be politically feasible, even if a very large parliamentary majority is required and in the absence of outside pressure, simply because the shift the Rawls-Machiavelli programme advocates does not fit standard party cleavages. On this point, the programme's radical instrumentalism is to be sharply distinguished from a partisan approach to constitutional engineering. Its 'Machiavellian' component does *not* start off checking which party's platform looks most conducive to social justice as defined by the 'Rawlsian' component, and next proceed to rig the rules of the game so as to favour its favourite party.[67] By promoting reforms which it believes it can justify using

---

67. Whether with or without public interest embroidering, this is the distinct form of instrumentalism that drives attempts by political parties to modify the rules of the game for their own benefit. This partisan instrumentalism is vulnerable in a way in which 'Machiavellian' instrumentalism is not. Think, for example, about transitions from 'first past the post' to proportional representation (PR). When Belgium became the first country to make the move in 1899, Vandenpeereboom's Catholic government first made a limited proposal that would have introduced list PR in the largest constituencies only – which happened to be industrial constituencies in which Catholics were the minority. This clearly partisan proposal aroused the indignation of opposition parties and led to the resignation of the government. A few months later, de Smet de Naeyer's (no less Catholic) government made the more radical but bias-free proposal of list PR in all constituencies. The proposal was adopted and proved stable, gradually spread to all levels of government and indeed, as from 1906, to many other countries (see Moureau and Goossens 1958). Similarly, 'the French Socialist Government's decision in 1986 to switch from their existing Two-Round System to PR

impartial arguments, it tries instead to shape the institutional framework in such a way that all parties, now and later, will be under pressure – as much as they can be made to be – to promote social justice. In certain historical contexts, these reforms may happen to strongly favour one party over another. But this is by no means necessarily the case. For example, introducing the family vote in Germany would induce a major shift in the political power of different age groups, but, judging from survey results, the immediate gains or losses to be expected by each of the four main parties are very limited[68]. Each can therefore hope to increase its following through designing and publicising policies better tailored to the new electorate. No comparison, therefore, with the strong resistance opposed by some European Social-Democratic and Liberal parties to the extension of suffrage to women on the basis of the (roughly correct) expectation that women would more than proportionally vote for confessional parties.[69] The absence of any clear partisan bias is possible and, when it applies, it makes things easier. But by no means does it constitute a necessary condition for successful reform, as this example of the introduction of female suffrage – or even more clearly that of universal male suffrage – clearly shows.

Although a change in the rules of the game may not be intrinsically impossible, it may still face a fatal dilemma if it is advocated, as the Rawls-Machiavelli programme requires it to be, on consequentialist grounds. If one is to gather a majority in favour of the parents' vote, for example, one needs a majority in favour of the policies which this change is designed to promote. But, as Claus Offe (1993: 20) puts it:

> If the latter majority obtains, then it is not necessary to change voting rights. If it does not, then it is not possible to change them.

Beyond the case of the parents' vote, this challenge can easily be generalised to any of the other proposals mentioned earlier for modifying the rules of the political game, and no less to the demographic policies advocated by virtue

---

was widely perceived as being motivated by partisan reasons, and was quickly reversed as soon as the government lost power in 1988' (Reynolds and Reilly 1997: 123), in sharp contrast, for example, with New Zealand's 1993 well-prepared switch from First Past the Post to list PR, also motivated by the expected consequences but in non-partisan fashion (Roberts 1997).

68. A survey conducted at the 1990 West German election showed that the electoral scores of Social-Democrats and Greens would go up slightly, while those of the Christian-Democrats and the Liberals would shrink slightly, if parents were given proxy votes for their children (Grözinger 1993: 1266). In contrast, a lowering of the minimum voting age to 16 would seem to have a more clearly favourable effect for Greens and Social-Democrats (Hurrelmann 1996).

69. Even in the 1980s, there would have been left majorities throughout Europe, had only males been allowed to vote! (Offe 1993: 20).

of their indirect effect on the outcome of the political process. But it can be defused by scrutinising each of the two horns of the dilemma.

Firstly, if a majority favours the sort of policy which it is the ultimate aim of the proposed reform to favour, there is still a point in bringing about this reform as long as one does not have full confidence that future electorates will similarly favour this sort of policy without the help that the reform would provide. This may be because the trends which undermine support for such policies are expected to develop further. Or it may be because the high-minded concern for future generations that one happens to be able to draw on for the time being is forthcoming only under exceptional circumstances. These possibilities make it safe to economise on future moral resources and restructure institutions so that less of these resources are required in the future to get the same sort of policies adopted.[70]

Secondly, if no majority favours the sort of policy which it is (from the programme's perspective) the ultimate aim of the proposed reform to favour, there may still be a majority in favour of this reform, though not, by hypothesis, because of the particular consequences the programme deems decisive. Take again the parents' vote.[71] Perhaps some women support it because of the extra recognition it gives to mothers or because of the further increase in women's electoral weight it implies. Perhaps the *Front national*'s leaders support it because they believe it will boost the native French population. Perhaps some people are attracted by the beautifully simple logic of 'one person, one vote, full stop'. Why should we care? Opportunities to get the right reforms through are few and far between. Hence, when one arises, it cannot afford the luxury of requiring a majority not only to support the appropriate reforms but to support these for the appropriate reasons. If the rhetoric of 'democracy' or of 'equality' or the appeal to some factional interests helps move things forward, it would be foolish to be fussy. As long as no counterproductive side payments need to be made, even unholy alliances and disreputable bedfellows are perfectly welcome. The proof, the programme says, is entirely in the pudding.

A third objection follows directly from Jon Elster's (1986, 1988) view that 'it is impossible to predict with certainty or even quantified probability the consequences of a major constitutional change'. Constitutional change – indeed any major institutional reform – can therefore only be justified on

---

70. Grözinger (1993: 1267) points out, in response to a similar objection to his proxy-vote proposal that it may be rational for a majority to bind itself through constitutional change in order to protect itself against the weakness of its will. This is another way of formulating the second case just mentioned.

71. See again Grözinger (1993: 1267), who similarly hints at the diversity of the reasons different categories of people may have for supporting his proxy-vote proposal.

non-consequentialist grounds, for example on the ground that the proposed institutions better express some notion of political equality, and not on the basis of more or less speculative conjectures about its likely lasting effects on the achievement of distributive justice. One can readily concede that the prediction of these effects is not always easy, and welcome Elster's reminder that global net steady-state effects, in which the Rawls-Machiavelli programme is primarily interested, should not be rashly inferred from local, partial or transitional effects. Indeed, as illustrated in the previous section, much of the programme's activity precisely consists in taking this reminder seriously, by tirelessly exploring the possibility of unanticipated consequences.

However, by no means should this awareness inhibit the firm advocacy of some specific change (or combination of changes) which one feels confident would significantly improve upon the status quo. True, this confidence will often rest on a complex set of convictions about facts and causal links, and may therefore have some difficulty spreading widely and motivating key political actors. But as illustrated above, there is no objection, in such cases, to mobilising the rhetoric of democracy or enlisting factional interests. From the standpoint of the Rawls-Machiavelli programme, it is essential that an adequate justification could be given for the reform, not that this reform should be driven by nothing but this justification. This is how Elster's challenge needs to be handled, not as an argument showing why the programme must fail, but as an explanation of why it is needed.

A fourth general objection can be gathered from Giovanni Sartori's argument – presented precisely to counter Elster's plea for non-consequentialist justice-based constitutional reform – to the effect that 'constitutions are, and must be, content-neutral. A constitution that takes upon itself to establish policies, i.e. policy contents, pre-empts the popular will and tramples upon the policy-making bodies' (Sartori 1994: 202). But even when they do not stipulate any specific policy themselves, some constitutional arrangements – if only those which specify who can vote and how campaigns are financed – obviously and massively affect the probabilities different policies have of being adopted. One can recognise the importance – stressed by Sartori – of assessing potential constitutional changes by anticipating the strictly political consequences of the induced changes in incentive structures (number of parties, government stability, accountability, etc.), while insisting that the operation of the political system is not to be judged exclusively by reference to standards internal to itself. There is no reason to regard purely political consequences as the sole relevant ones in a consequentialist evaluation of constitutional design. Indeed, the programme's central purpose is precisely to liberate the discussion of constitutional engineering from the narrow focus to which political scientists have tended to confine it.

Finally and most seriously, it may be objected that just-policy-motivated constitutional engineering is constantly at risk of overshooting. Convinced that the socio-economic policies in place are too favourable to the elderly or to the childless, one may endeavour to shift the balance of electoral power in favour of the young or of families with children. But once the reform is in place, the new majority may soon adopt policies that tilt the situation of the elderly or the childless below what justice requires. Given the inertia inherent in constitutional change, the pursuit of social justice through this type of means seems a very clumsy instrument that does not allow for much fine tuning. Consequently, not only must a direct appeal to what justice requires have sufficient power over the decision-makers at the constitutional stage, when the rules of the game are being designed or redesigned. In addition, there is no way, within the rules of the game thus adopted, for the sheer balance of power between suitably weighted interests to durably bring about what justice requires.[72] Conceding this – as I think one must – does not make nonsense of justice-instrumental constitutional engineering. But it invites us to pay special attention to those features of our democratic institutions – such as the maximum inclusion of all those affected or the firm regulation of campaign finance – which bring the actual objectives of key political actors closer to the demands of social justice. For this reason, disfranchising the elderly is definitely a bad idea, while the enfranchisement of younger people and the compulsory hearing of 'guardians' of future generations are more surely good ones.

In terms of the twofold test – ethical acceptability and strategic fruitfulness – to which the Rawls-Machiavelli programme is here being put, the concession just made is two-edged. On the one hand, at any rate by the standards of my own considered judgements, it gets rid of any lingering fear there might have been about the programme being morally repugnant. I feel morally embarrassed by none of the programme's implications disclosed in the preceding pages. Perhaps there are other implications that would make me feel far less comfortable. I would be grateful to anyone who could spell them out. On the other hand, the concession I made destroys any extravagant 'Machiavellian' hope I might otherwise have entertained about shrewd institutional reforms that would enable ordinary political life to dispense altogether with an active sense of intergenerational justice.

Yet, there is no principled reason why the programme should restrict itself

---

72. See Rawls (1971: 359–61): 'A peculiarity of the ideal market process, as distinct from the ideal political process conducted by rational and impartial legislators, is that the market achieves an efficient outcome even if everyone pursues his own advantage.' In contrast, 'there seems to be no way of allowing [citizens and legislators] to take a narrow or group-interested standpoint and then regulating the process so that it leads to a just outcome.' Does this mean that the same holds for Rawls as for Pascal's God: 'Un peu de pensée éloigne de [lui], beaucoup y ramène'?

to reforms that would serve the pursuit of social justice by strengthening an active sense of justice, spreading it more widely or tightening its grip over political decision-making.[73] There may sometimes exist quicker and safer institutional means for preventing serious injustice, for example along the inter-generational dimension. And if they exist, they must be used.

---

73. The absence of any such restriction distinguishes the radical instrumentalism defended here from a milder 'epistemic' variant that might be ascribed to David Estlund (1990) or Tom Christiano (1996).

chapter five | should the european union become more democratic?

In August 1996, Andreas Follesdal and Peter Koslowski organized in Oslo an international workshop on Democracy and the European Union (Follesdal and Koslowski (eds) 1997). This was the first time I participated in a meeting focusing on the political philosophy of European integration. The European Union had been officially created in 1992 by the Maastricht Treaty, along with the notion of European citizenship. The preparation of the 1997 Amsterdam Treaty, which would strengthen the role of the European Parliament, was well on its way. And the 'European democratic deficit' had become one of Eurospeak's most popular expressions. This seemed a good opportunity to reflect and debate on how my conception of the primacy of justice over democracy fitted into current discussions about the way the European Union should evolve. My chief conclusion was that the priority, in Europe, should not be more democracy, but a multi-dimensional shift from multi-national demoi-cracy to trans-national demos-cracy.

ॐ

1. CAN A DEMOCRATIC DEFICIT EVER BE A GOOD THING?

Does the European Union suffer from a democratic deficit? The answer clearly depends on what exactly counts as a 'democratic deficit', and hence also on what counts as 'democracy'.

Democracy is frequently linked to *accountability* – for example, in the European context, by Sverker Gustavsson (1997) and Philippe Schmitter (1997) – roughly understood as the need for decision-makers to justify their decisions in a persuasive way, or more explicitly as the conjunction of transparency (the provision of all relevant information to the controlling party) and responsibility (the serious risk of being sanctioned by that party). But there can be democracy without accountability – as in direct democracy, where the people are themselves the rulers – and there can be accountability without democracy – when the controlling party to whom accounts need to be given does not ultimately consist in the people of the entity concerned, but a foreign ruler for example. Leaving out the possibility – irrelevant on the scale of the EU – of generalized direct democracy, democracy should therefore be characterized, more specifically, as accountability *to the demos*, i.e. to the people expressing themselves through majorities emerging from free elections under universal suffrage.

If this is democracy, what is a *democratic deficit*? At the most abstract level, a democratic deficit is sometimes understood as less than maximal feasible democracy, and at other times as less than optimal democracy.[1] Under the former construal, it makes sense to ask whether a democratic deficit is a bad thing which one should attempt to get rid of. Under the latter construal, it does not. For a democratic deficit – on a par, presumably, with a democratic surplus – is by definition suboptimal. Whether there is a democratic deficit in the former sense is easily settled, as it is obvious enough that the complex amalgam consisting of the European Commission, the European Council, the Council of Ministers, the European Parliament, the European Court of Justice, the European Monetary Institute and their respective administrations is quite a bit less than maximally accountable to the relevant *demos*. The sheer opacity of many decision processes within the Commission's administration, the constant reliance on expert committees, the weakness of the democratic control over the activity of the European Council, the Council of Ministers

---

1. For my purposes, these abstract definitions are more appropriate than the common characterization of the democratic deficit in the EU context as a loss of democratic accountability at the national level unmatched by a corresponding gain of democratic accountability at the European level (see e.g. Dehousse 1995, Scharpf 1996, Gustavsson 1996). If there is a democratic deficit in this specific sense, it is nearly self-evident that there is also a democratic deficit in my first abstract sense ('less than maximal'), but by no means certain that there is also one in my second sense ('less than optimal').

and the European Commission – whether because of their mode of selection or because of the lack of a genuine arena for political debate – uncontroversially establish the existence of a democratic deficit understood as less than maximal democracy.[2]

But they do not *ipso facto* show that there is also a democratic deficit in the second sense – a suboptimal level of democracy. For whether there is such a deficit depends on what criterion of optimality one adopts, and this criterion cannot plausibly be, as a general rule, maximal democratic accountability. Why not? Let me just mention two possible sources of discrepancy. For reasons related to the general case for a separation between the judiciary power and the legislative power, it is arguably essential that the European Court of Justice should be sheltered from accountability to any *demos*. For reasons rooted in an analysis of the causes and effects of inflationary pressures, it is also arguably essential that the prospective European Central Bank should be an independent agency protected against political pressures. So, if optimal democratic accountability is not maximal democratic accountability, what is it? My answer is ruthlessly, unapologetically consequentialist.[3]

2. RUTHLESS CONSEQUENTIALISM

More explicitly, my claim is that the very existence of the European Union, the powers it is given and the way it is organized must be evaluated, criticized, shaped, on the basis of the conjunction of empirical conjectures about the likely consequences of alternative options and of a normative criterion for assessing these consequences. What should this criterion be? It should certainly incorporate considerations of security and prosperity – the two central concerns in the first two decades of the European Communities – but also of sustainability, diversity and solidarity. Can these considerations be integrated into an explicit, coherent and plausible conception of the overall goal? I believe they can, and have tried to systematically spell out and defend such a conception in *Real Freedom for All* (Van Parijs 1995). Being able to rely on a precise conception of this type presents great advantages. But only a rec-

---

2. See Dehousse (1995: 8–13) for a useful overview of the various dimensions of the 'democratic deficit' in this sense.

3. Unlike Knut Midgaard's (1997), for example, whose criterion of autonomy (everybody should be ruled by laws adopted by himself or his representatives) defines optimality by the extent to which the decision-making design satisfies some procedural feature, not the extent to which it fosters the achievement of some substantive goal. The purely instrumental approach to democracy on which I rely here is presented and defended more fully in Chapters 1–4.

ognition of the relevance of the broad set of considerations articulated in this conception, not the particular way in which it articulates them, is assumed in the argument which I am about to present, by way of an answer to the question of whether or not the European Union suffers from a democratic deficit.

The question can be rephrased as follows. If the overarching goal is the maximal feasible achievement of some substantive conception of social justice which incorporates the various considerations listed above, is there any strong reason to believe that the EU's current institutional situation is unsatisfactory and, if so, that enhancing the EU's democratic accountability would make things better, as far as the achievement of our overall goal is concerned?

3. NO OPTION BUT GOING FORWARD

Is the status quo satisfactory? Certainly not. Most fundamentally because the very existence of the single European market, added to the globalization of the economy, jeopardizes sustainability, the persistence of cultural diversity and, above all, the preservation and strengthening of solidarity. To clarify what I have in mind, let me just briefly illustrate this last dimension. At the national level, we used to be able to exert our solidarity in a variety of ways. For example, when publicly run bus services needed new buses, they could self-evidently select the single bus-manufacturing firm on it territory. This choice may turn out to be quite a bit more expensive than alternatives abroad, but it provides employment to a large number of workers, and hence the most rational thing to do, since the cost of unemployment benefits would far exceed the premium paid to the local firm. Moreover, state-owned firms or state-protected monopolies used to contain massive pockets of unprofitable activities and to apply rigid wage scales largely disconnected from any assessment of worker's actual productivity, thus implementing a large, though implicit solidarity in favour of the less skilled. As a result of the policing of public orders and the dismantling of monopolies by EU legislation, these two forms of solidarity are no longer available.

Never mind, one might say, all we need is replace these inefficient, untidy, implicit forms of solidarity by the more efficient, systematic and transparent transfers to the unlucky and the less talented provided by our tax and social security systems. But you then face another problem. For if in order to finance unemployment benefits or employment subsidies you attempt to impose high taxes or social security contributions on those firms, or on those owners of financial or human capital, who earn handsome incomes among other things because of the opportunities offered by the Single Market and globalization, then you soon realize that many of them move out − or credibly threaten to move out – to places where they face lower tax rates while retaining for their products unhindered access to the home market.

Consequently, both because of ongoing changes in the external economic environment ('globalization') and because of the gradual unfolding of the legal, economic and organizational implications of the single market, we cannot stop where we are. Since there is much to lose from going back to more autarkic economies, as well as from attempting to restore the inefficient and biased forms of solidarity illustrated above, we have no serious option but to move forward, by greatly increasing the powers of the European Union in matters that are directly and explicitly of a distributive nature. On the background of the diagnosis just sketched, this is required even in order to preserve current levels of solidarity within each member state.[4] It is obviously also required if one regards as desirable the strengthening of solidarity across member states. And it is further required to secure sustainability against downward environmental competition, to generate sufficient human capital against the downward spiral of free riding on the education and training provided by other countries and even to protect cultural diversity against the homogenizing pressure of a mad dash for competitiveness.

4. A MORE DEMOCRATIC UNION?

Granted that we need a more powerful Union for the reasons just mentioned, do we also need a more democratic Union? Let me say at the outset that I do not believe that this issue can be settled on the basis of a simple dichotomy between efficiency-oriented policies, which require no democratic accountability and can therefore be left to the Union as it is, and redistribution-oriented policies, which do require democratic accountability and should therefore be left under the control of the national *demoi*.[5] Competition policy and mon-

---

4. Scharpf (1996: 565–81) essentially shares this diagnosis, but he is rather pessimistic about the EU's political ability to remedy the national powerlessness brought about by the Single Market. His pessimism is rooted in the legal asymmetry between 'negative integration' (the effective dismantling of discriminating legislation by the Commission and the Court) and 'positive integration' (the laborious EU-level re-regulation by unanimous Council decisions), in the conflicting interests of member states with a developed and a rudimentary welfare state, in the ideological disagreement among the former group, and in the great institutional differences between social protection and industrial relations in the various countries. At the most fundamental level, these difficulties must be tackled through a combination of the political-institutional strategy sketched below and a basic-security approach to European social integration sketched elsewhere (Van Parijs 1996, 2000). These need not be incompatible with the less radical, shorter-term measures favoured by Scharpf (1995: 581–8; 2000).

5. As in (a rather rash interpretation of) Giandomenico Majone's (1996) position.

etary policy may be efficiency-motivated but they have massive distributive implications, and should therefore not be exempted, according to this very position, from democratic scrutiny. Deliberately redistributive policies, on the other hand, cannot be left, for the reasons just sketched, at the national level. Given this massive distributive relevance, should European policy-making, whether old or new, be made more democratic than it now is? Not necessarily. From the consequentialist perspective sketched earlier, the real question is rather how all relevant actors – rulers, officials, representatives, pressure groups and even voters – can be given the powers and the incentives to do the right thing, i.e. to do what is needed (given what the others do) for the best possible decisions to be made, as far as the achievement of social justice is concerned.

In the case of monetary policy hinted at before, this may well involve shielding the governors of the prospective European Central Bank against democratic accountability. Such shielding would not be justified by some alleged distributive neutrality of monetary policy, but by the presumption that accelerating inflation and political business cycles would jeopardize the sustainable fostering of the fate of the worst off. But what about the deliberate redistributive policies, which I claimed the EU should take on far more than it does now? How should the relevant decision-making institutions be designed? Should they be any more democratic that EU institutions currently are?

One cannot offer a sensible answer to this question without first looking at how generous the redistributive policies of various existing polities are, especially federal ones, and reflecting on whether the observed differences have anything to do with the design of their respective political institutions. As part of this exercise, it will be important to think, for example, about the reasons why the US welfare state is so much stingier that the typical West-European welfare state, despite comparable economic circumstances and a common cultural inheritance. Can this difference be attributed to greater internal heterogeneity, to the racial factor or to a greater openness to immigration, or rather to the presidential system, to the importance of money in the electoral process or to a majority system with large constituencies which prevents the underdogs from being represented in Congress?

From a casual exercise of this type, I derive the tentative conclusion that there is not much to expect from a European legislative body made up of representatives of the various governments – certainly if it is governed by a unanimity rule or by a wealth-weighted majority rule,[6] slightly less certainly if it

---

6.   As has apparently been suggested by President Chirac. Note that when the first European institutions were set up in 1951, Chancellor Adenauer was about to suggest that the weighting of each member state in the European institutions should be determined according to the size of its coal and steel production, when Jean Monnet, immediately endorsed by Adenauer himself, proposed

is governed by some unweighted or population-weighted majority rule. Why? Fundamentally because each government's representative at the intergovernmental table would be expected to bring back home at least the *juste retour*, at least the equivalent of what (s)he is giving away, and the closer one gets to a purely distributive issue, the more likely possible moves are likely to be blocked by one (unanimity) or more (majority) countries whose interests are perceived to be damaged. Even if, under unweighted or population-weighted majority, there turned out to be enough countries to gain from the redistributive measure, they may well refrain from pushing their advantage for fear of creating alienation, frustration, indignation in the countries which stand to lose. It is only if the discussion could be sufficiently shielded from scrutiny by the national media, parliaments and electorates and/or if it could remain sufficiently ignorant or quiet about the trans-national distributive consequences that the governments' representatives would not lose face (and by the same token a few points in the opinion polls) if they returned home with a bad deal. But if it can only be purchased at the cost of such a large 'democratic deficit', this possibility would unavoidably remain shaky, as it would falter should media attention suddenly seize the issue.

5. SINGLE-CONSTITUENCY PARLIAMENT, PUBLIC COUNCIL, ELECTED PRESIDENT?

Are things hopeless then? They need not be. But it is essential that the crucial legislative body should be made up not of the representatives of the various countries or their governments, but of subsets of their populations. The most obvious way of achieving this would consist in greatly extending the scope and strength of the legislative powers of the European Parliament, at least partly at the expense of the Council[7]. This preference for the Parliament is by no means based on the fact that each country's representation and weight at the Parliament is far more sensitive to the size of its population than it is at the Council. Not only could this in principle easily be done at the Council too,

---

that each of the three larger countries (France, Germany, Italy) and the three smaller countries together (Belgium, Luxembourg, the Netherlands) should each have the same weight. (See Monnet 1976: 413–15.)

7. This could probably be done most effectively by giving the Commission the power to propose legislation in the relevant area and the Parliament the power to approve, amend or reject it. By introducing co-decision by the Parliament and the Council of Ministers on some acts, by requiring Parliamentary approval of both the President and the members of the European Commission, by synchronizing (at a six-month interval) European elections and choice of a new Commission, the Maastricht Treaty has gone quite a long way in this direction.

as is actually put forward in some of the reform proposals made in preparation of the Intergovernmental Conference.[8] But it is also, for our purposes, of rather minor importance. What matters is rather, first, that the representation should be structured along ideological or social rather than ethnic or territorial lines, so as to allow for alliance or indeed party formation across the national borders. What also matters greatly is, next, that the representation should not be significantly affected by wealth, whether as a result of making the number of representatives (per capita) a function of a nation's GNP (or some other correlated variable), as a result of allowing campaign expenditure to significantly affect election outcomes or as a result of the *de facto* or *de jure* disenfranchisement of a significant proportion of the poor.

This may not prove enough, however. For one key factor in explaining the viable generosity of European welfare states is bound to reside in the existence of a nation-wide forum of political argument and competition in which an appeal to the common interest, or to the interests of 'the weakest among us all' can make sense. For something analogous to happen at the European level, despite linguistic barriers and cultural differences, more institutional help may be needed. One could, for example, imagine that a portion of the membership of the European Parliament, say 50 members, be chosen on Europe-wide lists, under a system of proportional representation with the possibility of multiple voting on each list.[9] Featuring on such lists would be attractive to major politicians, as there has probably never been as large an electoral constituency anywhere (not even for the US Presidential election). More importantly, such a system would force candidates to acquire a European profile, and hence to care about as much about their presence and image in the press of other European countries as in their own. It would of course also force them to collaborate closely across national borders on the programme and make up of the list. As a result, even the candidates for the remaining, nationally allocated, seats (more than 90 per cent of the total) would be far more closely connected cross-nationally than they currently are. Above all, the politicians' and the media's discourse will gradually be reshaped so as to construct 'our' interest on a Europe-wide scale.[10]

---

8. For example in August 1993 by the German Member of Parliament Karl Lamers, who suggested that Council decisions be taken with a double majority of 4/5 of the member states and 4/5 of the populations they represent; or in February 1994 by the Institutional Committee of the European Parliament, who proposed a simple majority of both the member states and the populations represented by them. (See Franck 1995: 41 for a survey of relevant proposals.)

9. A (timid) step in this direction was made in Maastricht, when allowing each citizen of a member state to take part in European Parliament elections, whether as a voter or as a candidate, in any European country.

10. An analogous proposal is to be found in Dewatripont et al. (1996: 17, 165–7) and in Roland

An alternative, less obvious and more hazardous way of pursuing the same objectives consists in modifying the other legislative bodies – European Council and Council of Ministers – in such a way that it can develop the same dynamic. One might think, for example of the radical conjunction of three changes: replacing unanimity by (not too qualified) majority, making the discussions public and adding, in the case of large or heterogeneous countries, representatives from their regional governments. This last element may be conceived in such a way that each country ends up with a weight that more or less reflects its population size. But this is not crucial.[11] What matters is that the combination of these three changes would take us quite some way from the diplomatic logic of hidden bargaining to the parliamentary logic of public argument, analogous to the one that prevails in the German or Austrian *Bundesrat*, or even in the US Senate or the Swiss *Conseil général* (with the significant difference, however, that in the latter two cases it is the voters, rather than the governments, of the federated units that are represented). However, the key element of cross-national alliance would be far more difficult to sustainably achieve under this set-up, as there would be a tendency for representatives from various parts of the same country either to systematically gang up together or to bash the traitors who defect to the opponents. Moreover, no electoral competition for votes from countries other than one's own would be put into place. Hence the incentive to construct the interests one is mandated to defend as trans-national would remain weak and the rise of a Europe-wide debate would hardly be fostered.[12]

---

et al. (1997).[See also the parallel defence of a country-wide constituency in an ethnically divided country in Chapters 9–10.] One may object that this pan-European list system does not guarantee representation from all areas and involves a strong bias in favour of politicians from larger countries. One might think of countering this (1) by imposing constraints on the national make-up of each list and attaching a significant electoral advantage to being high up on the list, or (2) by making votes attracted from outside one's country count more heavily for the individual candidate (not the list). More wisely perhaps, one can simply rely on the nationally allocated seats to guarantee representation from all member states (and even most regions), with some overrepresentation of the smaller ones (as is the case now) to compensate for the disadvantage their politicians may have on the Pan-European ballot.

11. Indeed, making power a function of population size, for example by requiring a high qualified majority (4/5 as in the Lamers proposal mentioned earlier) of the populations represented, would be counterproductive from my standpoint, as it would give, or be near to giving, a veto power to the large countries, and thus take us back to the bargaining dynamics from which it is essential to break away.

12. Note that it is precisely because of the lack of such a debate that Sverker Gustavsson (1997) finds it justifiable to give the same voting power or at any rate a fairly equal voting power to each nation at the Council level, as well as to secure a position in the Commission to at least one person from each member state. The underlying concern is with getting all arguments properly listened to, rather than with giving due weight to the interests of all. This argument makes sense. But the solution it suggests must be viewed as a poor and transitional Ersatz to building a well-

In order to achieve these further objectives, one could think of supplementing the reform of the Council – while disposing by the same token of its unsatisfactory rotating presidency – by having the President of the Council elected through a pan-European election.[13] To prevent the contest from degenerating again into a divisive conflict between nations or groups or nations, one could restrict eligibility at each election to the citizens of particular countries, with a rotation among fairly equally populated groups of countries so that each of them has its turn, say, every twenty years. Here again, we would have major politicians forced to adopt a high European profile, enter a highly publicized Europe-wide debate, strengthen cross-national political alliances and above all compete with a platform that caters to the general interest (or to the interest 'of the weakest among us all'), rather than to national interest. The experiment, however, may bring nothing but frustration if the elected President has no other power than to chair a Council that remains governed by international bargaining, or even to appoint a Commission whose initiatives are entirely submitted to approval by such a Council. Hence, even with this addition of an elected President – which may be a defensible idea in its own right – the Council version of the strategy is far less promising that its Parliamentary version.[14]

---

functioning European public realm – an admittedly difficult task for which electoral reform of the type sketched above for the Parliament and the uninhibited acceptance of English as the medium of debate provide two important preconditions. Moreover, an 'alarm bell mechanism' (see Dehousse 1994: 121–3), which makes it possible for the veto of a number of countries to postpone the decision (so as to give them time to make their case), would probably be a better tool for screening out fair arguments from sheer interests.

13. As proposed, for example, by former French President Valéry Giscard d'Estaing (see Franck 1995: 41).

14. Dehousse (1995: 19–25) contrasts the partisan, majoritarian logic of parliamentarism, which is meant to provide 'democratic legitimacy' to the EU, and the representative, pluralist logic of federalism, which is meant to provide it with 'state legitimacy'. He argues against a shift from the latter to the former on the ground that it would jeopardize the EU's authority and stability. In his view, an adequate balance between the two logics would rather require the Commission to remain non-partisan and be accountable on all issues to the Council of Ministers turned into a real second Chamber. I have two main objections to this interesting analysis: (1) Authority, stability, legitimacy and the like do not form the ultimate objective – save perhaps for the rulers themselves – but only conditions for the pursuit of broader goals. All we need is 'enough of them'. This enough may be quite a bit less than is achievable but nonetheless better for the sake of what we ultimately need the EU for – which should be, as it is in the present contribution, the point of departure. (2) Which policies and institutions can be stable depends on how the interests are constructed, which in turns depends on how the institutions are structured. Highly centralized and powerfully redistributive national institutions can be stable when interests are not primarily constructed along regional lines, which in turn is powerfully affected by the way in which political institutions have been shaped. Put crudely, my point is that we should start with the policies we want, next ask which EU institutions we need to get them and finally scrutinize the conditions under which these institutions can be made sufficiently viable, rather than start with an analysis

6. DEMOS-CRACY VERSUS DEMOI-CRACY

Would the adoption of this strategy amount to making the EU more democratic? This is by no means obvious. For the crucial change that is being proposed in this policy area is not an increase or decrease in the degree of democracy, but a shift from *demoi-cracy* to *demos-cracy*, a shift from accountability to the separate peoples of Europe (if redistribution were a purely national or intergovernmental matter) to accountability to the people of Europe as a whole.[15] This shift is not justified because *demos-cracy* is always better than *demoi-cracy*, but because in the case of (much of) redistribution under contemporary economic conditions, raising the scale of the democratic game and changing its rules along the lines indicated can be expected to lead to far better decisions, as far as the overall goal of social justice is concerned, than those to which national governments would be driven by the interaction of economic and political mechanisms.

So, does the EU suffer from a democratic deficit, from a suboptimal level of democratic accountability? It is certainly not good in the long run that some officials in charge of decisions that deeply affect the citizens' lives should carry out their jobs unchecked by them or their representatives. But we have seen that there are ways in which increases in democratic accountability may make matters worse. The question whether there is a democratic deficit, i.e. whether we need more democracy, is therefore dangerously underspecified. For the key question concerns the type of democratic accountability we need, and above all whether it is more *demoi-cracy* or more *demos-cracy* that is required.

---

of current stability or legitimacy conditions and try to make EU institutions, whatever they are, as stable or legitimate as possible.

15. On one definition of federalism, demoi-cracy would simply be democratic federalism, while demos-cracy would turn Europe into a non-federal, unitary state. (See for example King's (1982: 77, 143; 1993: 94) characterization of a federation by reference to the entrenched representation of the federated units in the legislative process of the federation.) But there is another conception of a federal system of government, that emphasizes the constitutional entrenchment of regional decentralization, rather than of regional representation. See e.g. Follesdal's (1997) characterization of federalism in terms of a sharing of final authority over different competences, or indeed Belgium's official claim to being a federal state (since the 1993 constitutional reform), despite the absence of any explicit representation of the federated units in decision-making at the central level. In this second sense, even if the Council were scrapped, even if the whole Parliament were elected in a single constituency, and even if Europe's fundamental law took the form of a Constitution to be approved and altered by the European Parliament alone (rather than that of a set of Treaties), Europe could still be a strongly federal (as opposed to unitary) state. Indeed, it would be of the greatest importance that it should remain so.

chapter six | power-sharing versus border-crossing in ethnically divided societies

In January 1998, I took part in San Francisco in the annual meeting of the American Society for Political and Legal Philosophy devoted that year to the topic 'Designing Democratic Institutions' (Shapiro and Macedo (eds) 2000). I was asked to be a discussant for a paper on the design of democratic institutions for ethnically divided societies presented by Donald Horowitz, from Duke University's Law School. I had just spent part of a sabbatical at All Souls College, Oxford, thinking more systematically than I had ever done before about Belgium's predicament, and even writing the draft of a small book on the subject which, for various reasons, I never completed. The San Francisco meeting provided a wonderful opportunity to connect the international theoretical literature on how best to organize the politics of ethnically divided societies not only with the fieldwork I had been conducting unwittingly for several decades in my own country, but also with a close look at the origin and impact of constitutional reforms that account both for the relative peacefulness and the relative alacrity of Belgium's ethnic relations, starting with the pioneering introduction of proportional representation in 1899. The outcome of this attempt was published in the proceedings of the meeting, where it was preceded by a written version of Horowitz's presentation (Horowitz 2000a) and followed by a rejoinder (Horowitz 2000b).

ॐ

Donald Horowitz's 'Constitutional Design: An Oxymoron?' (Horowitz 2000a) is an exceptionally instructive and gloomy contribution to our thinking about how best to design electoral institutions for ethnically divided societies. I found its instructiveness particularly pleasurable, because it helped me see in a completely new light whatever I knew about the subject, not, as it happens, by virtue of any expertise I might possess in political theory, but rather by virtue of having lived for most of my life in what can plausibly be characterized (as argued below) as a severely divided society: Belgium. Less predictably, the paper's gloominess too was a source of pleasure as I prepared this comment, not at all because I enjoy learning that things go wrong, let alone understanding that they are bound to go wrong, but – quite the contrary – because the little I knew and understood about the subject implied, I thought, that I had some good news for the author. For his paper's central message I understood as follows: while we can get a pretty definite image of the coherent constitutional package needed by a severely divided multiethnic society, there are deep-seated reasons why such societies will adopt instead incoherent hybrids, which will do them no good. The good news will take the form of an argument to the effect that this grim message needs to be drastically qualified. Unsurprisingly (coming from a philosopher), it will rest on two small exercises in conceptual clarification, the crucial relevance of which will be illustrated by my reading of Belgium's constitutional development and debate.

1. WHAT IS A SEVERELY DIVIDED SOCIETY ?
RED SPOTS AND RED SPHERES

First of all, what is it, in Donald Horowitz's view, that makes a poly-ethnic society qualify as severely divided? By definition, it is being prone to (acute, violent) conflict between ethnic groups. Let us take for granted that the notion of an 'ethnic group' is clear enough and concentrate on the concept of 'conflict-proneness'. Conflict-proneness is clearly a dispositional property of the society concerned. But for our purposes, the term 'society' is crucially ambiguous. Do we mean 'society' in a comprehensive sense that encompasses a country's current constitutional arrangements? Or do we mean it in a lean sense, which counterfactually strips a country of these arrangements? In either case, a society's characterization includes the specifics of its territory and its economy, its ethnic features, including their geographical and social distribution, the overall level and distribution of income and wealth, etc. But unlike the first interpretation, the second one excludes 'constitutional design', understood roughly and pretty narrowly as those rules that directly organize the distribution of political power.

The comprehensive interpretation makes the notion of a severely divided society fairly simple, while the counterfactual definition makes it unavoidably tricky. Nonetheless, choosing the comprehensive interpretation would be most unwise, for present purposes. It would soon prove a recipe for despair, as it would turn into an oxymoron, not constitutional design as such, but any successful constitutional design for a severely divided society: the very success of the design would disqualify the society as a severely divided one.[1] Therefore, unless one takes some perverse pleasure in pursuing the logically impossible, there is no sensible way out of some variant of the counterfactual definition.

But what does it mean to abstract counterfactually from a country's constitutional design? Does a poly-ethnic society count as severely divided if, and only if, it would be torn by acute ethnic conflict if it had no constitutional design at all, or perhaps if, and only if, there exists at least one (sufficiently absurd) constitutional design under which the society would be prone to acute ethnic conflict? Under such characterizations, any poly-ethnic society – indeed, presumably, any society under a sufficiently broad definition of an ethnic group – would count as severely divided. On the other hand, if a society were severely divided only if it was prone to acute conflict whatever its political institutions, we would be back to making successful constitutional design an oxymoron. The appropriate definition must obviously lie somewhere in between. Here is one way of making it precise.

Consider a particular society at a particular time, as characterized by the current values of its non-constitutional parameters (in a sense that matches the definition of constitutional design adopted above), and think of the set of all logically possible constitutional arrangements for this society as a multidimensional hyperspace, each point in which represents such an arrangement. To make this more concrete, think of this space as a sphere, with each constitutional arrangement represented by a small spot within this sphere, and specified by the values taken by three continuous variables – for example, what percentage of the total vote is required for representation in the Parliament, how much veto power there is for ethnic minorities, and how strong the government is with respect to the Parliament. Next, colour in red any spot that represents an arrangement under which acute conflict is likely, while leaving in white any point that represents an arrangement under which acute conflict is most unlikely, and colour the rest in shades of pink.

Under the comprehensive interpretation of what 'society' means in that expression, a severely divided society would be one that happens to be in a

---

1.   A conceptual choice of this sort must underlie Horowitz's (2000a) dismissal of consociational arrangements as irrelevant: 'they are more likely the product of resolved struggles or of relatively moderate cleavages than they are measures to resolve struggles and to moderate cleavages'.

red area of the sphere. Under the absurdly broad version of the counterfactual interpretation, it would be one whose sphere has at least one red spot: under a sufficiently broad conception of imaginable arrangements, any society, however safely lodged in the middle of a large white area, is severely divided in this sense. Under the self-defeatingly narrow version of the counterfactual interpretation, on the other hand, a severely divided society would be one whose sphere is completely red: no conceivable institutional arrangement could alleviate its conflict-proneness and only the delicate, often painful surgery of secession may enable the red to recede, as the one sphere is turned into two or more. Finally, under the intermediate counterfactual interpretation I propose to adopt, a severely divided society is defined as one whose sphere has a large red area: it is conflict-prone under a large proportion of the constitutional arrangements. The redder the sphere, the more severely divided the society: like fragility or vulnerability, severe division is a dispositional property that admits of degrees. For some countries, the red spots may be so few that the sphere looks white. The desperate cases are those in which red is all over and deep down. Constitutional engineering for deeply divided societies is concerned with the intermediate case, in which there is a serious risk of being in the red area, but also a serious chance of sticking to the white one.

On the background of this conceptual clarification, I can now try to express my first bit of good news. In the dispositional interpretation for which I have argued above, there are far more severely divided societies than is revealed by overt conflict. The United States is hardly less deeply divided than South Africa, or Holland than Ulster. It just so happens that some countries have chosen or stumbled upon institutions that have kept them safely in the white area. Compare the Netherlands and Northern Ireland, for example. Both were carved out of a larger territory (the Spanish Lower Countries, British Ireland) in which Catholics were an overwhelming majority, to form a territory in which the Protestants came to form roughly two-thirds, and the Catholics roughly one third, of the remaining total. By the beginning of the twentieth century, both had a history of pretty ruthless domination by the Protestant majority and of anti-Catholic discrimination. But in 1917, the Netherlands adopted a Pacification settlement that introduced proportional representation, protected both Protestant and Catholic school systems and ended discrimination against Catholics in access to public sector positions (see Lijphart 1968). In Ulster, instead, no such pacification deal was struck. Discrimination and domination continued, at least partly as a direct effect of the political institutions. Proportional representation (in the form of Single Transferable Vote) was introduced by Lloyd George in 1920 and kept in place in the Republic of Ireland, where the Protestant minority soon dissolved, politically speaking, into a number of Catholic-majority parties. But it was repealed in Ulster in 1929 by the Protestant prime minister James Craig, precisely in order to hinder trans-confessional parties (see Farrell 1997: 112–15). The good news, for Donald Horowitz and his profession, which is illustrated by this contrast is of course not, as such, that there are more severely divided societies than they think, but that constitutional design (whether deliberate or not) can be so successful in some societies that one loses sight of the fact that they are just as severely divided as others in which conflict rages. Once severe division is interpreted, as it must, as a reddish sphere (of potentialities) rather than a reddish spot (in which one happens to find oneself), constitutional engineering holds great promise.

2. SHIFTING STAINS

The goodness of this news should not be overstated, however, and the illustration I just gave is not meant to suggest that there are quick fixes. The job is promising but it is not easy. The constitutional engineer's first task obviously consists in locating with some precision the red and white areas, whose sizes and shapes will vary a great deal from one society to another. When naively advocating the import of a ready-made package of rules that has proven its value through years, the clumsy Western do-gooders stigmatized by Horowitz (2000a) are simply oblivious to this fact: a point safely located in an immaculate area of the sphere associated with one country – for example, a presidential system with an Assembly elected by first-past-the-post – may be deep inside a dark red portion of the sphere associated with another, in which the ethnic set-up is crucially different. The fact that the red patterns vary from one sphere to another does not mean that countries cannot learn from one another. Quite the contrary: there is a lot to be learned from other countries' successes and failures, providing one does not make conflict-proneness an attribute of isolated constitutional devices, nor even of whole constitutional frameworks, but of a combination of a system of devices and the background non-constitutional conditions. Even though no two countries are anything like identical along these dimensions, insight into the mechanisms that underlie conflict-proneness and conflict-inhibition in one country can help guide choices in another. This is exactly what is at work when Horowitz ventures to say, for example, to South Africa: 'Don't go there, it's red. Go there, you'll be safe.'

The job does not stop at identifying the contours of the red and white areas, however, for the wisest recommendation is not always that one should move to the nearest white spot. Often reaching the red area will require moving along two or more dimensions at once. If one moves along one of these dimensions and gets stuck, one may end up in a darker red area than the one one was trying to steer away from. When making recommendations, one should therefore anticipate the possibility that one may be able to go only part of the way. One must also try to guess what the winds and slopes will be, driving the reform further or pushing it back to where it started.

All this seems hard enough. But there are more sophisticated tasks still.[2] For the contours of the red area are not fixed. Demographic or economic changes, for example, may upset the ability of current institutions to keep conflict-proneness under check, and constitutional engineering should antici-pate such shifts of the red area and design institutions accordingly.[3] As a very simple illustration, take a country, such as Belgium, in which the constitu-tion can be changed only with a two-thirds majority. If the majority ethnic group represents 60 per cent of the population (which is currently the case in Belgium), this rule protects the minority group against a constitutional change unilaterally imposed by the majority. But if demographic trends lead to the majority ethnic group forming more than two-thirds of the population, then the current arrangements, without undergoing any change themselves, may suddenly find themselves in the turbulent red area.[4]

---

2. Even if one were only concerned, as I shall suppose throughout is the case, with conflict-proneness. But there is no reason why the consequentialist evaluation of political institutions should confine itself to their impact on acute ethnic conflict or even, more broadly, on democratic stability – even though there are no doubt circumstances in which there are good reasons to give this dimension top priority. Among locations that are outside the red area, there is no good reason to decree that they are all equivalent or that the optimal one is the one most remote from the red border. A just or good or decent society is not simply one in which ethnic groups do not kill one another. It may also be one, for example, in which the interests of younger or future generations are not sacrificed to older or present ones, and the design of political institutions might be of crucial importance in this respect (see Chapter 4). Or one may be dissatisfied with a system that secures ethnic peace but at the same time disempowers some ethnic minorities, thus preventing them from defending their material interests as much as the sustainable achievement of distributive justice would require. The balance between two poly-ethnic political conglomerates stabilized by the US plurality system, for example, may be quite effective to keep the country out of the red. But, as argued by Lani Guinier (1994), this may come at a heavy cost for the weaker, underrepresented minorities. If a broader (and more defensible) view is taken of the overall objective, as is the case in the other chapters of this volume, even reforms that take the risk of moving into a pinkish area would be fully justified if this were the price to pay for leaving a very dark area in terms of social justice.

3. The contours of the red area are not only not fixed, they may also be responsive to the nature of the constitutional arrangement itself. Hence, constitutional engineering should not only anticipate exogenous movements of the stain but also try to bring about its endogenous shrinking. Presum-ably, the maxim 'if you want peace, pursue justice' is relevant here, or the recommendation that, in multilingual societies, one should not go for some fuzzy bilingualism (as was tried in Belgium and Canada), but for a firm application of the territorial principle, as was in place from the start in the Swiss confederation (see e.g. Donneur 1984: 25–52; Papaux 1997: 131–4.)

4. Note that Switzerland, with a Germanic majority of more than three fourths, has a different rule, which requires approval both by an overall majority and by majorities in a majority of cantons

Or take the following, slightly more complex illustration, also taken from the history of Belgium. Throughout the nineteenth century, Belgium is marked by a sharp contrast between its mainly rural North (Flanders) and its far more industrialized South (Wallonia), with the result that, from 1884 onwards, Flanders sends 100 per cent of Catholics to Parliament, and Wallonia a majority of liberals. In 1893, the country moves from highly restricted male suffrage (only taxpayers vote) to universal male suffrage with plural voting (one additional vote for married taxpayers, one or two additional votes for the educated), using a plurality type of electoral system with small multi-member constituencies and a double ballot. As a result, the newly created Socialist Party obtains representation in Parliament, where Liberals and Socialists together win 40 of the 62 Walloon seats, while the Catholic party wins all 90 seats in Flanders and Brussels at the 1894 national election.[5] Obviously, the Catholics can retain power with a comfortable, overwhelmingly Flemish parliamentary majority. The government, which had no Walloon member at all in the 1880s, will have no more than one in the 1890s (see Wils 1992: 190, Mabille 1996: 41). As the population of Flanders kept growing faster than that of Wallonia, while Wallonia remained far more industrial, there was no prospect of a change in the underlying situation.

It may therefore be tempting to claim that, by the end of the nineteenth century, severely divided Belgium was well into the red area, and to understand in this light the bold, unprecedented leap Belgium ventured in 1899, when it became the first country to adopt proportional representation (PR). Thus, David Johnson (1991: 194) asserts that 'the list-proportional system was introduced in Belgium in 1899 to remedy some of the irreconcilable differences between the Walloons and the Flemish', while David Farrell (1997: 61) conjectures that what drove the move was Belgium's desire 'to adopt an electoral system which could equalize the representation of the different communities involved'. Such interpretations derive from the false presumption that if an area is red now, it must always have been so.[6] In fact, the 1899

(see Moser 1996: 43).

5.   The population is then overwhelmingly French-speaking in the South (Wallonia), with a German-speaking minority in the South-East; it is overwhelmingly Dutch-speaking in the North (Flanders), with French spoken by part of the urban middle classes; it is mainly and increasingly French in Brussels, the capital of the kingdom completely surrounded by Dutch-speaking territory.

6.   Analogous interpretations seem far more relevant for the introduction of list PR a few years later in Finland (1906) and of the Single Transferable Vote in the Republic of Ireland (gradually from 1918). In Finland, 'all parties except the Swedes [a comparatively privileged ethnic minority strongly represented in the former Estate of the nobility] were in favour of a unicameral system, and when the Swedes realized that this would probably prevail they held out for a system of PR for the unicameral parliament, as the only guarantee of the continued representation of minorities in parliament.' (Carstairs 1980: 113). In the first Irish election under home rule (1918), First

reform was not motivated by the desire to alleviate an ethnic conflict, nor did it result in extinguishing an ethnic tension, which simply did not exist. However, whatever it was driven by and whatever it achieved at the time, it certainly helped Belgium stay clear of the red area as the latter expanded through the following decades. Let me spell this out.

The history of proportional representation in Belgium starts with the creation of the *Association réformiste pour l'adoption de la représentation proportionnelle* (1881). One of its founding members is Victor D'Hondt, author of the first books advocating the list variant of PR (1878, 1882), as opposed to the Single Transferable Vote variant advocated by Thomas Hare (1859) and John Stuart Mill (1861). An international conference was organized in Antwerp in 1885 to discuss the relative merits of STV and list PR. It closed with a motion advocating the D'Hondt system and asserting 'that proportional representation is the only means of assuring power to the real majority of the country, an effective voice to minorities, and exact representation to all significant groups of the electorate' (Carstairs 1980: 3). Note that the 'minorities' referred to are ideological, not ethnic minorities. The results of Belgium's 1894 election did come as a shock that noticeably strengthened the case for PR, but this had nothing to do with ethnic divisions. The fact that, with about 50 per cent of the vote, the Catholic Party could get nearly 75 per cent of the seats simply did not seem fair. Moreover, some of the most forward-looking Catholics could see that, if the 1893 reform was only a first step to a 'one man one vote' electoral system, there was a serious risk that the Socialist party, still in its infancy but growing fast, would end up squeezing out the liberal party altogether and obtain an absolute majority, as a result of industrialization and rural exodus spreading to Flanders. Hence, the Catholic prime minister Auguste Beernaert, a member of D'Hondt's association (and later a laureate of the Nobel peace prize), proposed list PR in 1894 but was defeated and resigned. There followed some unsettled years, culminating in strikes, physical violence inside the Parliament, further resignations and finally the adoption of list PR by a narrow majority on the 29th of December 1899 (Carstairs 1980: 49–56). As the average magnitude of the PR districts was small, larger parties retained a strong advantage, and the Catholics' absolute majority survived until the introduction of 'one man one vote' universal suffrage in 1919, but the reform did secure that all three parties were signifi-

---

Past the Post was used everywhere except for one constituency where the Single Transferable Vote variant of PR was proposed and adopted in order to encourage political participation by the Protestant minority. Sinn Féin won a dramatic victory except in that constituency, where Protestants obtained impressive results. The Unionists hailed STV as 'the magna carta of political and municipal minorities'. The principle of PR was then incorporated in the first Irish constitution (1922) and its STV variant chosen, more out of ignorance of other systems than as a positive choice (see again Farrell 1997: 112–15).

cantly represented in all three regions.

Throughout this period all sorts of arguments were used (see Moureau and Goossens 1959). Some were contingent upon the specific variants under consideration (e.g. the 'immoral' alliances for the second ballot) while others related to the essential difference between plurality and PR (e.g. the number of viable parties). Some were unashamedly partisan while others were overtly impartial. And among the latter, some were consequentialist (the long-term public interest resulting from inclusion or stability) while others were not (fairness, genuine democracy). But nowhere is there a trace of any reference to 'the irreconcilable differences between the Walloons and the Flemish'. Why not? Because at the time Belgium was still run by a Francophone elite that was ruling throughout the country. Even when there were only Flemings in the national government, the language they spoke at government meetings was exclusively French (as it remained well beyond the middle of the next century), and the fact that Wallonia was in effect run by an exclusively or overwhelmingly Flemish government was not perceived, as such, as a serious problem.[7] The fundamental cleavage, so threatening that the national motto had to be 'L'union fait la force', was still the country-wide ideological divide between Catholics and liberals, not the ethnic divide between Flemings and Walloons.

Yet, it became true, half a century later, that had the old plurality system been kept and thereby the ideological minorities deprived of any representation in whole regions, 'the regional polarity would have been made more acute, hence nation-wide agreement would have been made harder to achieve and the unity of the State, indeed of the country itself, would have been endangered' (Moureau and Goossens 1958: 387). Owing to the steady progress of the 'Flemishization' of the Flemish territory and its elites throughout the twentieth century, it had become correct to say, by the middle of the century, that 'majority voting, if it were introduced, would divide the state so deeply that its continued existence would be in doubt' (Carstairs 1980: 57). Though not driven at the time by any concern with ethnic conflict, the move made in 1899 (and carried further later on through an increase of effective district magnitude) had kept the country for decades out of an area that was still white when Belgium left it but had gradually become dark red. The red

---

7. There were some faint, hardly audible noises on the Walloon side, for example the writer Albert Mockel suggesting in 1897, as a remedy to the antagonism between Walloons and Flemings, 'a complete administrative separation between Flanders and Wallonia, with a Parliament for each of them': Flanders would have a conservative Catholic government and Wallonia a liberal-socialist one, and the constant clashes of interests between the agricultural North-West and the industrial South-East would be avoided. But it is only from 1912, when Catholics unexpectedly retained an absolute majority, that a real autonomist movement got off the ground in Wallonia (Destrée 1923: 181–2, Wils 1992: 193–5).

stain, however, kept expanding further and by the 1960s – culminating in the expulsion of the French section of the Catholic University of Louvain from the Flemish town of Leuven in 1968 and the subsequent splitting of all three national parties along ethnic lines – it was clear that further constitutional reform was urgently needed to steer clear of the red. Belgium was then gradually turned into a federal state (1994), with significant regional autonomy, with veto powers for both linguistic communities in the form of supermajority requirements on touchy issues, and with guaranteed equal representation in the federal government. Concern with the red stain, by this time, was clearly on everybody's mind.

3. WHAT IS A COHERENT PACKAGE? CONSOCIATIONALISM AND ITS RIVAL

This extended example was introduced in order to illustrate the difficulties that arise – both when looking backward in order to explain and when looking forward in order to advise – when the red stain shifts, that is, when the extent to which a society is severely divided changes through time. The last episode of the example, however, leads naturally to the second conceptual issue I want to raise: what counts as a coherent constitutional package, and hence what is the relationship between the competing views of what this package should be? For jointly with proportional representation, the three features introduced in Belgium from the 1970s to alleviate the ethnic conflict are precisely the features listed by Don Horowitz (2000a) as the defining features of consociationalism.[8] Hence the arrangement currently in place in Belgium would seem to offer a paradigmatic example of what he presents as the main rival of the 'incentives approach', which he himself advocates. But is it really? Some doubt is bound to arise, as one considers Horowitz's (2000a) two main objections to consociationalism. One is that it is unable to mitigate conflict, because it generates no electoral support for ethnic compromise – an objection that is certainly not lacking relevance in the Belgian context and to which I shall return shortly. The other objection is that consociationalism 'provides no room for a feature vital to democracy: opposition' – an objection that can only strike me as bizarre, not because I do not believe in the importance of opposition, but because I fail to see why consociationalism, as characterized and hence as illustrated by Belgium, should rule it out. Belgian politics displays daily both the salience of the four characteristic features of consociationalism and the presence of an active, vocal opposition: the government is made

---

8. See section 2 of Chapter 9 for a less sketchy description of Belgium's consociational set-up.

up of an equal number of Flemings and Francophones, but backed only by a subset of the parties in Parliament – currently the Socialists and Christian-Democrats – leaving a diverse opposition made up of liberals, ecologists and nationalists from both linguistic communities to vigorously challenge the government from all sides. To sort this out, some further conceptual clarification is in order.

If one is to keep conflict-proneness under check in poly-ethnic societies – that is, if one is to keep clear of the red area –, there are basically three methods one could think of using. The first one – devolution – consists in reducing what is at stake at the level of the country as a whole. Since Karl Renner's (1902: 67–85) pioneering advocacy of institutional devices for accommodating diverse nationalities, it has come in two varieties: territorial federalism and personal federalism. How much the former can help depends on the separability of territories, that is, on the extent to which ethnic groups are concentrated in territorially contiguous areas or on the contrary dispersed throughout the country. How much the latter variety can help depends on the separability of competencies, that is, on the extent to which ethnically contentious policy areas can meaningfully be assigned to a decision-making body distinct from the one in charge of competencies with an irreducibly central spatial dimension.[9]

If devolution in either variant could go all the way, nothing of significance would be left to decide at the central level, and the problem would not be solved but dissolved with the disappearance of the deeply divided society into two or more homogeneous societies. Under most conditions, this is not possible, and some arrangement must therefore be devised for poly-ethnic governance of whatever is left at the centre. There are two basic methods for trying to foster accommodation and compromise at this level. One is commonly called 'consociationalism'. It consists in making political *power-sharing* between ethnic groups possible, or rewarding, or even compulsory. It has been advocated most systematically by Arend Lijphart (1969, 1977, 1995, 1996), but is traced back by himself to the 1979 British Nobel laureate in economics Arthur Lewis (1965). The other is sometimes referred to as the 'incentives approach'. It consists in making political *border-crossing* between ethnic groups possible, or rewarding, or even compulsory. It is being advocated most systematically by Donald Horowitz (1985, 1991, 1993, 2000a), but was anticipated in Seymour Martin Lipset's (1981) emphasis on the importance of cross-cutting cleavages for the political dynamics of the United States.

Note that even though these two methods will unavoidably lead to different specific institutional proposals in given historical conditions, they are not

---

9.   See sections 4–5 of Chapter 7 below for a discussion of these two varieties of federalism.

defined by specific institutions. This was stressed from the outset by Lijphart (1969: 213):

> The grand coalition cabinet is the most typical and obvious, but not the only possible, consociational solution for a fragmented system. The essential characteristic of consociational democracy is not so much any particular institutional arrangement as the deliberate joint effort by the elites to stabilize the system.

Analogously, Horowitz (2000a) notes:

> The incentives approach does not require specific structures. It is, for example, at home with different electoral systems, depending on the context, provided that the system is strongly conducive to interethnic moderation in the appeal for votes [...].'

This interpretation of both consociationalism and its alternative as methods rather than as specific institutional blueprints should help us sort out the puzzle with which we started about the relationship between consociationalism and opposition.

For one way in which power-sharing can be organized is by treating ethnic groups as sub-polities and using ethnically-based parties as the building blocks of central politics. This corresponds to a narrower characterization of consociationalism, which Horowitz (2000a) sometimes adopts. If power-sharing can only be institutionalized using such ethnic blocs, in the form of a guaranteed presence in the legislative and the executive, mutual veto powers, etc., then there is a serious tension between consociationalism and a lively opposition. But power-sharing between ethnic groups can also operate with either poly-ethnic parties – as it does in Switzerland – or poly-ethnic families of mono-ethnic parties – as it does in Belgium.[10] These variants of consociationalism can still impose ethnic constraints on the composition of the executive or the assembly, or require separate majorities on certain issues. It is perfectly compatible with a lively opposition, including on interethnic issues, though not with one consisting of the whole of one ethnic group. Hence,

---

10. The relationship between consociationalism and opposition is not the only issue that the Belgian example should help clarify. See e.g. Barry (1975a: 135): 'But would it be a contribution to social harmony if each ethnic group were represented by a single monolithic organization? If it were so in Belgium, then Belgium would be, as far as I know, unique in the annals of human history. Except where it is the prelude to peaceful scission of the state, a situation in which conflicting ethnic groups are mobilized behind monolithic organizations is a situation of potential civil war or of civil war averted by effective oppression by one group of the other.' Barry's forceful indictment of a mono-ethnic-party-based consociationalism, as advocated for example by Kenneth McRae (1974) for Canada and Ulster, is not an indictment of consociationalism (qua power-sharing) as such (see Barry 1975b: 139, 145).

the objection that rests on the claim that opposition is essential to democracy is quite relevant to the ethnic-bloc variant of consociationalism, but not to consociationalism as such.

4. BORDER-CROSSING FOR A POWER-SHARING SOCIETY

Conceptual clarification, on the other hand, can do nothing to counter the other objection Horowitz raises against consociationalism. As confirmed by the political history of Belgium – especially since, in the aftermath of the Louvain affair, all national political parties split up along ethnic lines – consociationalism does nothing to generate electoral pressure toward ethnic compromise. Admittedly, compromise needs to be reached at a post-electoral stage, whether because of the need to form a government or because of the mutual veto powers conferred by super-majority requirements. But this is consistent with electoral pressure that drives mono-ethnic parties to try to outbid one another in terms of ethnic toughness and intransigence. This generates a structural discrepancy between the platforms parties are driven to propose to their mono-ethnic electorates and the compromises power-sharing rules force government parties to settle for. The political forum does not construct a common interest. Instead, the whole of political life is essentially perceived as a strenuous bargaining between the distinct interests of the ethnic groups, with the government parties invariably selling out to the other side.

As an observer of the strain thus systemically generated by Belgium's current variant of consociationalism, I can only be favourably predisposed to the alternative, border-crossing approach, which emphasizes the importance of incentives for 'pooling votes across ethnic lines', for 'luring votes across group boundaries' (as Horowitz puts it). Indeed, I am convinced that conflict-proneness would be far better checked – that Belgium would dwell at a safer distance from the red stain – if arbitration between ethnic groups were done, not *ex post* between the sharply diverging platforms that mono-ethnic parties committed themselves to defend, but *ex ante* within the platforms of poly-ethnic parties put forward to poly-ethnic electorates. The final settlement would then be (perceived as) the outcome of a confrontation between rival views of the general interest, rather than a painful compromise between the particular interests of ethnic groups. And this obviously requires that one should make at the very least possible, preferably also rewarding, and perhaps even compulsory, the fishing for votes across ethnic borders. It is therefore not surprising that a number of Horowitz-like proposals have recently sprung up in the Belgian context.

Thus, the Flemish political scientist Wilfried Dewachter, who had long been advocating on independent grounds the double-ballot direct election of the prime minister (Dewachter 1968, 1992), has recently opted for a variant in which both the prime minister and the deputy prime minister are directly elected, with the constraint that one should necessarily belong to one linguistic group and the second one to the other (Dewachter 1996). It is of course of the utmost importance that the Flemings should not elect one and the Francophones the other, in the way the Greek and Turkish Cypriots elected the president and vice-president, respectively, in Cyprus's short-lived 'consociational' constitution of 1960–63 (see e.g. Shugart and Carey 1992: 99–100). The candidates must come in bilingual tickets (in Dewachter's proposal, only at the second ballot) with ethnic groups lumped together in a single constituency.[11]

One problem with such a proposal is analogous to the one pointed out by Horowitz (2000a) in connection with the 1978 Nigerian constitution. It is fine to build border-crossing incentives into the election of the executive. But if the executive needs the confidence of an assembly subjected to the same old incentives, precious little may have been gained. A natural response, for advocates of the above proposal, is to extend the double ballot single-member system to parliamentary elections. Of course, most of the corresponding single-member districts will be mono-ethnic. But as the party system adjusts to the direct election of the executive, one can expect two cross-ethnic party blocs to form and to compete country-wide on the basis of platforms consistent with the one put forward for the crucial election of the prime-ministerial ticket. Unfortunately, for reasons spelled out above in the discussion of PR, this would be a most risky move for Belgium to make, as the emerging pattern of representation is likely to be very different in the North and the South, with the result that the elected executive is likely to enjoy dangerously slender parliamentary support from one of the two linguistic groups.

The alternative is to stick to both parliamentarism and proportional representation, while forcing vote-fetching across the linguistic border at the elections for the House of Representatives (the only chamber in which the government needs a majority in Belgium's bicameral Parliament). One option, inspired by an aspect of the system currently in place in Mauritius and recently proposed by the constitutional lawyer Francis Delpérée, consists in giving each elector two votes at these elections. One would be used, in the usual way, to elect, say, 130 of the 150 representatives in relatively small multi-member constituencies. The second one would be used to fill the remaining 20 seats by asking voters of each of the two communities to choose ten

---

11. A similar proposal had been sketched by the (then) director of the Flemish liberal party's study centre Stefan Ector (1993). The idea of a mixed co-presidential ticket is also suggested for divided societies by Shugart and Carey (1992: 101–2, 219).

representatives among candidates from the other community (see Delpérée 1998: 45–50, Delpérée and Dubois 1998). Border-crossing will thus be institutionalized, and the House of Representatives will comprise members of both communities whose task will be to represent – in the way they vote and even more importantly in the explanation of their vote to the community to which they belong – the interests of the other community.

This is an interesting proposal that is worth pondering about. As far as the creation of centripetal forces is concerned, here is the most serious difficulty I believe it raises. Clearly, the impact of the scheme would be at best negligible, at worst seriously counterproductive, if candidates for the special seats could be 'pseudo-members' of the other community – say, Flemings living in Wallonia and defending Flemish-nationalist positions or Francophones living in Flanders and belonging to a single-issue party defending their own interests. For there is then a serious risk that campaigns would soon focus on concentrating votes on these Trojan horses instead of 'wasting one's vote' on 'real' members of the other community. The Francophones of Brussels' Flemish periphery – less than 1 per cent of Belgium's population – might then end up with 10 out of 150 representatives. To prevent such derailing, one can hardly put much hope in a language test (let alone a blood test!) or in a substantive screening of electoral platforms in order to prevent the special seats from being usurped by non-members of the relevant community. But it is possible to have the lists of candidates for the special seats endorsed by their own communities. This could be done quite simply by requiring these lists to be presented by the parties competing for the electors' first vote and by allocating the special seats of one community exclusively to those parties that obtain more than, say, 5 per cent of the first vote in the constituencies of that community: no hope then, for single-issue Francophone parties in Flanders or single-issue Flemish parties in Wallonia, and competition for the special seats will really be between the parties of one community for the votes of the other community.

The next question is whether the role thus given to political parties may thwart the impact hoped for. The people elected to the special seats may well want to be re-elected. But they will beware of diverging too markedly from their party's line, since they can be re-elected only if endorsed by their party, whereas if their own voters are disappointed and therefore unlikely to re-elect them, their party may still offer them, as a reward for sticking to the line, a potentially victorious position in the election for the standard seats. The personal action of the holders of the special seats is therefore unlikely to have a great impact, especially as one cannot expect a party's big names to accept being relegated to one of them. However, the parties themselves will factor into their strategies what they may lose as a result of disappointing the voters from the other community. The smaller the number of special seats, the more rewarding a tough line will remain, and the more damaging a conciliatory stance. But as their number rises, parties cannot ignore this source of potentially crucial gains and losses, and it will have to care, to an extent unimaginable in the present context, about developing an appropriately inclusive discourse and recruiting a political personnel able to address the other community in its own language. As the share of special seats increases, however, the intrinsic tension with the proportionality principle grows, which may jeopardize the scheme's legitimacy in the eyes of the community that is losing out.[12] This trade-off may not be fatal, but it invites a search for alternatives.

A second, quite distinct way of trying to engineer vote-fetching across the linguistic border at parliamentary elections relies on the creation of a country-wide constituency. As such, this measure is both too much and too little. Too much, because it would abolish any guaranteed representation for any part of the country, and each group's fear of being seriously underrepresented would therefore secure the persistence of mono-ethnic parties. Too little, because overbidding by nationalist parties will still make it a losing proposition for country-wide parties to form again with platforms designed to appeal to both ethnic groups. Some versions of the proposal, however, may avoid both difficulties. Here is one.

Introduce a German-style dual system, with each voter casting two votes for the election of the members of the House of Representatives. Using the first of the two votes, keep allocating 100 of the 150 seats with a list PR system in fairly small multi-member constituencies (for example 11, corresponding to the provinces, instead of the current 20), so as to make sure every part of the country is appropriately represented. Using the second vote, allocate the remaining 50 using open list PR, with the possibility of multiple votes on the same list, in a single country-wide constituency. The allocation of the first category of seats is made using the D'Hondt formula, with no *apparentement*

---

12. If the number of standard seats in each community is proportional to its size, the scheme generates overrepresentation either of the smaller community itself (if the special seats are distributed in proportion to the sizes of the populations they are meant to represent) or of its interests (if they are distributed in proportion to the sizes of the populations from which their incumbents are drawn) or both (under any intermediate formula). This is bound to look unfair to some members of the larger community, especially if the proposal is coming from the smaller one. The only way of circumventing this dilemma consists in abandoning proportionality for the standard seats at the expense of the smaller community. For example, with 60 per cent of Flemings and 40 per cent of Francophones, a 10/10 division of the 20 special seats can be reconciled with overall proportionality (in terms of both which community the representatives belong to and whom they represent), that is, a 90/60 division of the 150 seats, if the standard seats overrepresent (in both senses) the bigger community (80/50 instead of 78/52). As soon as the number of seats is no longer marginal, serious departure from proportionality along one of the three dimensions mentioned may start jeopardizing the legitimacy of the scheme.

across provinces – which amounts to a variant of PR that is quite favourable to (locally) large parties. The allocation of the second category of seats, on the other hand, is made so as to achieve maximum proportionality in the House as a whole, with no overall threshold, among those parties that have achieved, say, at least 0.5 per cent of the vote in each of the eleven provinces or maybe 3 per cent of the vote in each of the three regions.[13] Seats obtained by these parties in the provincial constituencies are taken into account in the overall proportional allocation. Seats obtained in the provincial constituencies by parties which do not present candidates in the country-wide constituency or fail to reach the quota in at least one of the provinces or regions, are retained by them.

The parties' best responses to these new rules is obvious enough: the former country-wide parties will reunite, or at least form common lists with single platforms at the federal level, and with candidates who will try to appeal to voters of both groups. The nationalist parties are also welcome to bid for votes in the country-wide constituency, but obviously they stand a chance only if they manage to gang up around a common platform – which may be easy enough if the key issue is autonomy, but is altogether out of reach if borders and net transfers are the key issues. In the latter case, nationalist parties are not excluded, but will have to narrow down their hopes to reaching the provincial constituencies' pretty high effective threshold. The central purpose, however, is not to get rid of any specific parties, but to reshape political competition and rhetoric, so that these will consist again in confrontation, not between the interests of mono-ethnic blocs, but between alternative versions of the common good.

---

13. The idea of country-wide constituencies for either the House or the Senate is also defended in Vansteenkiste, (1993: 8); and Roland, Vandevelde and Van Parijs (1997: 111–12). In the absence of regional or provincial quotas, however, the incentive for parties to provide platforms that are appealing to both ethnic groups is far too weak, as the individual candidates' desire to gather preference votes across the border will be constantly thwarted by their party's concern not to lose out to more nationalist competitors. Regional quotas need to be set higher than provincial ones to avoid the risk of their being satisfied by the vote of linguistic minorities in border areas (a sharply Francophone party could conceivably collect 1 or 2 per cent of the votes in the Flemish region by mobilizing the Francophone minority living in the part of Flanders around Brussels). [A moderate variant of the proposal discussed here (10 per cent of the seats, no provincial or regional thresholds, linguistic quotas) was later elaborated by the so-called Pavia Group (www.paviagroup.be) and widely discussed by Belgian academics, medias and politicians. See Chapters 9 and 10.]

5. 'INCOHERENT': HYBRID OR CENTRIFUGAL?

The various proposals thus briefly presented illustrate, for the severely divided society I am most familiar with, what the second, border-crossing approach might look like. But given the extent to which this society already uses, as mentioned earlier, paradigmatically consociational, power-sharing devices, is this not, at the same time, a crystal-clear illustration of an 'incoherent' package? Horowitz (2000a) 'want[s] to insist on coherence as a virtue of constitutional design for severely divided societies', and the requirement of 'coherence' or 'consistency' keeps popping up throughout his contribution. But what is 'coherence'? Horowitz repeatedly suggests that a coherent package is the opposite of a 'hybrid' package, as illustrated by the Fiji Islands or Ulster, that is, a package that puts together bits of consociationalism, of the incentives approach, of simple majoritarianism, etc. Under this interpretation, coherence requires us to choose between the power-sharing approach and the border-crossing approach, and therefore the vote-pooling measure suggested above would by definition make Belgium's constitutional design 'incoherent' and should therefore be rejected.

But there is another way of understanding 'coherence' or 'consistency'. The reason Horowitz (2000a) says he 'want[s] to insist on coherence as a virtue of constitutional design for severely divided societies' is that 'their centrifugal forces are so strong that without equally strong, consistent, centripetal institutions their divisions tend to become acute.' A coherent package, on this second interpretation, is not by definition one that is not a 'hybrid', but rather one whose components interact so as to be 'centripetal', so as to produce accommodation and compromise. Under this interpretation, there is no reason to suppose that coherence requires us to make an exclusive choice between the three methods of conflict mitigation – devolution, power-sharing or border-crossing –, which does not mean that specific devices may not turn out to be incompatible. For example, a variety of consociationalism organized around mono-ethnic parties with mono-ethnic electorates is obviously incompatible with the possibility, let alone the encouragement or obligation of vote-pooling. But these are not only formally compatible with power-sharing devices such as proportional representation, supermajorities or guaranteed presence of ethnic groups in the executive. They may well combine, as suggested above, to produce a more centripetal outcome. In this sense, a 'hybrid' package can be more coherent than a 'pure' one. The requirement of coherence then simply reflects, rather than a fixation on 'purity' (with a given nomenclature of ideal types), a down-to-earth search for a set of rules of the game that, taken as a whole, systematically defuse potential ethnic conflict.

No less than the first one (on 'divided societies'), this second exercise in conceptual clarification (on 'coherent packages') can be interpreted as good news for Donald Horowitz. For suppose he is stuck, as most of the time he seems to believe he is, with the first construal of the coherence requirement. What is needed in a severely divided society must then be either consociationalism, which is coherent but won't work, or the incentives approach, which is coherent and will work. But, for deep-seated reasons that Horowitz sketches and illustrates, opportunities for significant constitutional reform are rare, and often produce hybrids rather than coherent packages. No wonder therefore he sounds gloomy. But suppose we decide to drop all concern with coherence as ideal-typical purity, and interpret instead the coherence requirement in the second direction delineated above: what we are looking for is a set of rules of the game that jointly generate a conflict-mitigating dynamic. Territorial autonomy is then bound to help under circumstances in which ethnic groups are sufficiently concentrated. And so are some devices that make it possible, rewarding, or compulsory to share power *and* to cross borders. What and how much is required will depend on variable, though specifiable circumstances, but the three methods can certainly be combined, and not all features of any particular method need to be introduced in one go – even though, for reasons mentioned earlier, the order in which features are introduced must be carefully thought through.

This does not detract from the importance of Horowitz's observation that for any particular country, opportunities for significant reform are few and far between and that, when they occur, people often make a mess of it. But as the recent political histories of Italy, Japan or Eastern Europe show, situations that seemed completely frozen can suddenly come unstuck. And when this happens, well-intentioned insiders must be ready, duly equipped with principled and detailed proposals whose likely consequences in the relevant particular context have been properly thought through, at least in part thanks to the sort of perceptive and imaginative comparative research in which Donald Horowitz has been engaged. This message is nothing new. It is, for example, at the core of the *Memoirs* of Jean Monnet (1976), the man who changed the shape of Europe more deeply than Hitler, de Gaulle and Thatcher together, through shrewd, sometimes counterintuitive yet amazingly successful constitutional engineering for a severely divided continent. But whether new or not, I hope it will help Don Horowitz cheer up, shake off the despondency reflected in his paper. Gloominess is misplaced. 'Never doubt that a small group of thoughtful committed citizens can change the world: indeed, it's the only thing that ever has.' So at least Margaret Mead is quoted as saying on a bumper sticker that caught my sight on Berkeley's Telegraph Avenue while I was concocting my comment on Horowitz's paper.

chapter seven | must europe be belgian?

In November 2009, Herman Van Rompuy, Belgium's Prime Minister at the time, was chosen as the first President of the Council of the European Union. The Economist *reacted with an editorial entitled 'We are all Belgians now' and highlighting some emerging similarities between Belgian and European politics. In both title and contents, the article echoed a piece I had prepared over a decade earlier in a very different context and subsequently published in several languages.*

In September 1998, Quentin Skinner organized in Siena a conference focusing on the relationship between the European Union and the republican tradition. This was a good opportunity, not only to decrypt, under his expert guidance, the Palazzo Pubblico's Allegory of Good Government, but also to reflect of how good government could best be achieved in political entities that find it more difficult than others to regard themselves as 'republics'. The outcome was a more systematic treatment of the issues touched upon in Chapters 5 and 6 organized around the following central thesis: the institutions the European Union needs are not a replica of Belgium's current institutions, but something closely analogous to the institutions plurilingual Belgium is laboriously discovering it needs.

ॐ

'Let us once again cast a glance upon Belgium, our constitutional 'model state', the monarchical El Dorado with the broadest 'democratic' basis, the university of the Berlin statesmen and the pride of the *Kölnische Zeitung*.' Thus starts an article published in 1948 by Karl Marx in the *Neue Rheinische Zeitung* (Marx 1848: 333). Most of the article is devoted to documenting the growth of poverty and crime in the *Modellstaat Belgien*, the allegedly exemplary 'model democratic state of Belgium' and it persuasively suggests that, whatever its economic performance, there is also a seamy side to liberal capitalism. Although Marx's article could have been published under the title I rather frivolously proposed for this contribution, my purpose is rather different from his, and unlike his no doubt would have been, I am already warning you that my answer will be yes. Sounding more ludicrous, the claim I shall thereby be making is likely to arouse less concern than if in the question 'Belgian' had been replaced by 'German', or 'French', or 'British', or even 'Dutch'. Moreover, what I shall invite you to take seriously as a desirable institutional future for the European Union is not – arrogantly – Belgium's current Ego, but, as it were, its Super-Ego, not its present institutional structure, but what I believe it must urgently be moving towards.

More specifically, what I shall do in the bulk of this chapter is sketch two fundamental challenges to which Belgium's institutions need to respond in a coherent way. Finding such a response is by no means obvious, if only because the two challenges seem to generate conflicting demands. But the very survival of the country and – what is more important – the preservation of the combination of extensive freedom and generous solidarity, which the country has been able to develop, along with its neighbours, in the course of the twentieth century, hinge on identifying and implementing such a response. Very schematically, the discussion of possible responses to the first challenge will show how the demands of democratic citizenship foster the territorial partition, along linguistic lines, of what constitutes the last plurilingual sovereign remnant of the Habsburgs' multilingual Empire. But if citizenship is not to become vacuous in a globalised market, I shall next argue – even more briefly – in connection with the second challenge, we must resist this democratic impulse and attempt to restructure the country's institutions so as to make them lean but powerful, and durably compatible with the massive autonomy of essentially unilingual Regions. Against this background, I shall finally suggest that the European Union as a whole, though coming from the opposite direction as it were, increasingly faces the same predicament and I shall sketch how an analogous response needs to be thought about and put into place.

1. THE DEMOCRATIC CHALLENGE

The first challenge can be presented in many ways. I shall adopt the version given to it by John Stuart Mill (1861) in an ominous passage of the sixteenth chapter of *Considerations on Representative Government*. After having sympathetically noted that

> the Flemish and the Walloon provinces of Belgium, notwithstanding diversity of race and language, have a much greater feeling of common nationality than the former have with Holland, or the latter with France,

Mill pronounces his famous (near) indictment of multilingual democracies:

> Free institutions are next to impossible in a country made up of different nationalities. Among a people without fellow-feeling, *especially if they read and speak different languages*, the united public opinion, necessary to the working of representative government, cannot exist. The influences which form opinions and decide political acts are different in the different sections of the country. An altogether different set of leaders have the confidence of one part of the country and of another. The same books, newspapers, pamphlets, speeches, do not reach them. One section does not know what opinions, or what instigations, are circulating in another. [...] For the preceding reasons, it is in general a necessary condition of free institutions that the boundaries of governments should coincide in the main with those of nationalities. (Mill 1861: 291–4, emphasis added).

Leaving out a number of nuances and qualifications, I shall give Mill's claim the following stark formulation: 'No viable democracy without a linguistically unified demos.' This claim I shall here simply call *the democratic challenge*.

For a long time, the process described by Mill was hardly noticeable in Belgium, basically because the country was ruled, North and South, by a French-speaking elite. But it is now in full swing. Let me just mention three indicators. While the watching of Flemish TV by Walloons has always been very low, the watching of the French-language Belgian channels by Flemish viewers is now also down to 0.7 per cent of their TV time (BRTN 1996). Even in Brussels, 85 per cent of Francophones say they never read a Flemish newspaper (Fondation francophone de Belgique 1997: 23). And between 1954 and 1993, controlling for distance, the probability of moving from a Walloon commune to a Flemish commune or vice versa has dropped from one half to one third of the probability of moving from one commune to another within the same Region (Poulain and Foulon 1998: 55–6).

'The outcome', as sociolinguist Kas Deprez wrote in an opinion piece published in 1998 by the Flemish daily *De Standaard,* 'is that a genuine Belgian we-feeling is no longer possible'. Or again, in the equally Millian formulation of political scientist Wilfried Dewachter (1996: 136):

> The country's other community is practically a foreign people. It is rather difficult for a political system to keep functioning satisfactorily with such mutual ignorance and hence such lack of mutual understanding of the two halves of the country.'

No one who has been following Belgian politics in recent decades can deny that this is an increasingly serious problem. No one who has read Mill's analysis can fail to suspect that this problem does not arise from an idiosyncratic defect of Belgium's populace, but is paradigmatic for all multilingual democracies. With about 6000 living languages in the world, with 211 sovereign states to accommodate them, and with formal democracy slowly gaining ground, the problem is definitely worth more attention than the traditional focus on the 'standard' case of unilingual democracies has encouraged.

What can be done about it? How can Mill's condition of a unified demos be fulfilled? Before considering what can plausibly be regarded as the only four options, it is important to tease out a crucial ambiguity in the formulation I have given to our democratic challenge. As was neatly brought out in a controversy between Dieter Grimm (1995) and Jürgen Habermas (1995) about the European Union's democratic potential, a 'unified demos' can be understood either as a 'homogeneous ethnos' or as a 'common forum'. In the former interpretation, which can plausibly be traced back to Carl Schmitt (1926: 14), democracy is only viable for a homogeneous people, one which needs to possess, not racial purity, but a shared culture and identity. Language matters here as a central component of a people's culture. In the second interpretation, which I shall take to be the best construal of Mill's thought, democracy is only viable for a communicating people, one which may not share a single culture or identity in any thick sense, but which possesses a common space for discussion and decision-making. Language matters this time simply as a medium of communication. As the linguistic conditions for a common forum are likely be less stringent than the linguistic conditions for a homogeneous ethnos, this clarification may turn out to be crucial if one is not to unnecessarily foreclose some otherwise promising options.

2. GENERALISED UNILINGUALISM

The most obvious way of meeting Mill's condition for a viable democracy consists in adopting a single language throughout the country. There is no doubt that other countries have successfully pursued this strategy. Thus, in 1789, French was the mother tongue of less than 50 per cent of the population then living in the territory that now forms France. There is no doubt that part of Belgium's political elite was tempted to adopt an analogous strategy, toughly expressed in a quotation often attributed to Charles Rogier, one of Belgium's first Prime Ministers (1847–1852) and a powerful liberal politician throughout the first half century after Belgium's independence:

> The first principles of a good administration are based on the exclusive use of a language and it is obvious that the Belgians' sole language must be French. To achieve this outcome, it is necessary that, for a while, all civil and military functions should be entrusted to Walloons and Luxemburgers: in this way, being temporarily deprived of the advantages attached to these functions, the Flemings will be forced to learn French, and the Germanic element will be gradually destroyed in Belgium.[1]

I should add that there was at the time no lack of high-minded justifications for this tough approach. Friedrich Engels, for one, did not think much of the defence of weaker languages and cultures:

> By the same right under which France took Flanders, Lorraine and Alsace, and will sooner or later take Belgium – by that same right Germany takes over Schleswig; it is the right of civilisation as against barbarism, of progress as against stability.' (Engels 1848: 423)

And Mill himself cannot be said to have lacked sympathy for this first way of meeting the democratic challenge he so forcefully formulated:

> Experience proves that it is possible for one nationality to merge and be absorbed in another: and when it was originally an inferior and more backward portion of the human race, the absorption is greatly to its advantage. Nobody can suppose that it is not more beneficial to a Breton, or a Basque of French Navarre, to be brought into the current of the ideas and feelings of a highly civilised and cultivated

---

1. This text is often quoted (generally in French, which makes it sound more authentic) as if it had been written by Rogier himself (see e.g. De Ridder 1988: 106; Beelen et al. 1993: 19; Brans 1993: 25; Bouckaert 2008). But its only source is a passage in a 1866 lecture in Dutch which makes no claim to quoting Rogier literally (see Willems 1902: 59–69).

people – to be a member of the French nationality, admitted on equal terms to all the privileges of French citizenship, sharing the advantages of French protection and the dignity and prestige of French power – than to sulk on his own rocks, the half-savage relic of past times, revolving in his own little mental orbit, without participation or interest in the general movement of the world. The same remark applies to the Welshman or the Scottish Highlander, as members of the British nation. (Mill 1861: 294–5).

Yet, Belgium did not follow this path. Why not? Basically because there were sufficiently numerous, powerful and organised Flemish people who saw that it was in their collective interest to claim equal rights for their own language, or at any rate for a language far closer than French to their native dialects. There were therefore two competing processes of linguistic nation-building and one of them lost to the other. On one side, there was the central authority of an industrialising country with a strong interest in expanding an educated and mobile work force through a linguistically uniform administration, army and – above all – school system. This is the basic mechanism at work in the process famously described by Ernest Gellner (1983: 139–40) as a transition from Kokoshka to Modigliani, from a linguistic map of Europe that looks like a mess of coloured patches to one in which nearly uniform surfaces are neatly separated by thick black lines representing political boundaries. On the other side, there is the struggle to gain official recognition within a restricted area for a language so far unrecognised. To use Benedict Anderson's (1993: 615–17) illuminating metaphor, this works as a tariff, a customs barrier: to the people coming from the centre, the local people can now say: "Do come, trade, work, administer here, but henceforth you'll need the humility to learn and speak our language rather than expect us to speak yours." This amounts to the erection of new borders, to the drawing or strengthening of new lines, which does not prevent Modiglianisation but forces it to operate on a smaller scale. In this case, unlike many others, the resistance won. And it is right that it should have won. Why?

The answer is not straightforward. There is, after all, no lack of efficiency-based, and even equality-based arguments in support of linguistic homogenisation, of countries bulldozing out of existence their minority languages. My condoning of resistance does not rely on any alleged right for languages to survive, nor on the assumption that we owe our ancestors to preserve their culture, nor even on the aesthetic value of linguistic diversity. There are, I believe, only two types of arguments which can carry significant weight. One is consequentialist and relates to the long term. The other is justice-based and concerns the transition period only.[2]

There are undoubtedly strong efficiency advantages associated with the ease of communication and movement which linguistic homogeneity makes possible. But there are two effects of linguistic diversity which may plausibly, under some circumstances, more than offset these advantages. Given the nature and reach of present-day media, linguistic diversity is the firmest, and increasingly the only serious protection of cultural diversity, and the latter permits a diversity of experimentation in private and collective life, from which the general interest may well, in the long run, benefit. Secondly, in an increasingly globalised world, linguistic diversity is the firmest, and increasingly the only serious brake on the mobility of people. It is in this sense a precious population stabiliser, at any rate if one regards massive migration as undesirable, whether because of its propensity to dislocate local communities or because of its jeopardising the economic and political viability of institutionalised solidarity. The first of these two arguments is rather speculative, while the second one is contingent on a specific view of what counts as a good or just society. Both only apply to cases in which it is a less widely spread language that is losing ground.

The second, justice-based type of argument does not have those limitations, but it is necessarily restricted to the short term: it relates to what unavoidably happens in the transition from a situation of linguistic diversity within a territory to one in which one of the pre-existing languages is imposed as the official language. Having a mother tongue different from the one adopted as the official language puts one at a multiple disadvantage. People in that position have to bear the heavy cost of acquiring proficiency in a foreign language. They are handicapped, relative to natives of the official language, in economic and political competition. Most seriously perhaps, their self-respect is under pressure as a result of the subordinate, inferior status given to something as deeply associated with themselves (in other people's eyes and their own) as their mother tongue.

Admittedly, this injustice is limited to the transition period: native French-speaking Bretons and native English-speaking Irish people do not suffer from it. But if the transition is short, owing to some vigorous unilingualism policy, the injustice is very acute. And if the transition is milder, it will affect many generations. Admittedly too, the injustice could in principle be alleviated in various ways (though it seldom is in any of them). The native speakers of the dominant language could pick up at least the full financial burden of language learning. Reverse discrimination measures could secure a fairer access

---

2.   These two families of arguments are formulated more rigorously and discussed far more thoroughly in Chapters 2–6 of Van Parijs (2011).

to jobs and promotions to the speakers of the dominated language. But even if the cost of learning were fully compensated and discrimination fully neutralised, there would remain the serious *prima facie* injustice associated with the unequal respect manifested in the sharply unequal public recognition of the official and the subordinate languages. Of course, all things considered, this justice-based argument may sometimes need to give way, for example if the linguistic community concerned is very small, but it provides nonetheless the strongest and most general reason for condemning linguistic assimilation and justifying resistance to it.

Whether or not it is to be condemned, there is in any case no one in Belgium today, however attached to national unity, who still believes that this first strategy is the way to go – not even in the other direction. After all, over 60 per cent of Belgium's population now have Dutch as their mother tongue, and they are estimated to produce about 70 per cent of the national product. But even a very timid attempt by the Flemish regional government to slightly erode the Francophones' rights to receive administrative documents in French in six communes around Brussels has been met by fierce resistance, indeed was the subject of official complaints to the Parliamentary Assembly of the Council of Europe on the ground that it violated the fundamental rights of minorities. Hence, we might as well forget generalised unilingualism. Too bad! It would have made things so simple.

3. GENERALISED BILINGUALISM

The second strategy for meeting a bilingual society's democratic challenge consists in banking on bilingualism. It comes in two variants, profoundly different from one another, but both bound to fail, basically because of the conjunction of the same two trivial empirical facts: (1) For two people to communicate with one another, it is enough that one of them should know the other's language. (2) Learning a foreign language is a heavy, costly job, and getting unmotivated children or teenagers to learn a foreign language is a hopeless project.

In the soft or liberal version, bilingualism is required of the territory without being required of the people. This means that the administration, the courts, the political assemblies and above all the schools are required to function in either language throughout the country, depending on what the preferences of (a sufficient proportion of) the local population happen to be. However, this soft bilingualism is just a milder, slower, more covert but no less inexorable form of generalised unilingualism. This is so because of a process perceptively described by Jean Laponce (1984): the more kindly people behave towards one another, the more savagely languages treat each other. Languages can coexist for centuries when there is no or little contact. But as soon as people start talking, trading, working with each other, courting each other, having children together, one language gradually drives out the other one. The formal equality of Belgium's two languages officially recognised in 1898 did little to slow down the Frenchification of Brussels and other Flemish cities in the early part of the twentieth century. Spreading from the urban centres, the 'oil stains' kept growing steadily as a result of parents choosing the 'best' schools for their children and mixed couples choosing the 'easiest' language for internal communication. Hence, the hard, authoritarian, centralised, deliberate, top-down Gellner-type mechanism and the soft, liberal, decentralised, spontaneous, bottom-up Laponce-type mechanism are simply two very different ways of achieving in the end the same outcome, the gradual extinction of a linguistic community.

The same cannot be said about the hard, authoritarian version of bilingualism, the only one that takes bilingualism seriously as it requires the people, not only the territory, to become bilingual. To enforce a widespread real competence in the second language, one could think, for example, of making it a strict condition for graduating from secondary school or entering higher education of any sort, or a prerequisite for applying for all public sector jobs, possibly even some private sector jobs, throughout the country, whether or not the performance of the job is likely to involve a significant use of it. Jules Destrée, the historical leader of the Walloon and socialist movement, considered this possibility:

> It is in Brussels that the fabulous theory of full bilingualism was born. Belgium is a bilingual country, hence all Belgians must be bilingual. By teaching French to the Flemings and Flemish to the Walloons, we shall achieve the genuine national unity.

His assessment is unambiguous: 'This theory is imbecile.' (Destrée 1923: 127). This fierce hostility is not hard to understand. Firstly, against the background of the asymmetrical, soft bilingualism that was prevailing in Belgium in Destrée's time, it is clear that hard bilingualism would give a systematic advantage to Flemings, the natives of the dominated language, whose competence in the dominant language was (and still is) far greater than the Walloon's competence in Dutch. Secondly, Destrée could not fail to be aware of the massive, indeed prohibitive cost of motivating and teaching pupils, of motivating and training a sufficient number of teachers, for the learning of a language which there is little point in learning since the others will anyway be learning theirs. We are thus back to the double empirical fact mentioned at the start of our discussion of generalised bilingualism: it provides the fundamental reason why its hard version too is an unpromising prospect.

4. NON-TERRITORIAL SEPARATION

Let us not despair yet. For as we continue exploring the space of logical possibilities, we shall have no difficulty identifying a third straightforward way of satisfying Mill's condition of a linguistically unified *demos*. It consists in gathering all the people who speak the same language, wherever they live in the country, into a political entity, a *Gliedstaat*, and in devolving powers massively to this level. This is an extreme version of an idea put forward at the beginning of the century by Karl Renner, an Austrian social-democratic thinker and politician who became president of Austria after World War II. In his remarkable *Das Selbstbestimmungsrecht der Nationen* (1902, revised edition 1918), he tried to work out in detail – presumably for the first time in history – democratic institutions for an irreducibly multinational state. What he proposed was a combination of territorial federalism and what he called personal federalism. Each of the eight nations comprising the Austro-Hungarian empire (Germans, Czechs, Poles, Hungarians, Slovenes, Slovaks, Croats, Italians) were to be given their own Parliament and granted full autonomy in matters of culture, education and at least some aspects of social policy, with matters of common interest settled through negotiation between the representatives of the various nations.

The Austro-Hungarian Empire soon fell apart, and Renner's scheme was therefore never tried in the context for which it was meant. But some form of non-territorial federalism was tried elsewhere, for example in Estonia in 1925, in Cyprus in 1960 or in South Africa in 1984, never with great success. The only place where it subsists is precisely in Belgium, in the limited but still quite recognisable form of its federalism of Communities: next to its three Regions – Flanders, Wallonia and Brussels – Belgium has three Communities – Flemish (comprising all inhabitants of Flanders and the Dutch speakers of Brussels), German (comprising the 60,000 inhabitants of a handful of German-speaking communes in the East of Wallonia) and French (comprising all the other inhabitants of Wallonia and the French speakers of Brussels).[3] The very fact that Belgium is still in trouble shows that this scheme has not fixed it. But this might be because the variant of non-territorial segmentation it has adopted is not radical enough. One can easily think – and some people do – of further expanding the powers of the Communities, at the expense of either the Regions or the federal government. One can also think of simultaneously and massively expanding the territory whose inhabitants can belong to either Community, more precisely by making it possible not only for the inhabitants of Brussels (as is the case now), but also for those of the coun-

---

3.   See section 2 of Chapter 8 for a more comprehensive description of Belgium's current set-up.

try's other two Regions (Flanders and Wallonia), to be members of either the French or the Flemish community. What the existing weak version of non-territorial federalism cannot achieve, perhaps this more radical version will.

Not much reflection is needed to conclude that it will not. A first intrinsic difficulty can be compactly phrased in terms of a dilemma between linguicide and apartheid. For there can be a soft, choice-based conception of membership in a Community, and a hard, ascriptive one. In the former interpretation, each household is free to choose the Community it belongs to, as reflected, for example, in the choice of a school for its children. But there is then no reason why the weaker community should not feel under permanent threat – exactly like in the case of soft bilingualism, though with a major proviso: with economically unequal communities, the conversion speed from one community to the other may be further increased, as membership of the richer community is likely to come with a number of material advantages, but it may also be slowed down or reversed, if the community with the weaker language is the more affluent one.

There is of course a way of avoiding the strains generated by the fear of losing ground. It consists in depriving households of the right to choose which community they belong too. This is exactly what the hard version of non-territorial federalism does: which community you belong to – and hence which school you and your children attend, which health insurance package you receive, which sports facilities you have access to, which family law you are subjected to, etc. – is strictly determined by your native tongue. As one's native tongue is hardly less a matter of arbitrary luck than one's racial features, and as membership of different communities can be associated with very unequal packages of entitlements, it is clear that this ascriptive variant of far-driven non-territorial federalism is no less repugnant than the racial version of it imagined for South Africa in 1984.

This dilemma between (soft) linguicide and (linguistic) apartheid constitutes only one of two decisive difficulties for the strategy of non-territorial separation. The second one stems from the irreducibly spatial nature of any coherent, comprehensive project for a political community. There is a tremendous structural strain inherent in any set-up in which distinct political communities elaborate and discuss their own projects separately and then need to negotiate and compromise with each other on countless issues, because they happen to share the same territory. For this reason too, non-territorial separation is not that promising after all as a strategy for addressing our democratic challenge. Is there any other candidate? Reluctantly, it seems, only one: territorial separation.

5. TERRITORIAL SEPARATION

Underlying the rejection of each of the previous three options, there is not only the assumption that languages must be protected, but also that their protection requires enforcing some sort of territoriality principle. With some minor qualifications, this thesis is Laponce's (1984) central message. It also provides a plausible explanation for why relations between linguistic communities have on the whole been significantly better in Switzerland than in Belgium, Canada or Spain, let alone in Sri Lanka, East Timor or Kosovo. The territoriality principle amounts to telling any newcomer (whether by birth or immigration):

> Whatever your mother tongue, you are welcome to settle here. But if you do, you will have to learn the local language, which will be the exclusive language of public administration, of political communication and most importantly of publicly subsidised education.

Once this principle is firmly in place, our democratic challenge can be met through a massive devolution to suitably drawn Regions, at the limit through the territorial partition of the country. In contrast with non-territorial separation, there is here no dilemma between linguicide (languages are entrenched) and apartheid (all inhabitants of a territory belong to the same political community, with equal social and economic rights), nor does the irreducibly spatial dimension of projects and policies constitute a problem if boundaries are sensibly drawn.

For this solution to work smoothly, however, one obviously requires a significant degree of pre-existing linguistic homogeneity. For 99 per cent of Belgium's territory, this is not too bad, precisely because the territoriality principle has been in place, with some significant exceptions, since the language legislation of 1932. Regional unilingualism was then adopted for most of the territory outside the national capital, as a compromise between soft and hard bilingualism, to which, for the reasons sketched above, Flemings and Walloons were, respectively, bitterly opposed. The exceptions made by the 1932 compromise were at the source of further trouble. Some of them were later erased, most prominently when the borders were permanently fixed, instead of left alterable in the light of the linguistic census (1962) and when the Université catholique de Louvain, Belgium's largest French-language university, was expelled from the Flemish town of Leuven in which it had been located for over five centuries (1969). But the main exception persists.

As Jules Destrée (1923: 182) put it, 'When separatists are asked what will be done, in case of partition, with Brussels and the Congo, they are very embarrassed, and this is indeed the big stumbling block of any fully separatist scheme.' Congo has since taken care of itself – in this respect at any rate –, but what about Brussels? Has its linguistic situation evolved so deeply in recent decades that it no longer constitutes a stumbling block? I believe it has, and that the future lies, in this respect, neither in an absorption of Brussels, along with Wallonia and possibly the Grand Duchy of Luxemburg, into a re-drawn Belgique; nor in a 'reconquest' of Brussels by Flanders; but in a full recognition of the increasingly *sui generis* nature of 'the people' of Brussels. Rather than filling out the crucial details of this territorial devolution scenario, which I regard as the best response to Mill's challenge in the Belgian context,[4] I shall now turn, far more briefly, to the second challenge.

6. THE REDISTRIBUTIVE CHALLENGE

This second challenge can be formulated in very general terms by stating that a number of major, irreversible trends, most of them closely connected to so-called 'globalisation', have been converging to increasingly turn states into firms. States can no longer count on 'their' capital, 'their' workers or 'their' consumers, but they have to compete with each other to attract or retain savings and investment, skilled labour and the willingness to buy their products. As the pressure stemming from this competition intensifies, the pattern of public expenditure that can be sustainably achieved by each state is bound to be deeply modified. In particular, its ability to reduce the income inequalities that emerge from the operation of the market will be dramatically curtailed. This is our second challenge, which I shall call the *redistributive challenge*.

This is not the place to dwell on the general nature of the underlying trends, their causes and consequences. I shall restrict myself to indicating why the challenge is bound to take a particularly acute form in case Belgium were to fall apart, taking as a point of departure the following paradoxical fact. Among Belgium's eleven provinces (five in Flanders, five in Wallonia, and the Region of Brussels), the province of Brabant wallon, to the South of Brussels, is at the same time the richest and the poorest. It is the richest (*ex aequo* with Vlaams Brabant) in terms of average household income as recorded for income tax purposes. It is the poorest in terms of GDP per capita. The explanation is not that, since the Clabecq steel works were downsized, the province's biggest employer is one whose productivity might be suspected of being abysmally low, namely my own University. It is rather, quite simply, that the province in which one works need not be the province in which one lives. Therefore, many people who are currently earning high

---

4.   More is to be found on this territorial devolution scenario in Chapter 8.

incomes in Brussels or have done so in the past, can easily choose to retire in Brabant wallon or to commute daily into Brussels. Since Brussels is completely surrounded by the Flemish Region, note that the many people who do such commuting either by car or by train – many also from more remote Walloon provinces – travel every day through the three Regions which territorial partition would make formally autonomous.

This paradoxical fact and its explanation should suffice to enable you to imagine how acute fiscal competition would be in the vicinity of Brussels – and with efficient transport, the area within daily commuting distance of Brussels can easily comprise half of Belgium's population and three quarters of its GDP – if each of Belgium's three Regions were given a great degree of fiscal autonomy, and even more if they became as independent of each other as EU member states can be. Firms can choose to settle or relocate in any of the three Regions while hardly modifying the distance from their employees' residences or their business partners' sites. Households can also choose to stay in, or move to, any of the three Regions without a major impact on distances from their jobs, relatives or friends. There is therefore much to gain from a sharp and resolute lowering of tax rates in order to lure prosperous businesses and affluent taxpayers – and much to lose from sticking to high rates. It would therefore not take long for the fiscal competition triggered by fiscal autonomy to unravel the elaborate and comparatively generous redistribution systems slowly built up in the course of Belgium's history. The termination of trans-regional solidarity as a result of the partition process would thus be compounded by a fast erosion of intra-regional solidarity.

Of course, nothing would in principle prevent autonomous Regions from striking deals with one another in order to organise inter-regional redistribution and protect intra-regional redistribution at the levels that would have prevailed in the absence of partition. But the limits and fragility of such confederal systems are notorious. The authors of the *Federalist Papers* observed the workings of the confederal constitution of the United (Dutch) Provinces of their time and were not impressed:

> Such is the nature of the celebrated belgic confederacy, as delineated on parchment. What are the characters which practice has stamped upon it ? Imbecility in the government; discord among the provinces; foreign influence and indignities; a precarious existence in peace, and peculiar calamities from war. It was long ago remarked by Grotius that nothing but the hatred of his countrymen to the house of Austria kept them from being ruined by the vices of their constitution.' (Hamilton *et al.* 1788: 170).

There is no reason to expect a twenty-first century Belgian confederation to be any less 'imbecile' than the 'belgic confederacy' of the eighteenth century pilloried in the *Federalist Papers*.

7. A FOUR-PRONGED PACKAGE

Although far more would need to be said to show how serious this second challenge is and how hopeless it would be to try to tackle it through intergovernmental deals, enough has been said to see the emergence of a threatening tension. On the one hand, one cannot have a viable democracy in a multilingual society – this is the democratic challenge. On the other hand, one cannot have generous redistribution in a small open economy – this is the redistributive challenge. To make democracies more unilingual, and thereby alleviate the first difficulty, one needs to devolve power to linguistically more unified territories. But the more one decentralises redistributive powers, the tighter the economic constraints on redistribution, and hence the more acute the second difficulty. In a multilingual area, here lies therefore an undeniable tension, an unavoidable trade off between smooth democratic functioning and generous intra- and inter-regional solidarity. But there are also ways of softening the trade off. Imagining, implementing these ways is what I view as Belgium's central task in the years ahead. The guiding idea must be to strengthen the linguistic significance of borders while weakening their socioeconomic importance.

More specifically, what is needed in the case of Belgium is a coherent package of reforms including at its core the following four:

(1)   a vigorous protection of the linguistic integrity of Flanders and Wallonia (though not of Brussels);

(2)   a reform of (key sectors of) Belgium's welfare state that combines a central collection of resources with capitation grants to the three Regions, each in charge of the conception and management of its own health and education systems;

(3)   a reform of the electoral system that induces vote pooling across the linguistic border, instead of perpetuating the current state of affairs, in which unilingual parties fish for votes in only one of the two communities; and

(4)   the gentle fostering of a common forum of discussion which will increasingly be, not in French (the common medium in the past and the majority language in Brussels), nor in Dutch (the majority language in Belgium), nor in German (the third national language and the majority language in the European Union), but in the emerging first universal lingua franca.[5]

---

5.   The first of these four components has been motivated above and is developed in Chapter 5 of

I am convinced that this is also the sort of (four-pronged) package that Europe will, *mutatis mutandis*, increasingly need. In a nutshell, my diagnosis is as follows. On the one hand, the pressures of fiscal and social competition will build up, as savings, consumer demand, firms and high-skilled professionals become increasingly mobile. On the other hand, the strains arising from so-called asymmetric shocks and divergence within an economic and monetary Union will start making themselves felt as regional specialisation deepens, without labour migration providing an adjustment mechanism – as it does in the USA – because of Europe's linguistic diversity and the importance (argued for above) of preserving the latter. In this context, the need will develop for massive and systematic transfers across the borders of the EU's member states – at least if Europe does not want to perform even more poorly than the USA does today in terms of (freedom-friendly) solidarity. However, such transfers will only prove sustainable:

(1)   if they are consistent with the unilingual (sub)national polities' claim to organise the fine structure of their solidarity systems as they see fit;

(2)   if they take a very simple form that minimises moral hazard while preserving autonomy, typically capitation grants to governments or citizens, centrally funded out of a common tax base;

(3)   if they can rely on electoral institutions that structure the political game at EU-level along ideological rather than national lines, and

(4)   if they can be discussed and justified in a common forum of discussion using a language understandable all over Europe.

Belgium is coming from a situation in which redistribution was operating at the global level, but without adequate recognition of the consequences of having two separate democratic spaces. The task is to adequately accommodate this separation, while preserving the sustainability of global solidarity. In Europe, separate national democratic spaces have been recognised all along, but redistribution is not (more than marginally) organised at the global level. The task is to create the conditions for global solidarity, while protecting the autonomy of separate national democratic forums. For such global solidarity is required if the redistributive challenge is to be met under contemporary conditions. And if the democratic challenge is to remain satisfactorily met, this must go hand in hand with protecting linguistically homogeneous territories and their autonomy. It is therefore not surprising that the set of conditions spelt out above in the European case should bear close resemblance to the policy package advocated earlier in the Belgian case. If Belgium can successfully adopt such a package, then it will make it far more credible that Europe

---

Van Parijs (2011); the second one is spelled out in Van Parijs (2004); the third one is defended in Chapters 9 and 10 and the last one is inchoatively illustrated by the Re-Bel initiative (www. rethinkingbelgium.eu).

can and must move in this direction too.

This should have clarified in which sense it may not be altogether ludicrous to claim that Marx's *Modellstaat Belgien* will soon deserve to be, if not 'the University of the Berlin statesmen', at least a model worth thinking about and being inspired by for those who believe in the importance of preserving not only multilingualism and democracy but also social justice in today's Europe. So, must Europe be Belgian? In this rather qualified, somewhat far-fetched sense, yes indeed it must.

chapter eight | belgium re-founded

In December 2008, I was invited to give a public lecture within the framework of the Hogeschool Gent's Robert Vandeputte Chair. The bulk of this lecture consisted in a commentary of a sequence of graphs and maps that helped to understand why federal Belgium will survive us all – and why, therefore, it is worth devoting some effort to reforming thoroughly its institutions in order to make them better suited to the smooth working of a pluri-national democracy and to the efficient operation of a trans-national welfare state. The final part of the lecture sketched what this 'Copernican revolution' should look like. It updated and specified, in the light of an increasingly intense debate about Belgium's future, the four-pronged policy package advocated, for both Belgium and Europe, in Chapter 7. This part of the lecture was subsequently published in an English-language collection of Vandeputte lectures, followed by a critical comment by one of my hosts (Van Velthoven 2009).

ॐ

The conjunction of two simple claims explains why federal Belgium will survive us all.

(1)   Neither Flanders nor Wallonia can leave the Belgian federation while absorbing Brussels.

(2)   Neither Flanders nor Wallonia wants to leave the federation without remaining in control of Brussels.

What blocks the secession of one of the two main Regions with Brussels is that the other Region would not consent, that the Brusselers do not want it and that the European Union is not keen. What blocks the secession of one of the two main Regions without Brussels is that Brussels is at the core of the economic dynamism of the whole country (hardly more that 1 per cent of the country's territory accounts for one third of its wealth) and is inextricably linked to each of the other two Regions' wealthiest and fastest growing provinces (*Vlaams Brabant* and *Brabant wallon*).

Does it follow that we are stuck forever with a boring and painful status quo? Not at all. We urgently need a thorough reform of our federal state, a 'Copernican revolution' as some now prefer to say.[1] With what ingredients?

1. A FEDERALISM OF REGIONS.

First of all, we need to switch to a simpler and more efficient classic federalism, whose building blocks are the three Regions – or even the four Regions if the territorially defined German-speaking Community is given full regional status (it is admittedly fifteen times less populated than the Brussels Region, but also five times larger). The key feature of the 'Copernican revolution' we need is not the transfer of a handful of competences which the federal state still possesses. We need something far more radical. We need to move further away from the *Belgique unitaire de Bon-Papa* and get rid of the *Belgique bi-communautaire de Papa*. The Communities formed a useful stage in the evolution of our institutions, but it is now urgent to move beyond them. This is of little importance for Flanders, of greater importance for Wallonia and absolutely crucial for Brussels. A coherent, efficient decentralization of competences implies that decentralized governments should be made responsible for the impact of their policies on the welfare of their populations. But one will never seriously be able to make the Brussels Region responsible for the (lack of) prosperity of its population without allowing it to be in charge of its

---

1.   This expression was used by Kris Peeters, Minister-President of the Flemish Region to refer to a reform that would make the Federal State gravitate around the Regions and Communities, rather than the other way around.

education system. And education forms the bulk of the Communities' competences.

2. THE CAPPUCCINO MODEL

Secondly, what is the optimal distribution of competences between the various policy levels, from the communes to the European level and beyond? Should we aim, as is frequently demanded, for 'homogeneous packages'? Nonsense. Trying to gather at the same level of power all competences 'of the same genus', the environment, for example, or taxation, or mobility, makes no sense whatever. Optimality requires each policy domain to be intelligently broken down between the various levels, balancing in each case the respective demands of responsiveness to the situation and preferences of the people most directly affected and the need to handle efficiently positive and negative externalities. What must guide us is not a craving for homogeneity but the flavour and look of a cappuccino. Take child benefits as an easy example. By way of coffee, you get a strong and simple universal child benefit paid at the federal level, irrespective of family income, rank or age, to each child in a household subjected to Belgium's personal tax system. And let the regional governments, but also possibly the trans-regional mutualities, or individual firms, top this up with cream, cacao or sugar according to their own tastes and with their own resources. One Region may want to give a bit more to the third child, for example, another to single mothers, and yet another to unemployed parents. Let them do so. Regional governments will be able to experiment and boast with the cappuccino's most visible ingredients. But underneath, the strong coffee basis will be secured by the federal government and thereby protected against the risk of all cups running empty under the pressure of fiscal and social competition. In matters of health care or education, media or employment, the restructuring required is not always as simple, but the cappuccino model can and must keep providing the inspiration.[2]

3. LINGUISTIC TERRITORIALITY.

Next comes the general acceptance of the linguistic territoriality principle for Flanders and Wallonia. People who settle in Brussels will be able to get away more and more with knowing neither Dutch nor French: in addition to

---

2.   See Van Parijs (2004) for a discussion of this model in the domain of health care.

whatever languages they knew before leaving their many countries of origin, the knowledge of English, the *lingua franca* of the EU institutions and the European civil society, will increasingly suffice. But whoever wishes to settle permanently in Flanders or Wallonia will need to muster the courage and humility to learn Dutch and French, respectively: 'Europeans, Brussels is your capital, but Belgium is not your colony.' To achieve this, however, we shall need to get rid of the regime of 'permanent facilities' in six communes of the Brussels periphery that was introduced as a defective component of the 1963 settlement. This will require a new intelligent, honourable and courageous compromise, for example the one I have been defending along with my Ghent University colleague Etienne Vermeersch (make the four smallest of these communes part of the Brussels Region, and phase out the facilities in the remaining two) or perhaps one that consists in viewing the incorporation of all six of the communes concerned (69,000 inhabitants, 51 km²) into the Brussels Region as a fair *quid pro quo* for Wallonia accepting to lose the German Community (73,000 inhabitants, 854km²) through its transformation into a separate Region.[3]

4. ELECTORAL REFORM.

Finally, the 'Copernican revolution'we need also demands a modest but crucial reform of our electoral institutions. It would be good if part of the seats of the Flemish Parliament and part of the seats of the French Parliament were allocated in electoral districts that cover the whole of Flanders and of Wallonia, respectively. More important is that the separate French and Dutch electoral colleges for the Brussels Parliament should be abolished and replaced by a system that allows for linguistically mixed lists while securing a guaranteed representation for each language group. Most crucial, however, is the creation of a country-wide electoral district for part of the seats of the national Parliament, as proposed by the Pavia group (www.paviagroup.be) and now systematically defended by both liberal parties and both green parties, as well as by prominent members of both Christian-Democratic parties and both socialist parties.[4] At each level of government, we need political leaders who propose and defend programmes that are in the interest of all components of the population they purport to govern, and who are electorally accountable to the whole of this population.

---

3. See Van Parijs (2010)

4. This proposal is presented and defended in Chapters 9 and 10.

All this can go hand in hand with a strengthening of both the regional identities and the federal identity. We need Flemings, Walloons and Brusselers who identify with their Region and are proud of it. We need a strong Flemish, Walloon and Brussels patriotism, an inclusive one of course, based on place of residence and not on ethnic origin or mother tongue. This need not and must not be inconsistent with a strengthened and renovated federal Belgian identity. But such consistency is only achievable if we re-found our institutions in such a way that the federal state can better serve the Regions, that each of the Regions can better serve its citizens, and that Brussels can better play its role both as the leaner capital of a leaner Belgian federation and as the ever more significant capital of an ever more significant European Union.[5]

---

5.   On the future of Brussels, see Van Parijs (2007b) and Van Parijs (2008).

chapter nine | electoral engineering for a stalled federation: a country-wide electoral district for belgium's federal parliament
(with Kris Deschouwer)

In February 2005, a group of academics, mostly political scientists, from all Belgian universities, published an opinion piece in both the Dutch-language and French-language Belgian press under the title 'An electoral constituency for all Belgians '. We briefly argued that, given the division of all political parties along the language border, both the efficiency and the legitimacy of our federal government would gain much if its prospective leaders and their parties had to compete in a country-wide electoral constituency, rather than in linguistically far more homogeneous provincial constituencies. We soon realized that the idea could only have some chance of ever being implemented if it was worked out in detail and consistently supported in a linguistically balanced and non-partisan way. This led, in September 2005, to the creation of the Pavia Group (www.paviagroup.be), named after the Brussels street where it met, and coordinated by Kris Deschouwer (from the Vrije Universiteit Brussel) and myself. The group worked out a precise proposal and made it public in February 2007. Since then, the idea of creating a federal constituency for part of the seats of the House of Representatives has been consistently supported by both green and both liberal parties, as well as by top socialist and Christian-Democratic politicians. Much of the discussion of such a proposal is specific to Belgium. But some of it is of wider relevance. In the aftermath of a talk I gave on a related topic at the University of Pennsylvania in April 2008, Brendan O' Leary asked for a contribution on this proposal in a collective volume on power-sharing in divided places. Kris Deschouwer and I welcomed this opportunity to present the idea, its context and its rationale for an international audience. The piece that follows is the outcome of this attempt. It was written before the record-breaking governmental crisis that followed the federal elections of June 2010 and further illustrated the problem addressed by our proposal.

ॐ

On June 10 2007 a new Belgian federal parliament was elected. The next day the usual procedures for the formation of a new federal government were started. But it would be 176 days later before a new federal government was formed, just before the New Year of 2008, after several failures even to find an agenda or a procedure for fruitful negotiations. It was however only a care-taker cabinet, led by the head of the outgoing government, Guy Verhofstadt, leader of the Flemish liberal party *Open VLD*. In March 2008 Yves Leterme, the leader of the Flemish Christian-Democratic party CD&V, the largest party in Parliament after the June 2007 election, became the Prime Minister of a new, but again short-lived federal coalition government. In July 2008, as a result of no progress being made on some key demands made by his par-ty, Leterme offered the resignation of his government to the king. The offer was turned down, but the manoeuvre was used to transfer the negotiation of these demands to an *ad hoc* 'dialogue between Communities', i.e. Belgium's Dutch-speakers and French-speakers. The Leterme government plodded on for a few more months but could not survive the clumsy handling of some local manifestations of the global financial crisis. In December 2008, Yves Leterme was forced to resign, and his party comrade Herman Van Rompuy had to take over.

This story shows that the formation of a new government and its con-tinued functioning turned out to be an exceptionally laborious enterprise. It faced the usual challenge of bridging the different views and ideologies of the parties that have to govern together in a coalition. But the gridlock resulted from a clash between the conflicting demands of two sets of parties, each corresponding to one of Belgium's two main language groups. The Dutch-speaking political parties had promised their electorate that a government could only be formed on the condition that further devolution would be se-cured. On the other hand, the French-speaking political parties had promised their own electorate that they would not accept these new demands. Both tried as long as possible to stick to these electoral pledges, resulting in neither of them giving in.

This kind of governmental crisis is not a new phenomenon in Belgium. To the contrary: long and painful negotiations between the two language groups have become a normal feature of the system. The gradual transformation of the unitary Belgium into a federal state was a long and sometimes painful process. For example, between 1977 and 1981 there were no less than seven cabinets, all falling apart because they were not able to find an acceptable compromise about the institutional hardware of a new Belgium. When in 1993 the first article of the Constitution was changed to define Belgium as a federal state, political stability seemed to have been restored. Between 1991 and 2007 all four federal governments went to the very end of their term, without being torn apart by the tensions between Francophones and Flemings.

Yet the spectacular return of political gridlock in the aftermath of the June 2007 election suggests that there is still something wrong with Belgium's institutional capacity to deal with its linguistic and territorial divisions.

In this chapter, we argue that the design of the electoral system is one of the major problems, since it offers insufficient incentives to display the spirit of accommodation that is needed for a divided society to be smoothly governed. Section 1 offers a short background sketch of the basic ingredients of the Belgian divide. Section 2 describes the institutional solution that was gradually put into place at the end of the twentieth century. Section 3 identifies the solution as typically consociational, with full emphasis on segmental autonomy and power-sharing devices. However, emphasizing autonomy and inclusion of both groups in the decision-making process does not guarantee a smooth functioning and even less a high capacity for decision-making and change. Section 4 presents an electoral reform – a country-wide electoral district – that we have been advocating along with colleagues from all Belgian universities and that would go some way, we shall argue, towards remedying the shortcomings of Belgium's federal set up.[1]

1. BELGIUM'S LINGUISTIC AND TERRITORIAL DIVIDE

The conflict that led to the territorial transformation of the Belgian state is in the first place a linguistic matter. When Belgium was created in 1830 after seceding from the short-lived Kingdom of the Low Countries, the political elite of the new state spoke French throughout the country, and French was therefore also the obvious choice as the language of government and administration. However, the majority of the population spoke no French. Belgium is cut in two by an old language frontier that runs from west to east (Geyl 1962: 211). It divides the country into a southern area where French is spoken – now called Wallonia – and a northern area where Dutch is spoken – now called Flanders.

Nonetheless, the adoption of French as the sole official language was regarded as self-evident. Not only was French the language of the state-building elite – including those living in the north – but in 1830, French was also the language of modernity and liberalism, and the *lingua franca* of royal courts and diplomatic circles. Dutch, on the other hand, was the language of the northern Low Countries, i.e. precisely the country from which the new Belgium

---

1. For a far more comprehensive picture of Belgium's political institutions and their development through time, see Deschouwer (2009). The electoral reform we propose is discussed at length in many opinion pieces in French and in Dutch, by ourselves and by others, friendly and hostile, all downloadable from www.paviagroup.be.

had seceded, and it was also perceived as the language of Protestantism, the dominant confession in the northern Low Countries, whereas both the Dutch-speaking and French-speaking parts of the new Belgium were, if religious at all, homogeneously Catholic. It also went without saying that Brussels would become the capital city of Belgium. The city is, however, located north of the language frontier. Its role as the capital city of the newly independent state rapidly strengthened its predominantly Francophone character, and fed its gradual expansion into its historically Dutch-speaking hinterland.

These facts are the raw material for understanding Belgium's modern language conflict, and conflict it becomes when in the course of the nineteenth century the inhabitants of the part of the country where varieties of Dutch are the vernacular of the mass of the people started asking for the formal recognition of Dutch as a second official language of Belgium, and in particular for the right to use Dutch for educational, administrative and political purposes in the Northern part of the country. This process almost naturally led to a territorial solution (Murphy, 1988). From the 1920s onwards, the rules governing the use of language by public authorities and the language used as the medium of education relied on the creation – or rather the acceptance of the existence – of three linguistic territories: one for Dutch, one for French, and one – the Brussels area – where both languages can be used.

Obviously, a territorial organization requires the drawing of boundaries. This is seldom easy when ethnic, linguistic or religious tensions are present. Belgium has been no exception. Until today two conflicting principles have been invoked. One stipulates that the language to be used for official business is determined permanently on the basis of the historical distinction between the north and the south of the country. The alternative principle stipulates that official linguistic boundaries can and should be adjusted in line with changes in the composition of the population. According to this principle, the boundaries can shift in order to accommodate demographic movement and linguistic shifts. Whenever they did shift, they led to the transfer of historically Dutch-speaking territory into the bilingual area, and sometimes eventually into the Francophone area. Unsurprisingly, the historical principle has tended to be supported exclusively by Dutch-speakers, who feel that a safely protected territory is needed to safeguard their lower status language. French speakers, instead, tend to invoke the principle that official boundaries should track real-life trends, including the spread of the stronger language. The use of language has therefore gradually been organized on territorial premises, but without agreement on the operational principles for the drawing of the territorial boundaries.

Different languages, and different views on the way in which language shift needs to be given free rein or hemmed in, are not the only differences between the north and the south of Belgium. In terms of economic development, Flanders and Wallonia have differed from the very early days of the Belgian state. Industrialization came quite early, and was very much concentrated in the south, while the north remained agricultural for much longer. But after the end of the Second World War the steel-and-coal-based Walloon economy started declining, whereas Flanders attracted investments in new economic activities – for which the harbour of Antwerp was, and remains, a major asset. The economic balance of the country therefore shifted. In the early 1970s, GDP per capita became higher in Flanders than in Wallonia, and since then the gap has kept increasing. In 2006 GDP per capita was €21.559 in Wallonia and €29.992 in Flanders, while the unemployment rate was 5 per cent in Flanders and 12 per cent in Wallonia. This emphasis on Belgium's North-South economic divide is somewhat misleading, however, because well over one quarter of the country's GDP is produced in less than 1 per cent of its territory, in the Brussels Region and its immediate surroundings. But the dramatic shift in the balance of economic power between Flanders and Wallonia is nonetheless a crucial ingredient in Belgium's present situation.

By contrast, the political difference between North and South has remained relatively stable. As soon as all layers of the population were allowed to participate in parliamentary elections, the north and the south returned quite different results. At the first elections with some sort of universal male suffrage in 1894, the 72 Flemish seats and the 18 Brussels seats all went to representatives of the Catholic Party. Of the 62 Walloon seats, 14 went to the Catholic Party, 20 to the Liberal Party, and the remainder to the Socialist Party, which first entered parliament with 28 representatives, all elected in Wallonia. Although the differences did not remain as sharp – not least because of the introduction of proportional representation in 1900 – the two parts of the country still display significantly different electoral behaviour. Table 9.1 shows the results of the federal elections of 2007 for Flanders and Wallonia separately per party family. These reveal that for each party family the results are very different. However, these regional differences do not increase over time. They have always been important.

To these different electoral results one must add another crucial ingredient of the Belgian problem. The results in Table 9.1 are presented per *party family,* and not per party, because there are no country-wide parties any more. The traditional parties – Christian democrats, liberals and socialists – fell apart into two separate and unilingual parties between 1968 and 1978. The Greens and the populist radical right parties are younger, but have never existed as Belgian parties. They have developed in the party system of each of the language groups separately. For the federal elections, it is only in the central electoral district of Brussel-Halle-Vilvoorde (BHV) – which comprises the

Table 9.1: Results of the elections to the federal parliament in 2007 for Flanders, Wallonia and Brussels (percentage of the votes)

	Flanders	Wallonia	Brussels
Christian Democrats	29.6	15.7	16.5
Socialists	16.3	29.5	23.4
Liberals	18.7	31.1	34.7
Populist radical right	18.9	5.5	6.0
Greens	6.2	12.7	15.0
Others	10.3	5.5	4.4

Brussels region and 35 Flemish municipalities – that the parties of the two language groups compete with each other.

2. THE INSTITUTIONS OF THE BELGIAN FEDERATION

The unitary Belgium of 1830 is now long gone. Several constitutional reforms have rebuilt the Belgian state into a federation. The linguistic regions that were created to regulate the use of language provide its building blocks, albeit in a fairly complex way. Belgium is both a federation of three territorial regions and three languages communities. The regions are called Flanders, Wallonia and the Brussels Capital Region, with clear (though not uncontested) territorial borders. They have been given a broad set of powers, e.g. over environmental policy, public works, public transport, housing, and important aspects of economic policy. The three language communities are called the Flemish Community, the French Community and the German-speaking Community. The communities basically offer services to individuals in the areas of education, culture and welfare policy. The Flemish Community offers these services in Flanders and in Brussels. The French Community offers them in Wallonia and in Brussels. Hence, in the territory of the Brussels Region the operations of the two main language communities overlap. The German-speaking Community, composed of some 73,000 people living in two areas next to the German border (transferred from Germany to Belgium after the First World War) offers its services in those areas, which are part of the Walloon Region. The twofold nature of the federation is rather awkward, but it is a subtle compromise. At a first level, it often presented as a deal between pro-Community Flemings – who prefer a one-against-one conflict – and pro-Region Francophones – who might be advantaged by a two-against-one configuration. At a deeper level, it constitutes an attempt to articulate two types of concerns. The 'Community' component should assuage, at least for the time being, both many Flemings' fear that they will lose all control over Brussels, where the Flemish residential presence keeps shrinking, and many Francophones' fear of a weakening of the solidarity between Brussels and Wallonia. On the other hand, the regional component reflects some awareness of the fact that efficient policy making requires all decentralized powers to be exercised by one government, responsible to all those sharing the same territory.

The first constitutional reform of 1970 laid down this double structure, but it was only in 1989 that Brussels was given the status of a Region, and only in 1995 that the roof was put on the house with the first direct election of the three regional parliaments. The constitutional reform of 1970 was also extremely important for the changes it introduced in the functioning of the central state. The rules laid down at that time define the way in which decision-making operates at the federal level today, as well as the way in which the constitution can be further modified. Two principles were then deeply enshrined into the Belgian political system: a neat separation between the language groups, and an obligation to govern together.

The separation between the language groups was introduced both into the parliament and into the government. All members of the House of Representatives, whatever their origins, belong to either the Dutch or the French language group. That membership is defined by the territory in which the members of parliament have been elected. Those elected in constituencies of the Flemish region belong automatically to the Dutch language group and those elected in Wallonia belong automatically to the French language group. For MPs elected in the central BHV district the language in which they take their oath defines the group to which they belong. The full separation of the party system into Francophone and Flemish parties actually predefines the choice that these MPs will make. Subsequent reforms of the electoral system and of the parliament, have only reinforced this split and the role ascribed to the descriptive representation of language groups. Since 1995, the Senate has been elected in two electoral districts: one for Flanders and the central BHV district, and one for Wallonia and the central BHV district. The Belgian members of the European Parliament are elected in the same way and, as in the Senate, with a fixed number of seats available for each language group and an overlap in the territory of BHV, where voters can choose for either of the two districts.

The members of the federal government also clearly belong to one of the two language groups. Again, the split party system leaves no doubt about the membership. Since 1970, therefore, not one single politician formally represents voters outside of his or her language group. Politicians might claim to do so, but their position in the institutions gives them a clear and unambiguous label.

The neat separation of the language groups allows for the organization of the second principle: the obligation to include both groups within the federal decision-making process. This is done in a variety of ways. First, the federal government (i.e. Belgium's cabinet) has to be composed of an equal number of Francophone and Dutch-speaking Ministers. Only the Prime Minister is supposed to be 'linguistically *a-sexué*' (as the semi-official terminology puts it), even though the party to which he belongs leaves no doubt about his linguistic status. Since 1970 all Prime Ministers have been Dutch speakers, except for a one year period in 1972–73, and a two months period in 1978. The rule of decision-making in the federal government is unanimity. The cabinet never votes. This linguistic 'parity' assures the governing of the country by the two major language groups.

In the parliament, the Flemish group is larger than the Francophone one, reflecting the 60: 40 per cent demographic ratios. It can, however, not use that majority to impose its will on the minority. The normal rule of decision making for the federal House of Representatives is simple majority, but the minority has a veto power. It is called the 'alarm bell procedure'. Whenever three quarters of a language group declares that a proposal might be accepted that harms the interests of that group, it can activate the alarm bell. The parliamentary procedure is then suspended for thirty days, during which the government needs to find a solution. And with parity in its composition and unanimity as the decision-making rule, the solution of the government can only be one that is acceptable for both language groups. If no solution is found, the government will have to resign. But to form a new government, possibly after electing a new parliament, both language groups will still need to find a compromise. Moreover, to change the constitution a two-thirds majority is needed. Yet for most articles that define the political institutions of regions and communities, and for the so-called Special Laws that implement these basic principles, a majority is needed in each language group, i.e. a concurrent majority, as well as an overall two-thirds majority.

The same logic of strict separation of the political personnel into language groups and the obligation to govern together and to avoid a veto by one of the language groups has been built into the institutions of the Brussels region. It has indeed become a fully-fledged Region, as the Francophone parties requested, but, institutionally speaking it has not become a Francophone region, as the Flemish parties feared. Dutch-speaking parties are guaranteed 17 out of the 89 seats in the regional Parliament, and two out of the four ministerial positions in the regional government, while the minister-president is supposed to be, like the federal Prime Minister, linguistically *a-sexué*. To some extent, this picture is a mirror image of the federal institutions. The Brussels institutions display the Belgian logic of separation and inclusion. This logic is a consociational logic, albeit one in which the parity principle usually outweighs the proportionality principle. With two actors, the proportional distribution of power and resources is not the most important device. The common agreement needed for governing lays far greater stress on the right of both actors to be present in the decision-making process and hence on the veto power of each language group.

3. CONSOCIATIONAL BELGIUM

In a piece written nearly three decades ago, Arend Lijphart (1981: 1) left no doubt as to how he wanted to label Belgium: 'What is remarkable about Belgium is not that it is a culturally divided society – most of the countries in the contemporary world are divided into separate and distinct cultural, religious, or ethnic communities – but that its cultural communities coexist peacefully and democratically. What is more, Belgium can legitimately claim to be the most thorough example of consociational democracy, the type of democracy that is most suitable for deeply divided societies.' If the Belgian federation – still very much in the making when Lijphart was writing – is consociational, it needs prudent leaders willing to accommodate and to govern with the leaders of the other language group. The devolution of powers to the Regions and Communities, however, has taken away from joint decision-making quite a few powers for which the formulation and implementation of a common policy has been, or would be difficult. For the remaining federal powers a common policy is required and therefore an agreement is needed. That is obviously also the case for all matters relating to the state structure itself. Only an agreement between elites willing to compromise can offer a way out.

Functioning consociational democracy requires prudent leadership. Prudence may result from a learning process, from the awareness that a conflictual attitude leads to total gridlock, and possibly even to violent clashes (Lijphart 1977: 99). Prudent leaders are willing to bridge the gap over the possibly deep differences which divide the population. Functioning consociational democracy also requires that the elites want to keep the political system alive and value the latter's survival above the interests of their own groups. It means that they are willing and able to play a double role, to be advocates on behalf of their own rank and file and compromise seekers at elite level. Compromising therefore needs to come at an acceptable price. If compromising leads to a substantial loss of trust (and hence votes) from the followers, prudent leadership is not likely to develop (Horowitz 1985: 347).

This is indeed one of the major problems for the functioning of Belgium. If we look back at the last fifty years, we can observe the capacity to find compromises when needed. It was never easy, but exactly at times when terms like 'regime crisis' were being used by political commentators, a new, often unforeseeable, compromise was found. It is important to note though that these agreements were reached in a political system that was not yet a fully-fledged federation. Political agreements had to be found in the central government (and parliament). The absence of an agreement acceptable for both language groups meant the end of the current central government, or the non-formation of a government. That situation could go on for a while, but the longer it took, the more problematic it became for all parties. The very high systemic price to be paid for the absence of an agreement – for instance in terms of pressure on the currency or public sector deficits – provided the incentive for the elite to be both creative, and accommodating, and hence to concoct an acceptable compromise that could keep the system going again for a while.

This institutional environment has changed in ways that have tended to reduce the pressure to find a compromise, and increased the probability of long and enduring political crises. Since Belgium has become a federation, it has more than just a federal government. Many powers are now in the hands of the regions and communities. As a result, the formation or survival of the federal government is less important. In other words: the pressure to display an accommodating attitude in what used to be the only centre of power is far weaker than it was before (Jans 2001; Swenden & Jans 2006; Deschouwer 2005; 2006). This is also the case because of the expansion of the powers of the European Union. The melting of the Belgian franc into the euro, for example, strongly limits the dangers of a financial crisis when the country is not able to produce or to keep alive a working government. As a result of federal powers having shrunk from above and from below, it is both less important and more difficult to form federal governments and to keep them in place.

No less relevant have been the changes in the pattern of party competition. For a long time – actually until the end of the 1990s – there were two dominant parties in Belgium. Christian-Democrats were by far the largest party in Flanders, and therefore almost always a governing party. The Socialists were by far the largest party in the south. The most natural coalition was therefore one between the Christian-Democratic and the Socialist families. Since the turn of the century, however, this domination has gone. In each of the two party systems party competition is very high. All potential governing parties are very much afraid of losing votes. Even a slight electoral decline can have quite important consequences. Consequently, party elites are more scared than ever of having to pay the electoral cost of the compromises they accept.

This increased electoral competition happened to materialize precisely when the electoral cycles for the different levels of the federation became desynchronized. In 1995 and 1999 the federal and regional parliaments were elected on the same day, but since then they have developed their own rhythm of five years for the regional parliaments, and four years for the federal parliament. In the absence of country-wide political parties, distinct from the linguistically defined parties that compete for the regional elections, the federal elections and the regional elections are not really different.

As explained earlier, by the late 1970s all three Belgium-wide parties had divided into two separate parties, one Flemish and one Francophone. Consequently, whatever the type of election, the same parties compete for the electorate of their own language group. The next election for all parties is not the next election at the same level, but the next election *tout court*. There have been elections in 2003 (federal), 2004 (regional), 2007 (federal), 2009 (regional), and 2010 (federal). This is driving all political parties into a nearly permanent state of electoral campaign. As a result, the likelihood of an accommodating attitude on the part of politicians governing, or wanting to govern, at the federal level has been dramatically reduced.

4. A TRULY FEDERAL PARLIAMENT FOR A TRULY FEDERAL GOVERNMENT

There is definitely something wrong with the functioning of the Belgian federation. Its federal governmental level lacks decision-making and problem-solving capacity, and most suggestions to improve the functioning of the federal state defend a further devolution of powers to the regions and communities: if the federal government does not work, it should be given less work to do. This thinking fits in neatly with the trend that has characterized Belgium's institutions since the 1970s: the gradual hollowing out of the powers of the central government. Suggestions to improve the decision-making capacity of the federal governmental level are seldom heard. There is, however, one idea that cropped up now and then in the last couple of decades, was worked out in some detail shortly before the 2007 federal election and soon became the subject of a lively debate: the idea of creating a federal or country-wide electoral district for the federal elections.

When in 1979 Belgium had to decide on the procedure for the election of the Belgian members of the European Parliament, the idea of a country-wide electoral district appeared for the first time. It was suggested by the Flemish Christian-Democrat leader and then Belgian Prime Minister Leo Tindemans, who was hoping to score highly among both linguistic groups.

His Francophone coalition partners were diffident, and the government opted instead for an election of Belgian MEPs in two separate unilingual community-wide electoral districts, in line with the classical 'splitting' logic outlined earlier. The idea reappeared in the 1990s, as Belgium was becoming a true federation, but this time applied to federal elections. It did not arouse much interest, however, until a group of academics, known as the 'Pavia Group', drafted a detailed scheme, tested it among politicians and lawyers, and then presented it to the press on February 14, 2007[2]. The proposal was picked up by some parties, fiercely attacked by others, and eventually made it to the institutional agenda.

The basic idea is simple and straightforward. Of the 150 members of the federal House of Representatives, 15 should be elected in an electoral district that covers the whole territory of the Belgian state – henceforth called the federal district. So far the federal House is elected in 11 districts, coinciding with the provincial boundaries, except for the central BHV district, which encompasses the whole of the Brussels Region and part of a Flemish province. Almost all MPs are therefore currently elected in unilingual districts where the parties of only one language group compete.

Once a federal electoral district is created, voters will have two votes. Their first vote will be cast for one of the lists – or some of the candidates featuring on one of the lists – presented in a provincial electoral district. The distribution of seats among these districts will be distributed, as now, in proportion to the population of each province. A second vote will be cast for one of the lists – or one or more of the candidates featuring on one of the lists – presented in the federal district, common to all voters, irrespective of where they live.

Any candidate will be allowed to stand both on a provincial list and on a federal list. And most, if not all, of the candidates on a federal list can be expected to do so, for the following reasons. They may not be sure of being among the fifteen elected in the federal district, and therefore it is a safety call for them to be in a good position on a provincial list. Or, they are certain to be among the fifteen elected, but if they enjoy such popularity their party would be foolish not to also place them on a provincial list.

Thus fifteen out of the 150 people elected to the House will have a claim to being truly federation-wide MPs. But a far greater proportion of the 150 eventually elected, in all likelihood a significant majority among them, will have been candidates in the federal district. To win as many votes as possible

---

2. See www.paviagroup.be for the Pavia Group's original proposal, its defence and critical discussions; Deschouwer and Van Parijs (2007, 2008) for a synthetic account; section 4 of Chapter 6; and Buruma (2011: 40) for an outsider's assessment of the prospects of the Pavia Group's proposal for remedying Belgium's recurrent blockages.

in this district, it will be in their interest to campaign also in the other language group, with a fair chance of success if they manage to highlight their commitment to causes that are not divisive along linguistic lines. This will hold, in particular, for the top politicians of all the parties with the ambition to form and lead the federal government, those whose promises and declarations will be most binding for the action of the next government. Not only will their total personal vote affect, as it does now, their pecking order in their party and in the country, but this vote and the way it is distributed across the country will affect the legitimacy with which they will claim and exercise the functions to which they aspire.

For this reason, the number of seats to be allocated in the federal district is not that important. It could conceivably be increased beyond fifteen. But if this is done without a corresponding increase in the total size of the House, the district magnitude in the provincial districts would drop and that would create higher thresholds for the smaller parties. The degree of proportionality would be severely reduced, while the Constitution requires the electoral system to be proportional. On the other hand, increasing the number of seats in the federal House would be an unpopular measure, unless combined with an appropriate compensation. Bear in mind that the full implementation of the federal structure in 1995 increased the total number of parliamentary seats – federal and regional – from 369 to 503. However, increasing the number of seats in the House might possibly be compensated by a reduction of the number of seats in other assemblies. The most attractive and most probable version of such compensation would consist of scrapping the direct election of part of the senate – 25 Dutch-speakers and 15 French-speakers – thus leaving a Senate composed exclusively of people elected to the regional parliaments.

Whether fifteen or more members of the federal House are elected in the newly created federal district, the reform sketched would significantly alleviate the democratic deficit from which Belgium's federal system suffers. The current organization of elections without federal parties does not offer the possibility of a true dialogue between the governing elite at the federal level and the population of the federation as a whole. All those competing seriously in the federal district will face incentives to propose mutually acceptable solutions for institutional matters, instead of simply expressing the demands of their own language group. A federal district would re-introduce *pre-electoral incentives* – absent since the Belgium-wide parties fell apart – to display a disposition to compromise that is needed to govern, in power-sharing fashion, at the federal level. The proposal aims thereby to strengthen the potential for prudent leadership and political accommodation, by compensating for institutional developments that have dramatically weakened it. Given the absence of federal political parties, the emergence of a federal system that reduced the importance of the central government has seriously reduced the capacity of the country's political elites to promote or at least accept the principles of power sharing.

5. THE COUNTER-INTUITIVE IMPORTANCE OF LINGUISTIC QUOTAS

As is often the case with institutional engineering, however, it is crucial to anticipate the various political actors' response to the proposed set up, and to fine-tune the latter so as to avoid perverse effects. For this reason, the Pavia Group's proposal fixes before the election the number of seats allocated to each language group in the federal district. The proportions simply match as closely as possible the proportions of members of the House belonging to the two language groups in the previous legislature. If 15 seats are to be allocated, this means that 9 will go to Dutch-speakers and 6 to French-speakers. The lists put forward by the various parties in the federal district will accordingly consist of a maximum of 6, 9 or 15 names. Only lists containing 9 Dutch speakers and 6 French speakers can present 15 candidates.

Some simple and sufficiently uncontroversial criterion for recognition as a French speaker or a Dutch speaker will be required. In the light of past experience, and bearing the threat of political sanctions in mind, sponsoring by three members of the relevant language group of the previous House should do the trick. The allocation of seats between the lists and the candidates can proceed using the standard D'Hondt system, under the constraint of the linguistic quota. That means that a list can have its next candidate elected, as long as he or she belongs to a language group for which the quota has not yet been reached. If this quota has been reached, the seat is allotted to the next candidate on the same list from the other language group. If the list is unilingual, the seat is allotted to the next list that can claim the seat and has candidates from that language group (see Table 9.2).

Imagine three lists are participating in the election. List A is a list with 6 candidates, all French-speaking (FR). List B is a list with 9 candidates, all Dutch-speaking (NL). List C has 15 candidates of which 6 are French-speaking and 9 are Dutch-speaking.

The proportional distribution of seats between the lists – using the D'Hondt divisors – gives list A 6 seats (numbers 1, 3, 5, 8, 10, 13), List B 6 seats (numbers 2, 4, 6, 9, 12, 14) and List C 3 seats (7, 11 and 15). On each list, the candidates are ranked according to their preference votes. That defines the order in which they can be elected. Seat number 16 also has to be allocated, since seat number 13 could not be filled by list A. List A thus loses one seat because it is unilingual. An extra seat goes to the bilingual list C.

Table 9.2: Simulation of seat distribution for a federal electoral district

	List A	List B	List C	Quota	
				NL	FR
Seat 1	First candidate				1
Seat 2		First candidate		1	
Seat 3	Second candidate				2
Seat 4		Second candidate		2	
Seat 5	Third candidate				3
Seat 6		Third candidate		3	
Seat 7			First candidate (assume FR)		4
Seat 8	Fourth candidate				5
Seat 9		Fourth candidate		4	
Seat 10	Fifth candidate				6
Seat 11			Second candidate – must be NL	5	
Seat 12		Fifth candidate		6	
Seat 13	Quota is full – seat cannot be filled				
Seat 14		Sixth candidate		7	
Seat 15			Third candidate – must be NL	8	
Seat 16			Fourth candidate – must be NL	9	
TOTAL	5	6	4		

The use of quotas might at first sight seem at odds with the spirit of the proposal. Yet it is not. The aim is to offer electoral incentives for politicians to campaign in both language groups. In the absence of quotas, there is a risk – indeed a certainty in the foreseeable future – that many voters will be reluctant to support a politician from the other language group for fear of contributing to a reduction in the representation of their own group in Parliament. In the absence of quotas, the federal election would quickly degenerate into a race between the language communities – which it now is to a large extent in the BHV electoral district, where such a regime is in place. That is exactly what the federal district must not be. In the version of the federal district proposed by the Pavia Group, catching a vote from the other language group will not alter the numerical parliamentary representation of the language group to which a candidate belongs. It will not decrease but rather increase considerably the incentive for parties and candidates to court the voters across the linguistic border. If parties and voters' strategies are no longer frozen by fear of disproportionality, there is far more to gain from making one's promises and actions more palatable to others. The quotas make it possible to leave intact the existing power-sharing devices. All members of the federal parliament will keep belonging to one language group. This is needed to protect the Francophone minority, and for the double majorities required for some institutional reforms. A country-wide electoral district is intended to strengthen the democratic legitimacy and the problem-solving capacity of the federal governmental level, but without destroying the existing power-sharing principles and devices. Its introduction would not ignore or attempt to erase the differences between the language groups. Nor is it intended to resurrect country-wide political parties.

It is precisely because there are no such parties that other devices are needed to link the federal politicians to the population of the federation as a whole. Parties belonging to the same ideological family might decide to form common lists for the fifteen federal seats. This would make them look better, as they could present a full list, and would also guarantee that they would never lose a seat in case one of the quotas is filled. Moreover, their leaders would be given a better chance of winning more votes across the linguistic frontier, as each voter can tick several names on the same list. Parties belonging to the same ideological family could also present separate lists, while deciding to pool their votes, as allowed in the Pavia Group's formula. In any event, they would still present unilingual party lists in the provincial electoral districts of both Flanders and Wallonia. Indeed, it cannot even be ruled out that, as regionalization deepens, separate Brussels parties may arise within each political family. The proposal of a federal electoral district is fully consistent with such developments. Its purpose is to provide an electoral set up that facilitates the government of a divided society in the absence of country-wide political parties.

6. POLITICAL STRATEGY

By way of conclusion, we offer two remarks, one strategic and one philosophical. It is seldom a piece of cake to get an electoral reform through, if only because those currently empowered to change the rules are in power thanks to the rules they are asked to change. The reform proposal described and motivated in this chapter is no exception. Its adoption requires small changes in two articles of Belgium's federal constitution, and hence a two-thirds majority in both the House and the Senate. Is it possible to convince two-thirds of Belgium's top politicians that a change of this sort is in their personal interest? We doubt it. Is it nevertheless possible to convince enough opinion leaders that this is a remedy the Belgian system urgently requires, to convince enough political leaders that there is something in it for them, if not for the sake of gaining power, at least for the sake of exercising it, and to put enough moral pressure on the rest, so that the required super-majority can be patched together despite the opposition of secessionist parties? The future will tell.

On the bright side, it may be noted that the Prime Minister who took over from Yves Leterme on the 30th of December 2008, Herman Van Rompuy, publicly expressed his support for the idea, and that his two deputy Prime Ministers in charge of institutional reform, the Francophone liberal Didier Reynders (MR) and the Flemish Christian-Democrat Steven Vanackere (CD&V) have been supporters of the Pavia proposal from the start. But it will be hard for the proposal to emerge from self-interested bargaining between the linguistic blocks of political parties. What is supposed to be in the general interest cannot be offered nor accepted as compensation for a concession on the most salient contentious issues, such as the splitting of the BHV electoral district or the expansion of the Brussels Region.

If there is hope, it comes from a linguistically well balanced pressure from 'civil society'. It was crucial for the proposal's prospects that it should be associated with a bilingual set of academics rather than with a linguistically tainted political party. And it is crucial that it should keep being supported by journalists, and other opinion leaders, from both sides of the linguistic frontier. The June 2007 federal election was won in a decisive way by Flemish Minister-President Yves Leterme. But it was won with votes garnered only on one side of the linguistic frontier, and celebrated only under Flemish flags. The government formation process that followed was extraordinarily laborious. The government it eventually produced reached no deal on the key divisive issues, remained undermined by mutual distrust and did not survive what should have remained a minor incident. If enough people are able to see in this sad sequence of events, not the failings or bad luck of individual people, but a major defect of the system in which they are caught, progress is not out of reach.

7. POLITICAL PHILOSOPHY

Finally, let us briefly turn from political strategy to political philosophy. Among the many critiques expressed against the Pavia Group proposal in the course of the rich debate it triggered, the most profound is perhaps the one best articulated by Bart De Wever, president of the New Flemish Alliance (N-VA), a Flemish nationalist party that formed an electoral cartel with Yves Leterme's Flemish Christian Democrats until its collapse in September 2008. Proposing a federal electoral district, from this view, is a form of 'creationism'. The Belgian state failed to create a Francophone Belgian nation in the nineteenth century. It gave up the idea of creating a bilingual Belgian nation in the twentieth century. The federal district is too weak an instrument, and it comes too late, to create a Belgian nation. All it can do, if anything, is hinder the process through which the Flemish nation and, if such a thing exists, the Walloon nation, can become fully-fledged states. Only with the consolidation of two states matching these two nations will the never-ending process of transformation of Belgium's institutions come to a rest.

The political philosophy that underlies the Pavia proposal is different. No one could deny that being able to function in one language makes life easier for a democratic polity. For this reason, devolution to linguistically more homogeneous entities was a wise decision. The survival of Belgium is no aim in itself, and if all matters could sensibly be devolved in this way, why not? But they cannot, essentially because any sensible management of Brussels and its hinterland requires them to be under a single authority, and because neither an absorption of the Brussels Region by either of the other two nor an absorption by the Brussels Region of its hinterland (namely the richest provinces of both Flanders and Wallonia) belong to the realm of the possible. Instead of wasting one's time dreaming about nation-states that will never and should never exist, one must design and implement institutions that improve the working of polities that are not and will never become nation-states, including for the sake of moving more smoothly, as Flemish nationalists wish, towards more thorough-going devolution.

Belgium is one such polity, and the European Union is another. Such institutional engineering is not a losing battle against the democratic imperative of linguistic homogeneity. It is an essential part of the piecemeal shaping of the sort of institutions that the countries and super-countries of today's world will increasingly need.

| chapter
ten | anything (even) better than the
pavia proposal?
(with Kris Deschouwer) |

The text of the previous chapter ('Electoral engineering for a stalled federation') was used as the lead piece of an e-book published in July 2009 within the framework of the Re-Bel initiative (www.rethinkingbelgium.eu). This e-book included comments by two of the most articulate Belgian critics of the Pavia Group's proposal for a federal electoral district – the political philosopher and director of the study centre of the Francophone Christian-democratic party (CdH), Laurent de Briey, and the openly Flemish nationalist political scientist, Bart Maddens – and two of the world's most renowned specialists of electoral systems for divided societies – Don Horowitz, from Duke University, and Brendan O'Leary, from the University of Pennsylvania.

The e-book also contained a reply which enabled us to clarify the purpose of our proposal and to spell out the reasons we have for believing that the Pavia Group's proposal offers a more promising way of serving this purpose than the alternative proposals made by our critics. This reply is reprinted below. It summarizes the main criticisms explicitly enough – and hopefully fairly enough – to make these intelligible. The full text of all four comments is accessible on www.rethinkingbelgium.eu, which also contains a written version of the additional remarks made by Rudi Andeweg (2010), Laurent de Briey (2009b) and Bart Maddens (2009b) at a Re-Bel public event organized around the e-book in December 2009.

☙

We are grateful to all four of our critics for insightful remarks that are bound to enrich the debate and move it forward. Most of these critical remarks challenge the Pavia Group's proposal of a federal electoral district as the most effective way of pursuing the objective we ascribe to it, while some challenge the objective itself.

1. WHY WE NEED A BETTER FEDERAL DEMOCRACY

For us and for our colleagues in the Pavia Group, Belgium is not, it hardly needs saying, an aim in itself. The objective of our proposal is to make Belgium's federal democracy serve better the interests of the population affected by the decisions it produces (or fails to produce) for as long as it exists and wherever its operation leads to. Among our four critics, only Bart Maddens (2009a) challenges this objective, because he has given up on federal Belgium and hence advocates as the best next step scrapping federal democracy altogether and restricting direct elections to the regional level or (even better in his view) to the community level, thus turning Belgium into a confederation of democratic communities.

This view does not lack coherence. Nonetheless, it is misguided. Even Bart Maddens should share our objective of making federal Belgium work better, for two distinct reasons. The most fundamental one, but possibly the one hardest for him to accept, is that any feasible version of the confederal path towards separation is undesirable in his eyes too. Why so? Because of the 'Brussels problem' about which he has the honesty of confessing some embarrassment. In a nutshell, the problem is that neither Flanders nor Wallonia could secede from Belgium taking Brussels with them and that the overwhelming majority of both the Walloons and the Flemings – including, we suspect, Bart Maddens – would not want to leave Belgium without Brussels. In the hope of dodging this dilemma, some have been dreaming of a formula whereby the Flemish Region would conquer its full independence while retaining control over Brussels, if necessary as a 'condominium' shared with Wallonia. Anyone sincerely believing (as distinct from pretending for tactical reasons) that this is a feasible scenario has lost all touch with major aspects of twenty-first century Brussels. If Bart Maddens has not, it should not be difficult for him to draw the relevant conclusion. If he has, more time and space would be needed to convince him than we could reasonably devote to it here.

There is, however, another reason for Bart Maddens and other sceptics to endorse our objective, one that requires far less fieldwork in order to be substantiated. Institutional reform, in the Belgian context, including – as the Brussel-Halle-Vilvoorde (BHV) saga demonstrated – those reforms that require in principle no more than a simple majority, cannot be imposed by one community on the other. The current combination of segregated electoral competition and the requirement of inter-community consensus for a federal government to get off the ground leads to the sort of spectacular stalemate that followed the June 2007 electoral victory of the CD&V/N-VA cartel. To those like (we trust) Bart Maddens who really want to catch the 'fat fish' of greater devolution to Flanders – rather than spend their time whining or sulking about its absence – it must have occurred that there is something structural about the frustrating lack of progress in recent years. If one is to prevent the pan from remaining desperately empty, there is bound to be a safer and quicker way than the current alternation of vociferation and bitterness.

This is the second reason why Bart Maddens should share our objective, which is precisely to provide a way for the federal government not only to exercise in a more efficient and legitimate way the powers currently entrusted to it but also to push through the institutional reforms which will enable our federal state to better serve our regions and our regions to work better, including of course by acquiring more autonomy.[1]

2. MADDENS' ELECTED HEAD OF STATE

In the service of this objective, however, the institutional reform advocated by the Pavia group may not be the most effective means. All four of our critics think that there may be more promising options. As we care far more about the objective than about the particular way of getting there, we would be delighted if they were right.

In addition to having the merit of making us think harder about our objective, Bart Maddens (2009a) takes the trouble of articulating an alternative constructive proposal. The latter consists in having the head of state elected by universal suffrage. Though most likely to be a Fleming, a candidate who

---

1. For this reason, it can be misleading to characterize the aim of the Pavia Group proposal as 'centripetal' versus 'centrifugal' – as de Briey (2009a) and O'Leary (2009) both do. Our proposal does aim to encourage citizens and politicians not to remain confined within their own community and instead to listen and talk to each other across the language border. This should help identify and implement win-win reforms. But there is no need to believe that a win-win concern should amount to concentrating as many competences as possible at the 'centre'. If only for this same reason, our proposal is also by no means more 'pro-Francophone' than O'Leary's (2009) alternative proposal (contrary to what he incidentally suggests). It is in every region's interest to have a federal government moving speedily towards win-win reforms, whether decentralizing or not, and more generally to have an efficient federal government. Only those Walloon rattachistes and Flemish separatists who believe Belgium will suddenly explode can feel served by the federal government's inefficiency, and in particular its inability to reform.

manages to get strong support on both sides of Belgium's ethnic divide will tend to enjoy a serious competitive advantage. The leading candidates will campaign throughout the country, shape their programmes accordingly and try to create a cohesive support base by linking like-minded political forma-tions in the three Regions. As a simple version of a run-off majority system in an ethnically heterogeneous district, such a proposal is bound to attract Donald Horowitz's sympathy. But for the desired dynamics to arise in a coun-try like Belgium, so Maddens suggests, it may not even be necessary to im-pose regional or ethnic thresholds, as in the Nigerian and Indonesian cases hinted at positively by Horowitz (2009) and negatively by O'Leary (2009).

Maddens' (2009a) proposal is of course not original (nor is it meant to be). Indeed, it is actually in use in a number of other multiethnic countries, from post-Soviet Bulgaria to the Democratic Republic of the Congo and the United States of America. A crucial question is of course how much power the head of state so elected would be given. If the function is essentially symbolic, as in the version Maddens has in mind, the associated dynamics will be too weak to offset the dynamics stemming from the mono-ethnic electorates on which parliamentary majorities and hence the choice of governments will keep de-pending – hardly better for our purposes, it seems, than the hereditary system now in place. If it is substantial, on the other hand, we are talking about a shift towards a presidential system, i.e. an institutional revolution incomparably more radical than merely scrapping the little that is left of the monarchy's powers or indeed than implementing our very modest proposal.

This is not the place to discuss the respective advantages of (more or less) presidential versus (more or less) parliamentary regimes. Jumping to a presi-dential regime may or may not have disadvantages that will more than com-pensate the undeniable advantage that well designed majoritarian systems tend to possess, with ethnically heterogeneous electoral districts, in terms of the dynamics we want to strengthen. The game in which we deliberately chose to play with our proposal is a pretty conservative one, which satisfies a strong constraint of short-term political feasibility as we see it. With the strong (and only relevant) interpretation of his proposal, Maddens is invit-ing us to a quite different game which implies a far more radical reform of Belgium's institutional architecture. This is by no means a sufficient reason for refusing to think about it. But the exploration of its many effects in the Belgian context will unavoidably need to be far more speculative than what is required by our modest proposal. Probably too speculative for this option to ever be proposed seriously, not only tongue-in-cheek. [2]

---

2. The countries in which the system is in place are sufficiently different from Belgium in a suf-ficient number of relevant dimensions for any inference to be made very cautiously. But they do provide a starting point for such speculation. Perhaps the closest case is that of the Republic of

3. O'LEARY'S PROPORTIONAL CABINET

No less revolutionary are Brendan O'Leary's (2009) two proposals, both inspired by the Northern Ireland consociational settlement which he helped bring about. His first idea is that we should have 'two co-equal prime ministers', respectively nominated by the largest Flemish party and the largest Francophone party, as an alternative to 'the convention of unanimity in the cabinet'. This convention – which can more aptly be said to apply to the *kerncabinet*, i.e. to the chief ministers of each party in the government coalition – is of course a sheer corollary of the government's need to retain the confidence of a parliamentary majority. Hence, dual premiership would not make that convention redundant. And as the premier function is not particularly in trouble, it is not clear what problem dual premiership would solve. Perhaps the reason why such a proposal makes sense in the Northern Irish context and not in the Belgian one is that it is far easier to be(come) linguistically *asexué* than religiously *asexué*. Jean-Luc Dehaene and Guy Verhofstadt, once in power, have quickly acquired strong popular support on the other side of the linguistic border.

More intriguing is O'Leary's second proposal, which he develops at greater length. Why not take D'Hondt to the very top of his homeland's political power? Why not use for the composition of the federal executive, and not only of the various legislative assemblies, the list system of proportional representation first articulated by the Belgian Victor D'Hondt (1878) and first introduced in Belgium (1899) before spreading in waves to many other countries throughout the world?[3] The fifteen minister positions in the federal government, with predefined competences, would be allocated sequentially to the various parties as a function of their share of the seats in the Chamber, using the formula currently used for the allocation of these seats to the lists as a function of the popular vote. This sequence would determine the order in which the various parties could choose portfolios. One likely consequence is that the biggest party would automatically get the Prime Minister position and

---

Macedonia, where the proportions of native speakers for the two main language groups are not that different from those that prevail in Belgium (64/25 versus 56/36) and where parliamentary elections see two sets of parties address two de facto separate electorates (of Macedonians and Albanians) under a multi-district PR system. At presidential elections, both Macedonian and Albanian parties present candidates in the first round. In the second round, the top two candidates are kept, both Macedonians predictably. Neither of them, so far, tries to appeal directly to the Albanian voters, whether from the start or in the second round. But they both try to strike a deal with the leadership of one of the Albanian parties in order to enlist its support. (See Bieber 2008 and Petrov 2009.) Not quite the dynamics aimed at in Maddens' proposal, nor perhaps the one that can be expected in the Belgian case.

3.   See section 2 of Chapter 6 for an account of why it was introduced.

the second biggest party the deputy Prime Minister position. This obviously provides an alternative to the parity principle as a way of securing a balanced representation of both communities in the federal government. It would also have the advantage, O'Leary argues, of enabling us to dispense with the unanimity rule and go for a less constraining majority rule.

However, when looking at O'Leary's application of his proposal to the outcome of the June 2007 election, these two features are not the first ones that will strike any Belgian observer, but rather a spectacular violation of the *cordon sanitaire* to which all 'democratic' parties have scrupulously stuck so far in order to keep out of power, at all levels, the extreme-right anti-immigrant party Vlaams Belang. Two leaders of the Vlaams Belang would be graciously offered two minister posts, with predictable consequences for the atmosphere at government meetings. This particular consequence illustrates the general defect of O'Leary's scheme in the Belgian context: overkill. It is essential to the good working of Belgium's federal system that both communities should be sufficiently represented in the executive, but not that all political tendencies should be present in it. As Guy Verhofstadt's two liberal-socialist governments (1999–2007) have shown, it is even no longer necessary for the government's legitimacy that the two sides of the old cleavage between Catholics and non-Catholics (the cleavage that prompted *L'Union fait la force* as the national motto in 1830 and later made Belgium a paradigm of consociationalism) should be represented in the government. It is true that O'Leary's scheme would make it conceivable to dispense with the unanimous agreement of all parties in the government. Indeed, this would be indispensable to prevent constant blockages. But there is no reason to expect qualified majority support among the large set of parties O'Leary wants to bring into the government to be easier to achieve than agreement among all members of the subset of parties that form the governmental majority (in the present situation). Our conviction, therefore, is that the cohesion of a government, its capacity to act and its electoral accountability are all better served under the present system of government formation, which requires simple majority support in the Chamber combined with the support of at least some significant parties in each language group.

All this, however, does nothing to undermine Brendan O'Leary's (2009) fundamental point, which his Northern Irish inspired proposals are only meant to illustrate. His point is that once a problem is identified, it is fruitful not to remain stuck with one pet idea and instead to seek inspiration from how other divided countries might have successfully solved analogous problems, possibly in a 'less backdoor way'. O'Leary emphatically dismisses 'the absurd spirit that what works in Northern Ireland works best everywhere else'. And it is in the light of a 'sensitively detailed knowledge of Belgium's historic and current dynamics', whose importance he stresses, that we believe his proposal would not fix our problem. The reason why O'Leary conjectured it might do is that it would make the formation of a government an automatic consequence of the parliamentary elections, instead of the outcome of the sort of protracted negotiation we witnessed after the June 2007 election. Such negotiation, however, is about the substance of the government's programme far more than about the distribution of portfolios and the reason why it happens before the new government taking office is to prevent constant blockages and governmental instability later on. What the Northern Irish formula would do is shift these tensions and blockages into the working of the government once formed and probably make them worse, because of the guaranteed presence of hardliners from both communities. The consequences are likely to be crippling, with the government basically reduced to a caretaker role far beyond the realm of inter-community issues. Or at least this will be the case as long as the prior electoral process keeps inducing parties from both sides to make strong and salient but incompatible promises to their separate electorates. This is the fundamental problem we face, and O'Leary's (2009) two interesting proposals do not address it.

4. DE BRIEY'S DOUBLE VOTE

Laurent de Briey's (2009a) proposal does address this problem.[4] It is, moreover, significantly less radical than either Maddens' proposal or O'Leary's, and is therefore a closer competitor to ours. Like us, de Briey wants all electors of the federal Parliament to have a second vote in addition to the one cast in their own provincial electoral district. But whereas in our proposal, the second vote is cast on a unilingual or bilingual open list presented in a country-wide electoral district, de Briey wants the second vote cast on a closed unilingual list from the other community.

In order to prevent one community from having too much of an impact on who represents the other (and in particular to prevent the Flemish majority from having more say than the Francophones themselves in determining who will represent the Francophones), the votes cast across the linguistic border lose three-quarters of their value on the way. In order to avoid many complications and by-pass the problem of insufficient information about individual candidates, on the other hand, the second votes are cast on closed party

---

4.   A significantly different version of this proposal, with open lists and no reduction coefficients, was presented by UCLouvain law professor and CdH senator Francis Delpérée (discussed in section 4 of Chapter 6).

lists and distributed across provincial electoral districts in proportion to the votes obtained in each of them by the parties concerned. Here again, as under Maddens' proposal, we can reasonably expect that parties on each side will pay significantly more attention to the other side than is the case under the present set up, at least if electors bother to use their second vote in significant numbers.

For the level of complexity of the voting system to remain manageable, this double-vote system is not realistically combinable with ours. The question is then whether there are any good reasons to prefer one to the other. The main advantage of de Briey's proposal is that his second vote, unlike ours, is wasted if it is not used across the language border. As most voters are likely to have at least some preference between the parties on the other side, many of them are likely to make use of this second vote, and anticipating this response (even with an impact dampened by the coefficient) will induce the leaders of the various parties to care more for the citizens and the media of the other community. In our proposal, it could be said that the guarantee is weaker, since the 'federal' vote of each citizen could be cast exclusively on candidates from her own community. We believe, however, that this advantage is more than offset by a conjunction of disadvantages which make the proposal of a federal electoral district both more realistic and more promising in terms of the dynamics it will trigger.

Firstly, in de Briey's proposal unlike in ours, there is no competition between individual candidates for the favours of voters from the other side. As a result, one of the expected effects of our proposal is given up: the encouragement of a selection and self-selection of candidates more suitable for responsibilities at the federal level. Secondly, like the coexistence of two electoral colleges (French-speakers and Dutch-speakers), de Briey's scheme prevents the formation of bilingual lists. It thereby rigidly asserts and tends to reinforce the priority of the dichotomic 'ethnic' political identity over all others, with ideological differences playing only a secondary role. Our own scheme, despite the linguistic quotas to which we shall return, is far less rigid. It makes room for (without imposing) bilingual lists which give precedence to ideological over linguistic identity, and could also easily be adjusted if regional identities started overshadowing linguistic identities. Finally, the asymmetry implied by the coefficients means that the members of the federal government are not equally accountable, electorally speaking, to each citizen of the country: the vote of a citizen from the other community matters to him four times less than the vote of someone from his own. In our proposal, each voter matters equally to each member of the government.

It may, however, be argued, that speculations about the possible consequences of de Briey's scheme are pointless because its political feasibility faces a decisive obstacle. Owing to his proposal's closed-list aspect (for which he argues convincingly), the bridging between communities will arguably tend to take the form, not of vote-fetching by individual candidates, but rather of deals between political parties. Each party will tell its voters to allocate their second vote to the party with which it managed to strike a reciprocal deal. If this is anticipated (whether correctly or not) by the various parties, the proposal will be strongly opposed both by those who will have no party to make a deal with (which would presumably be the case for the Flemish nationalist parties N-VA and VB) and by those who have only a comparatively much smaller one (which would be the case, under present conditions, for the Flemish Christian Democrats and for the Francophone socialists and greens). Especially if the proposal is coming from those parties that stand to gain most from the scheme (the Francophone Christian-Democrats CdH or the Flemish Greens) this proposal will therefore look *cousu de fil blanc* by all others, and unlikely to get anything like the required majority. As our proposal is consistent with each party standing alone and receiving its usual share of the votes, it does not create a similar obstacle.

Before concluding that the scheme we propose is definitely better than double vote schemes of the type advocated by de Briey, it is important to answer one important objection to be found in both de Briey's (2009a) and Horowitz's (2009b) comments. Both of them fear that the incentives triggered by the creation of a federal electoral district will remain weak, if only because of the relatively small number of seats involved in the Pavia version of the federal district proposal (15 out of 150) or even in the versions favoured by the political parties that support the federal district (30 to 40 out of 180 or 190).

In response, we need to stress three crucial points insufficiently appreciated, it seems to us, by our critics. Firstly, there is no doubt that all the party leaders and most likely members of the federal government to be formed after the election will be standing in this federal electoral district: it will be in the interest of their parties to put them on these lists simply because of the appeal they will have outside their province (not necessarily outside their region), and in an age in which TV appearance is more important than door to door canvassing, how weighty the 'federal' candidates are is far more important than how numerous they are. Secondly and for the same basic reason, even though most of the MPs will be elected in a provincial seat, most will have been candidates in the federal electoral district. Finally, the possibility of multiple voting on the same list, which is standardly offered in all Belgian elections, makes it far more likely that voters will seriously consider voting for a salient candidate from the other community providing (s)he stands on a bilingual list and thereby enables voters to vote simultaneously for him/her and for one or more candidates from their own community.

Contrary to a frequent and understandable interpretation to be found for example in O'Leary's (2009) comment, our argument is emphatically *not* that there will be a special category of MPs who will represent, and feel they represent, the whole of the country, while the others represent their region or their province. Our argument is rather that the leaders of all parties and most of the MPs (whether elected in the federal or in a provincial electoral district) will have something to gain – and not, as now, only to lose – by listening to voters from the other side and accommodating their concerns in the programmes they propose and the commitments they make.

5. HOROWITZ'S REGIONAL THRESHOLDS

Now, as Horowitz points out, it remains true that the reform we propose merely opens a possibility, without any guarantee that it will be used. If voters consider that they can only be truly represented by members of their own linguistic group – as de Briey (2009a) fears they will –, there will be nothing for politicians to gain from looking across the linguistic border. But is there any fundamental reason why voters should find it more difficult to feel properly represented by MPs belonging to the other linguistic group than by MPs belonging to the other gender or to another age group? It is arguably crucial that voters should feel that their representatives understand them and care for them. The lack of any shared language is admittedly a formidable obstacle to both the feeling and the reality of being understood, but a difference in native languages need not be such an obstacle: it only appears to be so when the institutions make it so. And if voters are to feel that candidates from the other language group care for them, enabling these candidates to gain from caring for them – which is precisely what our proposal does – should definitely help.

Nevertheless, if our proposal is to achieve its objective rather than be counterproductive, it is essential that voters should not feel that by giving their vote (or one or more of their votes for individual candidates) to someone from the other community, they risk contributing to their own community being underrepresented. As noted by Horowitz, the open list character of Belgium's PR system (which we wish to keep) opens the possibility of block voting on bilingual lists for candidates belonging to one linguistic community. The widespread occurrence of such block voting can be anticipated to trigger the collapse of bilingual lists and the spreading of active campaigning for voting for the unilingual lists of one's own community. Pre-established quotas, simply fixed by the ratio of the linguistic groups in the outgoing parliament, are therefore indispensable if this perverse dynamics is to be inhibited.

Unfortunately, with the exception of O'Leary (2009), our critics do not like our quotas. They seem to feel that they introduce an unwelcome impurity into our proposal: they turn the latter into an uncomfortable hybrid of consociationalist power-sharing (which relies on salient distinct identities) and transcommunity bridge-building (which strives to make these distinct identities less salient). We do not care about purity.[5] Nor do we care about whether our proposal can be regarded as truly 'consociationalist' or truly 'centripetalist'. What we care about is results in the country as it is. And this country is one in which linguistic identities are strong enough for most people to care about the overall representation of their community in the national parliament. But it is also one in which for most people these identities are not so strong as to make it unimaginable for them to vote for a congenial candidate from the other community. This is why quotas are essential to our proposal. This is also why, contrary to what is sometimes suggested, our proposal does not amount to swelling BHV (the electoral district of Brussels-Halle-Vilvoorde whose partition along the regional border has been a pressing and contentious Flemish demand for many years) to the country as a whole.[6] The fact that the electoral system within the current BHV electoral district does not involve quotas is precisely one major reason why federal elections there amount to something like a conflict-ridden linguistic census that drives communities against each other instead of building bridges between them.[7]

It is therefore correct to say that quotas are for us a way of creating, in Horowitz's (2009) words, 'preelectoral incentives for intergroup cooperation' by switching off the voter's defensive inhibition. Horowitz suggests that we should 'follow that idea to its logical conclusion', instead of clinging to what looks like a remnant of consociationalism. How? By including far more seats in the federal district so as to mitigate more effectively 'the tendencies emanating from the [provincially allocated] seats in which candidates are elected as representatives of ethnic interests'. But also perhaps, more imaginatively, by stipulating that 'lists could only be elected if they achieved some territorial distribution threshold that testified to their interregional appeal'.

The Pavia Group did discuss variants of this idea, for example imposing a list-level eligibility condition that prevented allocating seats to lists that do not reach at least 5 per cent of the vote in each Region (a percentage that

5. See the defence of 'hybrid' packages in section 5 of Chapter 6.

6. See de Coorebyter (2007) and Maddens (2007). For a more detailed argument on the importance of quotas, see Van Parijs (2006).

7. By contrast, the Brussels regional elections, which operate with a 17/72 pre-established quota, display less divisive dynamics. However, they are organized in two unilingual electoral colleges which prevent bilingual lists and turn border-crossing voting into an anomaly (see Van Parijs 2009). Some analogue of the Pavia Group proposal should be explored for the Brussels Region's electoral system in order to avoid this defect without lifting minority protection.

would need to be safely above the estimated percentage of Francophones living in Flanders), or perhaps at least 0.5 per cent of the vote in each of the eleven provincial districts.[8] Were a condition of this type to be imposed, the incentive to form a country-wide list would obviously be greater than under our proposal. But there is a big danger. Some parties may deliberately opt for sacrificing seats on that electoral district in order to denounce both the 'undemocratic' character of a system that denies representation to nationalist parties and the despicable collaboration of their competitors with the 'other camp'. Their success may easily be so great as to block any 'collaborationist' majority in the federal parliament. Of course, this could be prevented by allocating most seats to the multiple-threshold country-wide electoral district. But the discrepancy between parliamentary majorities in the federation and in (at least one of) the regions would then tend to become explosive.

On reflection, therefore, the Pavia Group opted for a milder variant that does not make it impossible for mono-ethnic parties to get candidates elected in the federal electoral district. Common lists are encouraged by the fact that unilingual lists, in our proposal, will look incomplete (only nine candidates on unilingual Dutch lists, only six on unilingual French lists) and by the premium given to bigger parties by the D'Hondt PR system, at least if district magnitude is not too large. True, our allowing vote pooling between distinct lists reduces this encouragement. But this optional pooling seems to us an appropriate way of creating solidarities across the linguistic boundary when the level of trust is not sufficient for the creation of common lists, while not preventing these solidarities from paving the way to the latter. Moreover, the ability to gather both components of a political family in single list will be an attractive prospect for political leaders who want to become federal prime minister, as they will thereby be able to attract far more easily large numbers of votes spanning the whole country, thereby gaining both greater authority within their own party and a more legitimate claim to leading the government of the whole country.

If our proposal is to be improved in a direction Horowitz should welcome, therefore, it may be by stipulating that the leader of the list that gains most votes in the federal electoral district should automatically be put in charge of trying to form the next government (instead of the choice being left to the king, as is now the case). Horowitz is likely to welcome this way of increasing the extent to which politicians with the ambition to rule a divided country are "made 'partially dependent on the votes of members of groups other than their own' (Horowitz 2009)". And Maddens is certain to do so. For in our

---

8. I argued for a variant of this sort in section 4 of Chapter 6, and explain here why I changed my mind.

own modest, conservative way – parliamentarian and proportional rather than presidential and majoritarian – we are thereby going a long way towards a direct election of the head of the government, while eroding the little that remained of the current head of state's political power. Yes, there is perhaps something better than the Pavia proposal. Warm thanks to our critics in any case for having moved the discussion forward.

REFERENCES

Abukhalil, A. (1994) 'Women and Electoral Politics in Arab States', in W. Rule and J. F. Zimmermann (eds) *Electoral Systems in Comparative Perspective. Their Impact on Women and Minorities*, Westport, CT and London: Greenwood Press, 127–37.

Ackerman, B. A. (1991) *We, the People. Foundations*. Cambridge, Mass.: Harvard University Press.

— (1993) 'Crediting the Voters. A New Beginning for Campaign Finance', *The American Prospect* 13, 71–80.

Anderson, B. R. O. (1993) 'Nationalism', in J. Krieger (ed.)*The Oxford Companion to the Politics of the World,* Oxford: Oxford University Press, 614–19.

Andeweg, R. B. (2010) 'Electoral Engineering or Prudent Leadership', contribution to the Re-Bel event of 17 December 2009, www.rethinkingbelgium.eu, 5p.

Annemans, G. H. *et al* (1998) *Een Keuze voor het leven.* Brussels: Vlaams Blok.

Aoki, R. (2011) 'Let children Vote', *The Economist*, 1 January 2011, p.11.

Arneson, R. J. (1993b) 'Democratic Rights at National and Workplace Levels', in D. Copp, J. Hampton and J.E. Roemer (eds) *The Idea of Democracy*, Cambridge: Cambridge University Press, 118–48.

Auerbach, A. J., Gokhale, J. and Kotlikoff, L. J. (1991) 'Generational Accounts: A Meaningful Alternative to Deficit Accounting', *Tax Policy and the Economy* 5: 55–110.

Barry, B. (1975a) 'The Consociational Model and its Dangers', *European Journal of Political Research* 3: 393–412. Reprinted in B. Barry*, Democracy and Power*, Oxford: Oxford University Press, 1991, 136–55.

— (1975b) 'Political Accommodation and Consociational Democracy', *British Journal of Political Science* 5: 477–505. Reprinted in B. Barry, *Democracy and Power*, Oxford: Oxford University Press, 1991, 100–35.

— (1977) 'Justice Between Generations', in P.M. Hacker and J. Raz (eds) *Morality and Society*, Oxford:Oxford University Press, 268–84. Reprinted in B. Barry, *Liberty and Justice*, Oxford: Oxford University Press, 1989, 242–58.

— (2001) *Culture and Equality*. Cambridge: Polity Press.

Barry, B. and Goodin, R. E. (eds) (1992) *Free Movement: Ethical Issues in the Transnational Migration of People and Money.* Hemel–Hempstead: Harvester–Wheatsheaf.

Bayer, A. (1997) 'Let's Give Parents an Extra Right to Vote', *New York Times* 4 May 1997.

Beelen, S., De Poorter, L., Haeyaert, P. and Vandenbroeke, C. (1993) *Geschiedenis van de Vlaamse ontvoogding.* Deurne: MIM.

Bieber, F. (2008) 'Power-sharing and the implementation of the Ohrid Framework Agreement', in F. Bieber (ed.) *Power Sharing and the Implementation of the Ohrid Framework Agreement*, Skopje: Friedrich Ebert Stiftung, 7–40.

Binstock, R. (1994) 'Transcending Intergenerational Equity', in T. R. Marmor, T. M. Smeeding and V. L. Greene (eds) *Economic Security and Intergenerational Justice. A Look at North America*, Washington, D.C.: The Urban Institute Press, 155–85.

Birnbacher, D. (1988) *Verantwortlichkeit für zukünftige Generationen.* Stuttgart: Reclam.

Blanchet, D. and Ekert-Jaffé, O. (1994) 'The Demographic Impact of Family Benefits: Evidence from a Micro-Model and from Micro-Data', in J. Ermisch and N. Ogawa (eds) *The Family, the Market and the State in Ageing Societies*, Oxford: Clarendon Press, 79–103.

Bouckaert, B. (2008) '*Leo Belgicus* op zoek naar zichzelf. Territorialiteit, regionalisme en confederale bestuurscultuur in de Lage Landen', *Fédéralisme et Régionalisme* 8(1).

Boulanger, P.-M. (1990) 'Vieillissement et gérontocratie dans une constitution démocratique', in M. Loriaux, D. Remy and E. Vilquin (eds) *Populations agées et revolution grise*, Louvain-la-Neuve: CIACO, 971–81.

Bourgeois, L. (1902) *Solidarité*, Paris: Armand Colin.

Bowles, S. and Gintis, H. (1998) *Recasting Egalitarianism. New Rules for Communities, States and Markets*, London: Verso.

Brans, M. (1993) 'High-Tech Problem Solving in a Multi-Cultural State: The Case of Brussels', *Dutch Crossing. A Journal of Low Countries Studies* 49: 3–28.

BRTN. (1996) *Continukijkonderzoek*, Brussel: BRTN Studiedienst, februari.

Buruma. I. (2011) 'Le Divorce. Why Belgium, Home of the European Union, Has Never Been So Disunited', *The New Yorker*, 10 January 2011, 36–40.

Büttner, T. and Lutz, W. (1990) 'Estimating Fertility Responses to Policy Measures in the German Democratic Republic', *Population and Development Review* 16 (3): 539–55.

Campiglio, L. (1997) 'Political Participation, Voting, and Economic Policy: Three Problems of Modern Democracies', in A. Breton, E. Galeotti, P. Salmon and R. Wintrobe (eds) *Understanding Democracy. Economic and Political Perspectives*, Cambridge: Cambridge University Press, 196–208.

— (2005) *Prima le donne e i bambini. Chi rappresenta i minorenni?*, Bologna: Il Mulino.

Carballo, M. (1981) 'Extra Votes for Parents?', *The Boston Globe* 17 December 1981, 35.

Carstairs, A. M. (1980) *A Short History of Electoral Systems in Western Europe*. London: George, Allen and Unwin.

Chesnais, J.-Cl. (1996) 'Fertility, Family, and Social Policy in Contemporary Western Europe', *Population and Development Review* 22 (4): 729–39.

Christiano, T. (1996) *The Rule of the Many. Fundamental Issues in Democratic Theory*. Boulder, Co and Oxford: Westview Press.

— (2003) 'Is Democracy Merely a Means to Social Justice?', in A. Reeve and A. Williams (eds) *Real Libertarianism Assessed. Political Philosophy After Van Parijs*, Basingstoke: Palgrave Macmillan, 172–200.

Cohen, J. (ed.) (1997) 'Procedure and Substance in Deliberative Democracy' in J. Bohman and W. Rehg (eds) *Essays on Reason and Politics: Deliberative Democracy*, Cambridge, Mass.: MIT Press, 407–37.

Curtis, G. (1998) 'The Unintended Effects of Japan's Electoral Reform', paper presented at Yale University, Department of Political Science, 25 February 1998.

Day, C. L. (1990) *What Older Americans Think: Interest Groups and Aging Policy.* Princeton, NJ: Princeton University Press.

de Briey, L. (2009a) ' A Federal Electoral System: Country-Wide Electoral District or Multiple Proportional Vote?', *Electoral Engineering for a Stalled Federation. A country-wide electoral district for Belgium's federal Parliament*, Brussels: Re-Bel e-book no.4, www.rethinkingbelgium.eu, July 2009, 21–4.

— (2009b) 'Could a federal electoral district be effective? ', contribution to the Re-Bel event of 17 December 2009, www.rethinkingbelgium.eu, 7p.

de Coorebyter, V. (2007) 'Een super B-H-V?', *De Morgen*, 18 januari.

Dehousse, R. (1994) 'Community Competences: Are There Limits to Growth?', *Europe After Maastricht: An Ever Closer Europe?,* Munich: Law Books in Europe, 103–25.

— (1995) 'Institutional Reform in the European Community: Are there Alternatives to the Majoritarian Avenue?', European University Institute: Robert Schuman Centre, Working Paper no.95/4, 33p.

Deliège, R. (1993) *Le Système des castes*. Paris: P.U.F.

Delpérée, F. (1998) *La Démarche citoyenne*. Bruxelles: Labor.

Delpérée, F. and Dubois, F. X. (1998) 'Le double vote ou le vote multiple', in Groupe Avenir UCL (ed.) *Des Idées et des hommes. Pour construire l'avenir de la Wallonie et de Bruxelles*, Louvain-la-Neuve: Academia-Bruylant, 69–84.

De Ridder, P. (1988) *Het andere Brussel. Een afrekening met vooroordelen.* Wommelgem: Den Gulden Engel.

Deschouwer, K. (2005) 'The unintended consequences of consociational federalism: the case of Belgium', in I. O'Flynn and D. Russell (eds) *Power sharing. New challenges for divided societies*, London/Ann Arbor: Pluto Press, 92–106.

— (2006) 'And the peace goes on? Consociational democracy and Belgian politics in the 21st century', *West European Politics*, 29 (5): 895–911.

— (2009) *The Politics of Belgium. Governing a Divided Society*, London: Palgrave-Macmillan.

Deschouwer, K. and Van Parijs, P. (2007) 'Une circonscription fédérale pour tous les belges', *La Revue Nouvelle* 4: 12–23.

— (2008) 'Een federale kieskring voor een gezonde federatie', *Samenleving en Politiek* 15(3): 43–52.

Destrée, J. (1923) *Wallons et Flamands. La Querelle linguistique en Belgique.* Paris: Plon.

Dewachter, W. (1968) 'De verdere democratisering van de Belgische politiek',

Res Publica 10 (2): 253–78.

—   (1992) 'Une nouvelle technique d'élection directe du gouvernement', Res Publica 34 (1): 75–85.

—   (1995) 'Changer la démocratie pour sauver la solidarité?', Université catholique de Louvain: Chaire Hoover d'éthique économique et sociale, 4 April.

—   (1996) 'La Belgique d'aujourd'hui comme société politique', in A. Dieckhoff (ed.) La Belgique. La Force de la désunion, Bruxelles: Complexe, 105–42.

Dewatripont, M., Giavazzi, F., Harden, I.Persson, T., Roland, G., Sapir, A., Tabellini, G. and von Hagen, J. (1996) Flexible Integration. Towards a More Effective and Democratic Europe, London: Centre for Economic Policy Research.

D'Hondt, V. (1878) Question électorale. La représentation proportionnelle des partis par un électeur. Bruxelles: Bruylant.

—   (1882) Système pratique et raisonné de représentaion proportionnelle. Bruxelles: C. Muquardt.

Donneur, A. (1984) 'Un nationalisme suisse romand est-il possible?', Vous avez dit Suisse romande?, Lausanne: Institut d'études politiques, 25–52.

Downs, A. (1957) An Economic Theory of Democracy. New York: Harper.

Dworkin, R. (1989) 'What is equality? Part IV: Political equality', University of San Francisco Law Review 22, 1–30.

—   (1996) 'The Curse of American Politics', The New York Review of Books 17 October, 19–24.

Ector, S. (1993) 'Federale burgerzin vereist een echte federale regering', De Standaard 7 August.

Elster, J. (1986) 'Comment on van der Veen and Van Parijs', Theory and Society 15: 709–22.

—   (1988) 'Arguments for Constitutional Change: Reflections on the Transition to Socialism', in J. Elster and R. Slagstad (eds) Constitutionalism and Democracy, Cambridge: Cambridge University Press, 303–23.

—   (2000) 'Arguing and bargaining in two constituent assemblies', University of Pennsylvania Journal of Constitutional Law 2(2): 345–421.

Engels, F. (1848) 'The Danish-Prussian Armistice', English translation in K. Marx and F. Engels, Collected Works Vol. 7, London: Lawrence and Wishart, 1977, 421–5.

Ermisch, J. (1988) 'Economic Analysis of Birth Rate Dynamics in Britain', Journal of Human Resources 23 (4): 563–76.

Estlund, D. (1990) 'Democracy without Preference', Philosophical Review 3: 397–423.

Farrell, D. M. (1997) Comparing Electoral Systems. Hemel Hempstead: Prentice Hall/ Harvester Wheatsheaf.

Feist, U. (1992) 'Niedrige Wahlbeteiligung - Normalisierung oder Krisensymptom?', in K. Starzacher et al. (eds) Protestwähler und Wahlweigerer, Köln: Bundverlag.

Follesdal, A. (1997) 'Democracy and Federalism in the European Union', in A. Follesdal and P. Koslowski (eds) *Democracy and the European Union*, Berlin and New York: Springer, 231–53

Follesdal, A. and Koslowski, P. (eds) (1997) *Democracy and the European Union*. Berlin and New York: Springer.

Fondation francophone de Belgique. (1997) *Etude sur l'identité francophone en région de Bruxelles-capitale*. Bruxelles, décembre.

Franck, C. (1995) 'Evolution institutionnelle de l'Union dans la perspective de la Conférence intergouvernementale de 1996', Université catholique de Louvain: Institut d'études européennes, working paper, 49p.

Gaspard, F., Servan-Schreiber, C. and Le Gall, A. (1992) *Au Pouvoir Citoyennes: Liberté, égalité, parité*. Paris: Seuil.

Gauthier, A. H. (1996) *The State and the Family. A Comparative analysis of Family Policies in Industrialized Societies*. Oxford: Oxford University Press.

Gauthier, A. H. and Hatzius, J. (1997) 'Family Benefits and Fertility: An Econometric Analysis', *Population Studies* 51 (3): 295–307.

Gellner, E. (1983) *Nations and Nationalism*. Oxford: Blackwell.

Geyl, P. (1962) 'The National State and the Writers of Netherlands History', *Debates with Historians*, Glasgow: Collins/Fontana.

Glyn, A. and Miliband, D. (eds) (1994) *Paying for Inequality. The Economic Cost of Social Injustice*. London: Institute for Public Policy Research.

Goodin, R. E. 'Enfranchising the Earth, and its Alternatives', *Political Studies* 44 (5): 835–49.

Grimm, D. (1995) 'Does Europe Need a Constitution?', *European Law Journal* 1 (3): 282–302.

Grözinger, G. (1993) 'Achtung, Kind wählt mit! Ein Beitrag zur allmählichen Aufhebung der Diktatur der Gegenwart über die Zukunft', *Blätter für deutsche und internationale Politik* 10: 1261–7.

Grözinger, G. and Geiger, H. (eds) (1993) *Zukunft wählen – Zusatzstimmen für Eltern?*, Bad Boll: Evangelische Akademie.

Guinier, L. (1994) *The Tyranny of the Majority. Fundamental Fairness in Representative Democracy*. New York: The Free Press.

Gustavsson, S. (1996) 'Preserve or Abolish the Democratic Deficit?', in E. Smith (ed.) *National Cornerstones of European Integration*, London: Kluwer, 100–23.

— (1997) 'Double Asymmetry as Normative Challenge', in A. Follesdal and P. Koslowski (eds) *Democracy and the European Union*, Berlin and New York: Springer, 108–31.

Gutmann, A. and Thompson, D. (1996) *Democracy and Disagreement*, Cambridge, Mass.: Harvard University Press.

Habermas, J. (1995) 'Remarks on Dieter Grimm's "Does Europe Need a Constitution?"', *European Law Journal* 1 (3): 303–7.

Hamilton, A., Madison, J. and Jay, J. (1788) *Federalist Papers*, New York: The New American Library of World Literature, 1964.

Hare, T. (1859) *Treatise on the Election of Representatives, Parliamentary and*

Municipal.London:Longman,Green,LongmanandRoberts,1861(2nded.).

Hartwick, J. (1977) 'Intergenerational equity and the investing of rents from exhaustible resources', *American Economic Review* 66: 972–4.

Hattenhauer, H. (1997) 'Über das Minderjährigenwahlrecht', in C. and K. Hurrelmann (eds) *Jugend und Politik. Ein Handbuch für Forschung, Lehre und Praxis*, Neuwied: Luchterhand, 238–59.

Hayek, F. A. (1960) *The Constitution of Liberty*. London: Routledge and Kegan Paul, 1976.

— (1973) *Economic Freedom and Representative Government*. London: Institute of Economic Affairs, Occasional Paper no. 39.

Hazlitt, H. (1968) 'Income without work', in J. H. Bunzel (ed.) *Issues of American Public Policy*, Englewood Cliffs, N.J.: Prentice–Hall, 108–11.

Holt, J. (1974) *Escape from Childhood*. New York: Penguin Books.

Horowitz, D. L. (1985) *Ethnic Groups in Conflict*. Berkeley: University of California Press.

— (1991) *A Democratic South Africa? Constitutional Engineering in a Divided Society*. Berkeley: University of California Press.

— (1993) 'Democracy in Divided Societies', *Journal of Democracy* 4 (4): 18–38.

— (2000a) 'Constitutional Design: An Oxymoron?', in I. Shapiro and S. Macedo (eds) *Nomos 41. Designing Democratic Institutions*, New York: NYU Press, 253–84.

— (2000b) 'Provisional Pessimism: A Reply to Van Parijs', in I. Shapiro and S. Macedo (eds) *Nomos 41. Designing Democratic Institutions*, New York: NYU Press, 296–320.

— (2009) 'A Federal Constituency for Belgium: Right Idea, Inadequate Method', *Electoral Engineering for a Stalled Federation. A country-wide electoral district for Belgium's federal Parliament*, Brussels: Re-Bel e-book no.4, www.rethinkingbelgium.eu, July, 25–8.

Hume, D. (1741) *Essays. Moral, Political and Literary*. Indianapolis: Liberty Classics, 1985.

Hurrelmann, K. (1996) 'Mit 16 Jahren an die Wahlurne?', *Reutlinger General Anzeiger,* 23 February.

— (1997) 'Für eine Herabsetzung des Wahlalters', in C. Palentien and K. Hurrelmann (eds) *Jugend und Politik* , Neuwied: Luchterhand, 281–90.

Hurrelmann, K. and Palentien, C. (1997) 'Jugendliche an die Wahlurnen! Argumente zur Verbesserung der politischen Partizipation der jungen Generation', *Diskurs* 2: 38–45.

Jaffrelot, C. (1993) *La Démocratie indienne entre archaisme et modernité*. Paris: Fondation Saint Simon.

Jans, M. T. (2001) 'Leveled domestic politics. Comparing institutional reform and ethnonational conflicts in Canada and Belgium (1960–1989)', *Res Publica* 43 (1): 37–58.

Jansen, M. (ed.) (1986) *Halbe-Halbe. Der Streit um die Quotierung*, Berlin: Elefanten Press.

Johnson, D. B. (1991) *Public Choice: An Introduction to the New Political Economy*. Mayfield, CA: Bristlecone Books.

Karmis, D. and Gagnon, A.-G. (1996) 'Fédéralisme et identités collectives au Canada et en Belgique: des itinéraires différents, une fragmentation similaire', *Canadian Journal of Political Science* 29 (3): 435–68.

King, P. (1982) *Federalism and Federation*, London: Croom Helm.

— (1993) 'Federation and Representation', in M. Burgess and A.-G. Gagnon (eds) *Comparative Federalism and Federation. Competing Traditions and Future Directions*, New York and London: Harvester Wheatsheaf, 94–101.

Kotlikoff, L. J. (1993) 'Justice and Generational Accounting', in L.M. Cohen (ed.) *Justice Across Generations. What Does It Mean ?*, Washington (DC): American Association of Retired Persons, 77–93.

Landry, A. (1949) *Traité de démographie*. Paris: Payot.

Laponce, J. A. (1984) *Langue et territoire*. Québec: Presses uniersitaires de Laval. (English translation: *Languages and their Territories*. Toronto: University of Toronto Press, 1987.)

Lasserre, H. (1873) *De la Réforme et de l'organisation du suffrage universel*. Paris: Victor Palmé.

Lefèvre, J. (1997) 'Le troisième âge: riche mais inexploité', *Le Soir* 5 August 1997, 15.

Levy, F. and Murnane, R. J. (1992) 'Orphans of the Ballot Box', *The New York Times* 6 February 1992, A23.

Lewis, W. A. (1965) *Politics in West Africa*. London: Allen and Unwin.

Lijphart, A. (1968) *The Politics of Accommodation. Pluralism and Democracy in the Netherlands*. Berkeley: University of California Press.

— (1969) 'Consociational Democracy', *World Politics* 21: 207–25.

— (1977) *Democracy in Plural Societies. A Comparative Exploration*, New Haven: Yale University Press.

— (1981) *Conflict and Coexistence in Belgium. The Dynamics of a Culturally Divided Society*, Berkeley: Institute of International Studies

— (1995) 'Multiethnic Democracy', in S. M. Lipset (ed.) *The Encyclopedia of Democracy*, Washington D.C.: Congressional Quarterly Press, 853–65.

— (1996) 'The Puzzle of Indian Democracy: A Consociational Interpretation', *American Political Science Review* 90 (2): 258–68.

Lipset, S. M. (1981) *Political Man: The Social Bases of Politics*. Baltimore: Johns Hopkins University Press.

Longman, P. (1987) *Born to Pay. The New Politics of Aging in America*. Boston: Houghton Mifflin.

Löw, K. (1974). 'Das Selbstverständnis des Grundgesetzes und wirklich allgemeine Wahlen', *Politische Studien* 213: 19–29.

— (1993) 'Verfassungsverbot Kinderwahlrecht? Ein Beitrag zur Verfassungsdiskussion', *Familie und Recht* 1: 25–8.

— (1997) 'Es gibt kein allgemeines Wahlrecht', *Frankfurter Allgemeine Zeitung* 11 July 1997.

Ludbrook, R. (1996) *Should Children Have the Right to Vote?*, University of New South Wales (Sydney): National Children's and Youth Law Centre.

Luykx, T. and Platel, M. (1985) *Politieke geschiedenis van België*. Vol. 2. Antwerpen: Kluwer.

Mabille, X. (1996) 'De l'indépendance à l'Etat fédéral', in A. Dieckhoff (ed.) *La Belgique. La Force de la désunion*, Bruxelles: Complexe, 19–46.

Machiavelli, N. (1517) *Discorsi sopra la prima deca di Tito Livio*, reprinted in E. Raimondi (ed.) N. Machiavelli, *Opere*, Milano: Mursia, 1969, 69–342.

Maddens, B. (2007) 'Un très grand B-H-V', *Doorbraak*, 26 mei.

— (2009a) 'Chassez le naturel...', *Electoral Engineering for a Stalled Federation. A country-wide electoral district for Belgium's federal Parliament*, Brussels: Re-Bel e-book no.4, www.rethinkingbelgium.eu, July, 29–31.

— (2009b) 'Thinking twice about the national constituency', contribution to the Re-Bel event of 17 December 2009, www.rethinkingbelgium.eu, 4p.

Majone, G. (1996) *La Communauté européenne: un Etat régulateur*, Paris: Montchrestien.

Marmor, T. R., Smeeding, T. M. and Greene, V. L. (eds) (1994) *Economic Security and Intergenerational Justice. A Look at North America*, Washington, D.C.: The Urban Institute Press.

Marshall, G., Swift, A., Routh, D. and Burgoyne, C. (1999) 'What Is and What Ought to Be: Popular Beliefs about Distributive Justice in Thirteen Countries', *European Sociological Review* 15 (4): 349–67.

Marx, K. (1848) 'The 'Model State' of Belgium', English translation in K. Marx and F. Engels, *Collected Works* Vol.7, London: Lawrence and Wishart, 1977, 333–6.

McRae, K. D. (1975) 'The concept of consociational democracy and its application to Canada', in J.-G. Savard and R. Vigneault (eds) *Multilingual Political Systems: Problems and Solutions*, Québec: Presses universitaires de Laval, 245–301.

Metje, M. (1994) *Wählerschaft und Sozialstruktur im Generationswechsel. Eine Generationsanalyse des Wahlverhaltens bei Bundestagswahlen*. Wiesbaden: Deutscher Universitätsverlag.

Midgaard, K. (1997) 'The Problem of Autonomy and Democracy in a Complex Polity: The European Union', in A. Follesdal and P. Koslowski (eds) *Democracy and the European Union*, Berlin and New York: Springer, 189–203.

Mill, J. S. (1861) *Considerations on Representative Government*, reprinted in J. Gray (ed.) *On Liberty and Other Essays*, Oxford: Oxford University Press, 1991, 203–467.

Möckli, S. (1994) 'Demokratische Struktur und Volksabstimmungen', in P. Füglistaler (ed.) *Hilfe, die Schweiz schrumpft*, Zürich: Orell Füssli, 13–25.

Monnet, J. (1976) *Mémoires*, Paris: Fayard.

Moser, P. (1996) 'Why is Swiss Politics So Stable?', *Swiss Journal of Economics and Statistics* 132 (1): 31–61.

Moureau, L. and Goossens, C. (1958) 'L'évolution des idées concernant la représentation proportionnelle en Belgique', *Revue de droit international et de droit comparé* 35: 378–93.

Murphy, A. B. (1998) *The regional dynamics of language differentiation in Belgium, a study in cultural-political geography*, Chicago: University of Chicago.

Nagel, J. (1993) 'Lessons of the impending electoral reform in New Zealand', *PEGS Newsletter* 3(1): 9–10.

Norman, W. (1990) 'Démocratie juste ou justice démocratique?', *Cahiers de philosophie politique et juridique de l'Université de Caen* 18: 109–24.

Offe, C. (1993) 'Zusatzstimmen für Eltern. Ein Beitrag zur Reform von Demokratie und Wahlrecht?', in G. Grözinger and H. Geiger (eds) *Zukunft wählen – Zusatzstimmen für Eltern?*, Bad Boll: Evangelische Akademie, 1–26.

Okin, S. M. (1996) Comment on Robert Dahl, 'Equality and Inequality: Facts and Causes in a Normative Perspective', APSA Conference, San Francisco, 31 August 1996.

O'Leary, B. (2009) ' Belgium and Its Thoughtful Electoral Engineers', *Electoral Engineering for a Stalled Federation. A country-wide electoral district for Belgium's federal Parliament*, Brussels: Re-Bel e-book no.4, www.rethinkingbelgium.eu, July 2009, 32–9.

Ordeshook, P. C. (1986) *Game Theory and Political Theory: An Introduction.* Cambridge: Cambridge University Press.

Palentien, C. (1997) 'Pro- und Contra-diskussion zu einer Veränderung des Wahlrechts', in C. Palentien and K. Hurrelmann (eds) *Jugend und Politik*, Neuwied: Luchterhand, 290–300.

Papaux, A. (1997) 'Droit des langues en Suisse: Etat des lieux', *Revue suisse de science politique* 3 (2): 131–4.

Perrin, J.-P. (1997) 'Un mollah outsider à la présidence de l'Iran', *Libération* 26 May.

Peschel-Gutzeit, L.M. (1997) 'Unvollständige Legitimation der Staatsgewalt oder geht alle Staatsgewalt nur vom volljährigen Volk aus?', *Neue juristische Wochenschrift* 43: 2861–2.

Peterson, P. E. (1996) 'An Immodest Proposal', *Daedalus*, 151–74.

Petrov, P. (2009) 'Is it possible to overcome the social exclusion of ethnic minorities through their political inclusion? The examples of Bulgaria and Macedonia', paper presented at the Euro-Balkan Institute conference 'Integrating Differences', Ohrid (Macedonia), 28–31 May 2009.

Pettit, P. (1999) 'Republican Freedom and Contestatory Democratization' in I. Shapiro and C. Hacker-Cordón (eds) *Democracy's Value*, Cambridge: Cambridge University Press, 163–90.

Phillips, A. (1995) *The Politics of Presence.* Oxford: Oxford University Press.

Poulain, M. and Foulon, M. (1998) 'Frontières linguistiques, migrations et distribution spatiale des noms de famille en Belgique', *L'Espace géographique* 1: 53–62.

Pratt, H. J. (1976) *The Gray Lobby.* Chicago and London: The University of

Chicago Press.

Price, M. C. (1997) *Justice Between Generations: The Growing Power of the Elderly in America*, New York: Praeger.

Rae, D. W. (1993) 'Proportional representation over gerrymandering', *PEGS Newsletter* 3(1): 13–14.

Rawls, J. (1971) *A Theory of Justice*. Cambridge, Mass.: Harvard University Press.

— (1993) 'The Law of Peoples', *Critical Inquiry* 20: 36–68.

— (1997) 'The Idea of Public Reason Revisited', *The University of Chicago Law Review* 64 (3): 765–807.

— (1999) *The Law of Peoples*. Cambridge, Mass.: Harvard University Press.

Rawls, J. and Van Parijs, P. (2003) 'Three Letters on the Law of Peoples and the European Union', *Autour de Rawls*, special issue of *Revue de philosophie économique* 8: 7–20.

Reeve, A. and Williams, A. (eds) *Real Libertarianism Assessed. Political Philosophy After Van Parijs*, Basingstoke: Palgrave Macmillan.

Renner, K. (1918) *Das Selbstbestimmungsrecht der Nationen, in besonderer Anwendung auf Oesterreich*. Leipzig and Wien: Franz Deuticke. (Revised edition of Rudolf Springer, *Der Kampf der österreichischen Nation um den Staat*. Leipzig and Wien: Franz Deuticke, 1902.)

Reynolds, A. and Reilly, B. (1997) *The International IDEA Handbook of Electoral System Design*, Stockholm: Institute for Democracy and Electoral Assistance.

Ringen, S. (1996) 'In a Democracy, Children Should Get the Vote', *International Herald Tribune* 14–15 December 1996.

— (1997) *Citizens, Families and Reform*. Oxford: Oxford University Press.

Roberts, N. (1997) 'New Zealand: A long-established Westminster Democracy Switches to Proportional Representation', in A. Reynolds and B. Reilly (eds) *The International IDEA Handbook of Electoral System Design*, Stockholm: Institute for Democracy and Electoral Assistance, 129–31.

Roland, G., Vandevelde, T. and Van Parijs, P. (1997) 'Repenser la solidarité entre les régions et entre les nations', *La Revue nouvelle* 105 (5–6), 149–57; reprinted in F. Docquier (ed.) *La Solidarité entre les régions*, Brussels: Deboeck, 1999, 99–115.

Rule, W. and Zimmermann, J. F. (eds) (1994) *Electoral Systems in Comparative Perspective. Their Impact on Women and Minorities*, Westport, CT and London: Greenwood Press.

Sartori, G. (1994) *Comparative Constitutional Engineering. An Inquiry into Structures, Incentives and Outcomes*, London: Macmillan.

Sauvy, A. (1945) *Bien-être et population*. Paris: Edition sociale française.

Scharpf, F. W. (1996) 'Demokratische Politik in Europa', *Staatswissenschaften und Staatspraxis* 6 (4): 565–91.

— (2000) 'Basic Income and Social Europe', in R. J. van der Veen and L. Groot (eds) *Basic Income on the Agenda*, Amsterdam: Amsterdam University Press, 154–60.

Schmitt, C. (1926) *Die geistesgeschichtiche Lage des heutigen Parlamentarismus*

(2nd ed.). Berlin: Duncker and Humblot, 1963.

Schmitter, P. C. (1997) 'Is it Really Possible to Democratize the Euro-polity?', in A. Follesdal and P. Koslowski (eds) *Democracy and the European Union*, Berlin and New York: Springer, 13–36.

Shugart, M. S. and Carey, J. (1992) *Presidents and Assemblies: Constitutional Design and Electoral Dynamics*. Cambridge: Cambridge University Press.

Schultz, H. (1992) 'Mit Familienwahlrecht Einfluß nehmen', *Sozialdemokratischer Pressedienst* 25 August.

Schumpeter, J. (1943) *Capitalism, Socialism and Democracy*. London: Allen and Unwin, 1976.

Scorer, R. (1994) 'The Extension of Democracy to Posterity', in E. Angius and S. Busuttil (eds) *What Future for Future Generations?*, University of Malta: The Foundation for International Studies, 231–9.

Shapiro, I. and Hacker-Cordón, C. (eds) (1999a) *Democracy's Value*. Cambridge: Cambridge University Press.

— (eds) (1999b) *Democracy's Edges*. Cambridge: Cambridge University Press.

Shaviro, D. (1997) 'The Minimum Wage, the Earned Income Tax Credit, and Optimal Subsidy Policy', *The University of Chicago Law Review* 64 (2): 405–81.

Skinner, Q. (1981) *Machiavelli*. Oxford: Oxford University Press.

Stewart, D. J. (1970) 'Disfranchise the Old', *New Republic,* 29 August, 20–22.

Stone, C. (1994) 'Should We Establish a Guardian to Speak for Future Generations?', in T. C. Kim and J. A. Dator (eds) *Creating a New History for Future Generations*, Kyoto: Institute for the Integrated Study of Future Generations, 128–39.

Swift, A., Marshall, G. and Burgoyne, C. (1992) 'Which Road to Social Justice?', *Sociology Review* 2(2): 28–31.

Suhr, D. (1990) 'Transferrechtliche Ausbeutung und verfassungsrechtlicher Schutz von Familien, Müttern und Kindern', *Der Staat. Zeitschrift für Staatslehre, öffentliches Recht und Verfassungsgeschichte* 29: 69–86.

Swenden, W. and Jans, M. T. (2006), 'Will it stay or will it go? Federalism and the sustainability of Belgium', *West European Politics* 29 (5): 877–94.

de Tarde, G. (1892) 'Le suffrage "dit" universel', *Etudes pénales et sociales* Paris: Masson, 411–21.

Toulemon, A. (1933) *Le Suffrage familial ou suffrage universel intégral*. Paris: Librairie du Recueil Sirey.

— (1948) 'Influence du vieillissement de la population sur la composition du corps électoral', *Actes des journées pour l'étude scientifique du vieillissement de la population*. Paris: Alliance nationale contre la dépopulation, 107–15.

Vallès, J. M. and Bosch, A. (1997) *Sistemas electorales y gobierno representativo*. Barcelona: Ariel.

Van Parijs, P. (1991) *Qu'est–ce qu'une société juste? Introduction à la pratique de la philosophie politique*. Paris: Le Seuil.

— (1993a) *Marxism Recycled*. Cambridge: Cambridge University Press.

— (1993b) Solidarité et responsabilité: une contradiction insurmontable?, *La Revue Nouvelle* 11: 58–64.

— (1995) *Real Freedom for All. What (if anything) Can Justify Capitalism?*, Oxford: Oxford University Press.

— (1996) 'Basic Income and the Two Dilemmas of the Welfare State', *The Political Quarterly* 67 (1): 63–6.

— (2000) 'Basic Income at the Heart of Social Europe? Reply to Fritz Scharpf', in R. van der Veen and L. Groot (eds) *Basic Income on the Agenda. Policies and Politics*, Amsterdam: Amsterdam University Press, 161–9.

— (2003) 'Hybrid Justice, Patriotism and Democracy. A Selective Reply', in A. Reeve and A. Williams (eds) *Real Libertarianism Assessed. Political Philosophy After Van Parijs*, Basingstoke: Palgrave Macmillan, 201–16.

— (2004) 'Just Health Care in a Pluri-National country", in S. Anand, F. Peter and A. Sen (eds) *Public Health, Ethics and Equity*, Oxford: Oxford University Press, 163–80.

— (2006) 'Pourquoi des quotas?', Pavia Group document, www.paviagroup. be, April.

— (2007a) 'International Distributive Justice', in R. E. Goodin, P. Pettit and T. Pogge (eds) *The Blackwell's Companion to Political Philosophy*, Oxford: Blackwell, Vol. II, 638–52.

— (2007b) 'Bruxelles aujourd'hui: dix paradoxes et cinq menaces', *Politique* 49: 20–7.

— (2008) 'Brussel morgen: vier scenario's zonder taboes en zonder illusies', *Wat met Brussel? Uitdagende perspectieven voor de hoofdstad*, Leuven: Davidsfonds, 91–102.

— (2009) 'Towards the end of ethnic parties in the capital of Europe?', *The Bulletin*, 18 June; also as 'Bientôt la fin des partis ethniques à Bruxelles?', *Le Soir*, 27 mai; and as 'Weldra het einde van de etnische partijen in Brussel?', *De Standaard*, 27 mei.

— (2010) 'BHV: Place à la sagesse et à l'ambition', *Le Soir*, 29 April, also as 'Wijsheid en ambitie voor ons land', *De Morgen*, 27 April.

— (2011) *Linguistic Justice for Europe and for the World*. Oxford: Oxford University Press.

Vansteenkiste, S. (1993) 'Staatsstruktuur moet via federale rol parlement versterkt worden', *De Standaard*, 2 September.

Van Velthoven, H. (2009) 'The Belgian and Brussels Model Reconsidered', in F. De Rynck, B. Verschuere and E. Wayenberg (eds) *Re-Thinking the State*, Mechelen: Kluwer, 103–11.

von Schoenbeck, H. (1980) 'Deutsches Kindermanifest', in U. Klemm (ed.) *Quellen und Dokumente der Antipädagogik*, Frankfurt am Main.

Westoff, C. F. (1978) 'Marriage and Fertility in Developed Countries', *Scientific American* 239 (6): 51–7.

Wils, L. (1992) *Van Clovis tot Happart. De lange weg van de naties in de Lage Landen*, Leuven-Apeldoorn: Garant.

Willems, L. (1902) 'Over twee antivlaamsche brieven toegeschreven aan Minister Rogier', *Verslagen en Mededeelingen der Koninklijke Vlaamsche Academie voor Taal- en Letterkunde*, Gent: A. Siffer, 53–90.

Wright, J. W. (1997) *The New York Times Almanac (1998)* New York: Penguin Books.

index

Curtis, G. 55 n.58
Cyprus 44, 92
Day, C. L. 36
de Briey, L. ix, 141, 143 n.1, 147–50
de Coorebyter, V. 151 n.6
de Gaulle, C. 46, 97
De Ridder, P. 103 n.1
De Rynck, F. viii
de Smet de Naeyer, P. 61 n.67
de Tarde, G. 46, 48, 49 n.45
De Wever, B. 140
Debré, M. 46
Dehaene, J.-L. 145
Dehousse, R. vii, 28 n.25, 68 n.1, 69
    n.2, 76 n.12, n.14
Deliège, R. 17 n.13
Delpérée, F. 92, 147 n.4
democracy
    as ideal 6, 16
        as instrument for justice 5–8,
        13–16, 19–21, 33, 61, 66 n.73,
        67, 69–70, 72
    consociational see under ethnically
        divided countries
    contestatory 23–9
    definition of 1, 7, 39, 68
    deliberative 19, 26–7, 65–6
    direct 68
    economic theory of 9 n.5
        global 2, 13–14, 18–21, 34
        optimal 1–2, 68–9, 84 n.2
democratic deficit 1, 67–70, 73, 77
demos 67–8, 77, 101–4, 108
Deprez, K. 102
Deschouwer, K. v, viii, ix, 123, 125
    n.1, 132, 134 n.2, 141
Destrée, J. 87 n.7, 107, 110–11
Dewachter, W. 91–2, 102
Dewatripont, M. 74 n.10
D'Hondt, V. 85, 86, 145
Donneur, A. 84 n.3
Downs, A. 9 n.5
Dubois, F. X. 93
Dworkin, R. 8, 14–15 n.9, 29 n.27
Dyba, J. 47

East Timor 110
Economist, The 31, 99
Ector, S. 92 n.11
Egypt 43 n.29
Ekert-Jaffé, O. 51, 52 n.49, 53 n.51
elderly 31–7, 45, 50 n.46, 57, 65
elections
    freedom of 1, 7
    funding of 44, 65
    see also universal suffrage, voting
electoral reform see children's vote;
    constitutional engineering; federal
    electoral constituency; proportional
    representation
Elster, J. 19 n.18, 63–4
Engels, F. 103
environment 18, 21, 30, 33–4
equality, political 3, 31–2, 34–7, 41–3
Ermisch, J. 53 n.53, 59 n.64
Estlund, D. 66 n.73
Estonia 108
ethnically divided countries 2, 44,
    79–97
    consociational/power-sharing
        approach 81 n.1, 88–91, 96–7,
        125, 130–2, 145–7, 151
    devolution and 89, 96, 140
    incentives/ border-crossing ap-
        proach 88–97, 144, 149–53
European Central Bank 69, 72
European Commission 68, 69
European Consortium for Political
    Research (ECPR) iii
European Council (of heads of govern-
    ment) 68, 75–6, 77 n.15, 99
European Council of Ministers 19
    n.17, 28, 68. 71 n.4, 73–4, 75
European Court of Justice 68–9, 71
    n.4, 72
European Monetary Institute 68
European Parliament 67, 68, 73–4, 76,
    77 n.15, 129, 133–4
European Union
    citizenship 67, 100
    democracy in 67–77

Moureau, L. 87
Murnane, R. J. 35 n.10, 36–7 n.15
Murphy, A. B. 126

Nagel, J. 17 n.12
Nasser, G. A. 43 n.29
Netherlands, The 82
New Republic, The 32
New Zealand, 17 n.12, 40 n.23, 61, 62
    n.67
Nicaragua 40
Nigeria 92, 144
Norman, W. 15 n.10
Northern Ireland 82, 145–7

Offe, C. 34 n.6, 39, 41 n.24, 45 n.31,
    49 n.43, 54 n.54, 56 n.59, 62
Okin, S. M. 29 n.27
O'Leary, B. ix, 123, 141, 143 n.1,
    144–7, 150
Ordeshook, P. C. 9 n.5
Ortega y Gasset, J. 8 n.3

Palentien, C. 40 n.23
Papaux, A. 84 n.3
parental proxy vote *see* children's vote
parliamentarism 26, 76 n.14, 144
Pavia Group v, 95 n.13, 120, 123,
    133–67
Peeters, K. 118
pension rights 34, 36
Perrin, J.-P. 40 n.22
Peschel-Gutzeit, L. M. 47, 49
Peterson, P. 47
Petrov, P. 145 n.2
Pettit, P. vi, 23, 24–9
Phillips, A. 39
population policy 50–3
Poulain, M. 101
Pratt, H. J. 35 n.10
presidential election
    in the European Union 19 n.16, 76
    in divided societies 92
        in Belgium 143–4, 153
presidentialism 144

Price, M. C. 35 n.9, 40 n.24
property rights 25
proportional representation
    in assembly, 35, 39, 61 n.67, 79,
        85–7, 92, 94–5, 127, 135–6, 145,
        150, 152
    in cabinet, 145–7
    see also Single Transferable Vote
Prussia 46

Rae, D. 18 n.14
Rawls, J. 1, 3, 8–10 n.4, 20 n.19, 31,
    32–3 n.3, n.5, 37, 38 n.17, 65 n.72
Rawls-Machiavelli programme 1–2,
    31, 37–8, 43, 55–6, 60–2, 64–6, 66
    n.73
    see also democracy, as instrument
        of justice
Re-Bel initiative 114 n.5, 141
Reagan, R. 32
redistribution 13 n.6, 28, 30, 36 n.12,
    52–3, 71–2, 77, 111–14
    see also taxation
Reeve, A. v, 25 n.23
Reilly, B. 39, 62 n.67
Renner, K. 89, 108
republicanism 23, 99
Reynders, D. 139
Reynolds, A. 39, 62 n.67
Ringen, S. 47–8, 49
Roberts, N. 62 n.67
Roemer, J. 38 n.18
Rogier, C. 103
Roland, G. 74–5 n.10, 95 n.13
Roulleaux-Dugage, H. 46, 48
Rule, W. 39
Russia 18, 61

Sartori, G. 64
Sauvy, A. 45 n.32, 46, 48
Scharpf, F. W. 68 n.1, 71 n.4
Schmitt, C. 102
Schmitter, P. 31, 68
Schultz, H. 47
Schumpeter, J. 14 n.9